DIRECTIONS IN DEVELOPMENT

The Economics of Involuntary Resettlement

Questions and Challenges

Edited by
Michael M. Cernea

The World Bank
Washington, D.C.

© 1999 The International Bank for Reconstruction
and Development / THE WORLD BANK
1818 H Street, N.W.
Washington, D.C. 20433

Cover: background, a rising reservoir from the El Penol Dam in Colombia
floods a village, and only the church is still visible (Juan Mesa Villa); fore-
ground, squatters construct housing in Lusaka, Zambia (World Bank photo).

Library of Congress Cataloging-in-Publication Data

The economics of involuntary resettlement:questions and challenges   /
      edited by Michael M. Cernea.
          p.   cm.   — (Directions in development)
      Includes bibliographical references.
      ISBN 0-8213-3798-X
          1. Economic development projects—Developing countries.
2. Developing countries—Economic policy.   3. Forced migration—
Economic aspects—Developing countries.   4. World Bank—
Developing countries.   I. Cernea, Michael M.   II. Series: Directions in
development (Washington, D.C.)
HC59.72.E44E285   1998
333.3'1'091724—dc21   98-34774
                                                          CIP

Contents

Acknowledgements

The ideas that led to the preparation of this volume have been much discussed by the anthropologists, sociologists, economists, and technical specialists who form the "thematic group" for resettlement issues of the World Bank's Social Development Family. We concluded—and set out to make this case here—that more economic research and analytical tools, in addition to sociological and anthropological knowledge, are necessary for understanding and effectively addressing the complex issues of involuntary population resettlement.

The authors of this interdisciplinary book acknowledge therefore with great appreciation the support of the Bank's Social Development Department led by Gloria Davis and of the resettlement thematic group led by Maninder Gill. We much benefited from the personal stimulating intellectual interactions with Dan Aronson, Cynthia Cook, Gloria Davis, Ashraf Ghani, Dan Gibson, Maritta Koch-Weser, Maninder Gill, Scott Guggenheim, Ayse Kudat, William Partridge, Robert Picciotto, Ellen Schaengold, Ismail Serageldin, Andrew Steer, and other colleagues whose ideas are abundantly reflected in this volume.

We also express our gratitude to the many development practitioners from various countries who helped us during our fieldwork to better grasp and define the intricacies of displacement and relocation. However, the ultimate source of whatever insights this volume communicates are the resettlers themselves. They shared with us their firsthand perceptions of what forced relocation is and cast the crude light of real life on the economic and financial aspects of displacement and recovery.

The authors and the editor are also indebted to many colleagues and outside readers who reviewed chapters in manuscript—in particular to Andrew Steer, Scott Guggenheim, and Maninder Gill—and helped enrich them. Warren A. Van Wicklin III, in the initial preparation phase, and Milan Lin-Rodrigo, in the last phase of readying the manuscript for publication, offered help that is much appreciated. Throughout the entire effort, Gracie Ochieng bore the brunt of processing and reprocessing the text, all done with her typical diligence and steadiness. Gaudencio Dizon ensured the professional desktopping of the entire volume. Alicia Hetzner initially, and Bonnie Bradford with Virginia Hitchcook over the previous year, ably coordinated the technical process of publication.

The background picture reproduced on the volume's cover was graciously contributed by the Colombian sociologist Juan Mesa Villa, who took it himself 20 years ago, in 1978, when he carried out one of the first resettlement studies in Latin America on the population displacement from the reservoir area of the El Penol Dam.

It is customary, and fully adequate in this case, to also recognize that whatever is missing or is not well stated in the argument developed in this volume is solely our own responsibility.

Abbreviations and Acronyms

ADB	Asian Development Bank
ADEL	Agencia de Desarrollo Local
CBA	Cost-benefit analysis
CDHU	Housing and Urban Development Company of the State of São Paulo
CEHAB	State Housing Company of Rio de Janeiro
CHESF	Companhia Hidro Eletrica do São Francisco
CIDA	Canadian International Development Agency
COHAB	State Housing Company of Minas Gerais
DAC	Development Assistance Committee
DDP	Development Discussion Paper
DfID	Department for International Development (UK)
EPZ	Export processing zone
FAO	Food and Agriculture Organization of the United Nations
GTZ	German Agency for Technical Cooperation
ICLARM	International Center for Living Aquatic Resources Management
IDA	International Development Association
IDB	Inter-American Development Bank
IIED	International Institute for Environment and Development
IIPS	International Institute for Population Studies
INCRA	Instituto Nacional de Colonizacae e Reforma Agraria
ISI	Indian Social Institute
IWGIA	International Work Group for Indigenous Affairs
kWh	Kilowatt-hours
LAC	Latin American and the Caribbean Regional Office of the World Bank
LEGOP	Legal Department—Operations
NGO	Nongovernmental organization
NORAD	Norwegian Development Agency
NRCR	National Research Center on Resettlement (China)
NTPC	National Thermal Power Corporation (India)
OD	Operational directive

ODA	Overseas Development Administration
OECD	Organisation for Economic Co-operation and Development
OECF	Overseas Economic Cooperation Fund (Japan)
OED	Operations Evaluation Department of the World Bank
OMS	Operation manual statement
PAP	Project-affected people
PAR	Performance audit report
PCR	Project completion report
PLN	National Electricity Authority (Indonesia)
PPF	Project preparation facility
PROSAM	Programa de Saneamiento
R&R	Resettlement and rehabilitation
RSP	Refugee Studies Programme (UK)
SA	Social assessment
SAR	Staff appraisal report
SEHAB	Housing Department of São Paulo
SfAA	Society for Applied Anthropology
TOI	*Times of India*
UGP	Project managing unit
UNHCR	United Nations High Commissioner for Refugees
UNICEF	United Nations Children's Fund
UNIDO	United Nations Industrial Organization
WTAC	Willingness to accept compensation
WTP	Willingness to pay

INTRODUCTION

Mutual Reinforcement: Linking Economic and Social Knowledge about Resettlement

Michael M. Cernea

Every important advance in development work yields lessons that point to new directions, fostering a dialogue between practice and research that encourages creative reexamination of past approaches. This volume is the product of such a dialogue on the complicated issue of involuntary population resettlement. The volume calls for overcoming an insular social perspective on resettlement and for building an "alliance" between economic and sociological research about resettlement. It examines the economic tools for planning resettlement and searches for ways to refine them.

Historically, the disciplines that have most explored resettlement processes and have informed resettlement policy and operations have been social anthropology and sociology. But for reasons discussed in this book, the anthropological analysis of resettlement has remained somehow isolated and insufficiently complemented by parallel inquiry in the economic disciplines.

Although involuntary resettlements are a prerequisite for some infrastructural projects and exact multiple undesirable costs, development economics has paid little attention to the economic and financial underpinnings of resettlement. Awareness about the serious economic consequences of displacement has kept increasing, yet the economic study of resettlement is unjustifiably still lagging. Evidence about the externalization of project costs to resettlers also has kept accumulating, yet the methodology of financial analyses has somehow failed to internalize them and to find effective remedies. This lack of integration has deprived many resettlement projects of the economic analytical tools and financial means necessary to succeed.

Two important conclusions emerge from both operational work and social research: first, involuntary resettlement programs need to be informed better by economic research and theory; second, in the routines of project design, the economic and financial analyses must be adjusted to address the complexities of displacement and recovery.

At this time, development thinking at large is intensely concerned with broadening the frameworks of knowledge and action, particularly with incorporating social dimensions—social transformation—into the development paradigm. This is the substance of the new "Comprehensive Development Framework," which proposes a ". . . more inclusive picture of development. We cannot adopt a system in which the macroeconomic and financial is considered apart from the structural, social and human aspects, and vice versa. *Integration of each of these subjects is imperative*" (Wolfensohn 1999; author's emphasis). The same social concerns are also at the core of the proposed "New Development Paradigm," which emerges from "both the failures of past conceptions and the changes in the world that lead to the necessity of a new conception" (Stiglitz 1998).

This volume participates in this broad policy and intellectual debate about reorienting the development paradigm toward social inclusion and social development by focusing on one aspect: the need to bridge the gap between economic and social knowledge in addressing an important challenge faced by many current and forthcoming development programs–population resettlement. The volume is devoted to the argument for a more direct and involved role for economics in studying the social and economic dimensions and effects of involuntary population resettlement.

The authors of this volume bring the perspectives of four different scientific disciplines—economics, sociology, anthropology, and political science—yet all converge in making the same basic case: they argue for an organic synergy and mutual reinforcement between economic and social knowledge in resettlement work. Bringing in the tools of economics to complement the sociological and technical analysis of resettlement processes is essential not only for *explaining* their anatomy better, but also for *guiding* decisionmaking and investments.

Informed by the perspectives of these disciplines, the volume's coauthors offer theoretical and methodological considerations, rein- forcing empirical evidence and lessons learned from actual projects. The studies explore broad policy issues as well as "project-kitchen" issues, such as the procedures of economic planning and analysis, valuation methods, cost identification, resource allocation, and benefit distribution.

The first chapter, written by the volume's editor, examines the current state of the art in both social and economic research on resettlement. From this angle, it builds up the argument for more specialized economic inquiry as well as for cross-disciplinary knowledge development. The chapter also highlights the limitations of cost-benefit analysis and the risks of impoverishment through displacement. The evidence shows that the underfinancing of resettlement is pervasive and that it undercuts project outcomes as well as the improvement of resettlers' lives. The author argues that the challenge to economics in projectizing involuntary resettlement is to shift from the shortsighted economics of merely compensating the displacees to an economics of support for resettlers' full recovery and for growth enhancement.

The second chapter, written by David W. Pearce, addresses key methodological issues in the economic and financial analyses required for involuntary resettlement. In examining existing economic methods and current practices, the author draws parallels with environmental economics, discusses the unsatisfactory treatment of externalities, and makes important recommendations for improving the economic and financial foundation of resettlement operations.

The third chapter, written by John H. Eriksen, takes the methodological analysis further by discussing the practicalities of resettlement planning. It is based on the most detailed comparative analysis carried out to date between voluntary resettlement programs and involuntary resettlement programs—particularly of rural populations. The analysis reveals unjustified disparities between the two categories of resettlement in the planning and financing of comparable projects cofinanced by the World Bank and points to recurrent undertreatment of the forced resettlement projects. The author documents the large potential for improving the planning and financing of involuntary resettlement by adopting methods already tested in voluntary settlements.

The fourth chapter, written by María Clara Mejía, is dedicated to the economic aspects of urban resettlement, based on experiences in several Latin American countries. It addresses numerous social, economic, and financial variables such as grants, subsidies, compensation issues, affordability of new houses, credits to resettlers, employment in the urban context, and so forth. It demonstrates that in urban resettlement—no less than in rural—difficult economic dilemmas must be weighed and resolved to allow the social reinclusion of those displaced.

The fifth chapter, written by Lakshman K. Mahapatra, focuses on poverty reduction in resettlements in India, testing the adequacy of the risks and reconstruction model of resettlement and applying the risk-focused framework to a vast body of empirical findings. The author discusses each of the major risks of impoverishment through displacement, showing how these risks convert into real impoverishment, then outlines the counteractions necessary for avoiding or mitigating economic and social risks. The chapter also highlights the contrast between India's vast social research and its limited economic research on involuntary resettlement.

The final chapter, written by Warren Van Wicklin III, explores the crucial issue of benefit sharing in projects entailing forced resettlement. The chapter demonstrates that contrary to widespread assumptions, financing resettlers' recovery can be accomplished not only through up-front preproject budgetary allocations, but also through explicit provisions for channeling some of the project-generated benefits to people adversely affected. The author examines the options for benefit sharing one by one and recommends employing them as one key strategy for increasing the financial feasibility of resettlement with development.

Together, the volume's seven sections aim to inform about unresolved methodological and operational economic issues, and to further stimulate research and theory, particularly cross-disciplinary economic and social inquiry.

The fundamental policy and goal, even where involuntary resettlement becomes unavoidable, must remain *inclusive development*. This means that resettlers should not be excluded from the benefits of the developments they make possible but should instead be explicitly included. In short, they should share in the gains, not just the pains, of development.

In pursuing a closer "partnership" and advocating mutual reinforcement among economics, anthropology, and sociology in resettlement analysis, this volume is only a beginning: once joint research expands, there will be more to explore than the issues we are raising here. The authors of this volume are firmly convinced that a more refined and deeper treatment of the complex economics of resettlement by all concerned is essential for achieving resettlement *with* development.

We hope that many researchers and practitioners will respond to this call for better information and comprehensive knowledge and will carry the effort further.

References

Stiglitz, Joseph E. 1998. "Towards a New Paradigm for Development." Presented as the 1998 Prebisch Lecture at UNCTAD, Geneva, October 19. Processed.

Wolfensohn, James D. 1991. "A Proposal for a Comprehensive Development Framework." Memorandum to the Board, Management, and Staff of the World Bank Group, Washington, D.C., January 21, 1999. Processed.

1

Why Economic Analysis Is Essential to Resettlement: A Sociologist's View

Michael M. Cernea

Editor's Note   This chapter examines the current state of the art in resettlement research, comparing the progress in socio-anthropological knowledge about resettlement with economic knowledge. The comparison questions whether the economic knowledge and the analytical methods used for planning and financing resettlement are adequate for achieving the goals of resettlement policy.

Historically, research on involuntary resettlement has emerged primarily within the fields of anthropology and sociology. *Economic* research on displacement and resettlement, the author argues, is virtually missing—but would be indispensable to improving resettlement outcomes.

Seven characteristics of recent progress in social research are defined and contrasted with the paucity of economic research on resettlement. Displacements impose major economic and social risks upon the affected people. Absence of economic research partly explains the obsolete methodology of economic and financial analysis employed for planning involuntary resettlements and thus accounts for some of the enormous difficulties and failures of such operations. The paper argues that the method of cost-benefit analysis, and the conventional project risk and sensitivity analyses used in projects entailing resettlement, are incapable of answering displacement's economic and financial challenges and in practice tolerate the structural underfinancing of resettlement operations.

The author calls for a constructive "alliance" between economic and sociological knowledge on resettlement and argues that

5

in-depth economic knowledge is indispensable to achieving two fundamental goals of resettlement policy: *reduced* displacement and *development* of resettlers' livelihoods, once they have moved.

The chapter concludes with a discussion of the areas in which economic research is called upon to make important contributions: valuation of losses, risk analysis, cost analysis, internalization of costs, poverty mapping, distributional inequities, design of safety nets, and rationale for financial investments in reconstruction. The author calls for a novel "economics of recovery and development", to replace the long outdated "economics of compensation" that still guides the majority of resettlement operations, particularly in projects financed only from domestic sources. Developing such a novel "economics of recovery" demands a much closer intellectual and operational partnership than currently exists among economists, sociologists, and technical specialists.

The primary goal of any involuntary resettlement process is to prevent impoverishment and to improve the livelihood of resettlers. To do this, governments and technical agencies must understand the economics of dispossession, impoverishment, and recovery and plan for growth at the relocation site. The key point of this chapter is that displaced populations face a *specific set of risks*. These atypical risks are not addressed in routine project economic analysis. Robust empirical evidence has shown that, in most cases, these overlooked and little understood risks result in cumulated deprivations and severe impoverishment.

Insularity versus Partnership

Decades of sociological and socio-anthropological research have generated a substantial body of *social* knowledge about resettlement. This knowledge has been translated into policy and operational prescriptions that have improved many involuntary resettlement operations.

However, by its very nature, anthropological research primarily focuses on *sociocultural* dimensions. It does not regularly use the tools of economic analysis to explore the economic and financial variables of resettlement. Nor does it explore how those variables are incorporated into project budgets. Research findings and lessons from practice indicate that far more focus on the economic and financial components of resettlement is needed.

Socio-anthropological knowledge, however important, is not sufficient alone to guide all the economic and financial steps involved in displacement and resettlement. Anthropologists should not claim resettlement as their "exclusive" territory and should stay clear of any attempt to monopolize the research on resettlement. More economic knowledge about resettlement is imperative for better addressing the financial and budgetary implications of forced relocation. It is also important to include the *political* analysis of resettlement events and the scholarly perspective of *human geography* on such processes (Cernea 1996b).

I had the opportunity in 1994 and 1995 to publicly signal the exaggerated pursuit of exclusive "professional jurisdiction" over substantive research areas in resettlement. My point was critical of the insular tendency to "colonize" resettlement issues as an exclusive domain for anthropology. In substantive terms, I argued, important dimensions of resettlement are

> in the court of our colleagues, the economists. Misunderstanding or sheer ignorance in many agencies and countries about the complex economics of displacement and recovery are simply appalling. Many pitfalls in current practice can be traced to the sorry state of the economic research on resettlement, to the flawed prescriptions for economic and financial analysis, and for planning in this domain. *Perhaps anthropologists and sociologists have too exclusively colonized resettlement.* We must become more inviting of complementary perspectives (Cernea 1995).

In this chapter I discuss in some detail the need for integrating the social and economic knowledge about resettlement. In my view, anthropologists and economists alike have yet to fully recognize this need. I also review the progress to date in *social* knowledge, pointing to the areas that require more *economic* research and project economic analysis. I argue that mutual reinforcement between the economic, financial, and social analyses of resettlement components in projects is indispensable for avoiding their failure.

Social Knowledge about Resettlement: Recent Progress

Progress in social research on involuntary resettlement has been nothing short of explosive during the past two decades. Anthropologists and sociologists started the study of these processes some six or seven decades ago, and they maintained a virtual monopoly in this area of inquiry. Though progress was slow and sporadic in the first four decades, it has picked up great speed, particularly after development agencies started to use social research findings in formulating their resettlement policies and operational activities.

The appendix to this chapter offers an overview of the recent effervescent developments in *social research* on resettlement. Drawing from this overview, I have identified seven principal characteristics of these recent developments in social knowledge:

1. Social knowledge about processes of involuntary resettlement is more *intensive and substantive*, "thicker" than ever before. The understanding of displacement's socioeconomic content has been considerably enriched, refined, and systematized.
2. Research on resettlement has developed *extensively* as well: it covers new sectors of the economy that involve forcible relocations (forestry, urban infrastructure, thermal plants, and so forth) and has been expanded to include previously unexplored geographic areas.
3. Resettlement research has multiplied its *products and services*, moving from descriptions to prescriptions, from academic analysis to operational research.
4. Research has *scaled up*, crossing the threshold from micro to macro, from case ethnographies on localized instances of resettlement to general—sectoral, national, and international—policy frameworks for resettlement.
5. To overcome the limitations inherent in narratives and "soft" methods, resettlement researchers are crafting more precise *measurements and indicators* for quantifying the magnitude and consequences of resettlement.
6. New *theoretical models*, based on the ever-growing bodies of empirical data on resettlement, inform the practical planning of induced resettlement more effectively and generate hypotheses for further research.
7. Resettlers' growing resistance to, and the political implications of, displacement are topically integrated into resettlement research and theory; resettlers' participation in the reconstruction process has started to be explored.

These seven characteristics reflect essential advances in the state of resettlement *social* research (see also bibliographic references in the appendix). Such knowledge gains may become gradually codified in new institutional procedures for managing resettlement, previously nonexistent, and have already led to improvements in resettlement programs.

Economic Knowledge: The Challenges Ahead

Contrasting with the progress in social research, economic research on the variables of resettlement is lagging far behind. Integration between socio-anthropological knowledge and economic knowledge about re-settlement has far to go, largely because such economic knowledge has yet to be developed.

Despite the better social understanding of resettlement, it is dismay-ing that, in practice, so many resettlements programs still go so wrong in so many places—to the detriment of such large numbers of people. Nearly every inquiry presents fresh evidence of "depriving the under-privileged," to use Pandey's forceful expression. And failure to improve or even restore resettlers' livelihoods is frequent. Fresh evidence of im-poverishment after displacement can be found in a series of field sur-veys recently published by the World Bank's Operations Evaluation Department (OED), covering India (Karnataka state), Togo (Nangbeto Dam), and Indonesia (Kedung Ombo) (OED 1998).

Why then—despite all the policies, studies, and public debates—is failure in resettlement still so frequent?

As in all complex situations, no single cause explains all outcomes. Here too there are several, but I want to focus on causes related to the state of economic knowledge about resettlement. We may consider this from two perspectives: as theory—how economics conceptualizes reset-tlement—and as methodology—how economic methods are applied for costing forced displacement and for determining the financial provisioning of sustainable relocation.

Basic research by professional economists on population displace-ments, to the best of my knowledge, currently is not carried out any-where. Development economics still has to respond in full to the challenge of analyzing not only the economic dimensions of dislocation, but also the economic content of other *social* costs of development. When one of the few books about the social costs of structural adjustment pro-grams came out (Cornia, Jolly, and Stewart 1987), it sent a virtual shock wave through development economics. Population displacement is just another one of those "social" costs; however, the economic book on dis-placements' costs has yet to be written.

The shortage of economic theory is mirrored at the practical level in a shortage of specialized *methods* or *techniques* to be used in the economic and financial analysis of resettlement operations at project level. Ex-isting general methods for such analyses have not been tailored to the specifics of displacement. Current methods were proved in projects the world over to be faulty in assessing both the costs and the benefits of re-settlement, yet corrections to these methods have not been worked out. The routine methodology of cost-benefit analysis obscures rather than highlights displacement losses (as shown further in this chapter and in the following chapters by Pearce and Eriksen).

Brief Review of the Economic Literature

In a seminal address about the "New Development Paradigm," Stiglitz (1998) forcefully argues that development economics must go beyond the narrowness of the past "Washington consensus" and defines development as "the transformation of whole societies." The alternative paradigm he proposes

> is based on a broader conception of development, with a concomitantly broader vision of development strategies. . . . Many previous development strategies have focused on pieces of this transformation, but because they have failed to see the broader context, they have failed, and often miserably. Most of these have focused narrowly on *economics* (Stiglitz 1998).

For this paradigm to be adopted and implemented, social processes—and the *social* outcomes of economic development—would have to command a much more intense analytical attention from the economic sciences. This should apply also to the "social costs" of development in general, not just to one such cost as involuntary resettlement is. More economic knowledge on social variables in development is becoming indispensable to understanding development scientifically, with its benefits and risks, and to influencing and managing change.

> Key to these changes—wrote Stiglitz—is the movement to "scientific" ways of thinking, identifying critical variables that affect outcomes, attempting to make inferences based on available data, *recognizing what we know and what we don't know* (Stiglitz 1998; author's emphasis).

Certainly, "what we know and what we still don't know" about the economics of resettlement is only a small fraction of the vast body of economic knowledge needed to inform induced development projects. Nonetheless, this particular body of knowledge becomes, in fact, decisive when governments plan and finance resettlements: the presence or absence of such economic knowledge, its adequacy or inadequacy, can spell success or failure in practice. And evidence shows that such knowledge is largely missing.

Leading economists and sociologists have explicitly called for bridging the overall disciplinary "gulf" between economic and sociological-anthropological studies (Lipton 1992; Ruttan 1988; Smelser and Swedberg 1994). For instance, pointing to the vast domain of community studies, a well-known Indian economist, Pradan Bardhan, incisively noted that the methodological gulf is particularly wide between econo-mists and anthropologists. I have often observed between the two groups an attitude of mutual indifference, or worse. On the rare occasions when they meet they usually talk past each other (Bardhan 1989, p. 7).

Supporting Bardhan's argument and comparing the same two disciplines, Michael Lipton suggests, in turn, that there is a

crying need for economists' survey techniques and theorizing to be based in anthropologists' study of socially mediated relation-ships.... Part of the way forward... is the grounding of mi-cro-economics in an anthropologically and politically researched understanding of intergroup, inter-role processes, not only in models of expected utility maximization (Lipton 1992).

Such insufficient theoretical and methodological "conversation" between economists and anthropologists is directly dysfunctional in certain research subareas, such as development-caused displacements and their impoverishing effects. The neglect of resettlement research by economists was specifically deplored by G. Edward Schuh:

Economists have tended to neglect the problems of what an-thropologists and sociologists often refer to as "oustees" or dis-placed people—those who have to resettle in the face of large development projects that wipe out the economic activities from which they have earned their livelihood. This neglect is somewhat puzzling. Perhaps it occurs because the resettlement problem tends to be viewed as a social problem, and therefore one to be dealt with by anthropologists and sociologists. These latter groups of social scientists have brought an important per-spective to such projects... But greater involvement of develop-ment economists should give more of a forward and dynamic perspective. It should also help put front and center the idea that it isn't enough just to re-establish those ousted from their previ-ous situations. Rather, the goal should be to re-establish the oustees in such a fashion that they can experience sustained eco-nomic growth in the future, or sustained increases in per capita income (Schuh 1993, p. 59).

David Pearce, a leading British economist credited as one of the cre-ators of environmental economics, notes that resettlement issues have been "something of a Cinderella issue" in the economic appraisal of de-velopment projects (see Pearce, this volume). In turn, John Eriksen has documented Pearce's severe assessment by demonstrating, project by project, the unsatisfactory quality of economic analysis of involuntary resettlement components (see Eriksen, this volume). The roots of this situation can probably be traced to the classic economic textbooks about development projects (Little-Mirrlees 1974), as well as to recent ones (Fabre 1997), which simply skate over population displacements by projects despite their frequency, as do many other manuals of development economics (Torado 1989).

Paradoxically, despite their valuable contributions to the economics of hydropower, economists have traditionally overlooked population displacements as a dysfunctional by-product of dam building. A clear example is the response given by a noted British economist, J. L. Joy, when he was asked "*What does an economist want to know about dams?*" Joy answered with a lengthy article, listing tens and tens of variables and categories of data that an economist "would want to know" for making economic analyses and planning decisions on dam-building options (Joy 1968). However, displacement by reservoirs, canals, and roads was missing from Joy's list. Except for a passing reference to general social aspects, all indicators were of an economic or technological nature. Whether forced displacement is of a magnitude that demands alternative investment options was an issue he never "wanted to know." Neither did he grant a place in his list to compensation of people's assets, to income restoration, or to economic reestablishment issues. Certainly not all economists think alike. However, sadly, it seems though that J. L. Joy's answer reflected a situation common at the time rather than only a personal opinion.

The net result of overlooking for decades the displacement effects of infrastructural investments is that economic *conceptualizations* of resettlement have remained skeletal. Consequently, the *methods* and indicators supposed to translate such understanding in prescriptions for the economic and financial analysis of resettlement at project level are unrefined. As long as such rudimentary methods continue to be used in economic analysis and planning, past errors will be recycled.

Two examples from India illustrate this situation. As recently as 1995, a book by four economists entitled the *Economic Dimensions of the Sardar Sarovar Project* (Alagh and others 1995) undertook a reappraisal study of the economics and financing of this now famous project. The book includes interesting new data on the dam, the canal network, power and irrigation benefits, and environmental costs and benefits, including over 100 pages of tables. Yet resettlement is covered by only a few mentions (pp. 96–98) and some annexes. For a project noted worldwide for its flaws in policy and execution, a project with over 200,000 people slated for displacement and at severe risk of impoverishment, no analysis is made in the book of the costs incurred by the displaced people or the investments required for their economic recovery. Not even baseline data on resettlers' preproject incomes and economic condition is reported. No projection of sustainable farming models or of alternative strategies is provided to guide the restoration and improvement of the oustees' incomes.

Another example is the manual *Economic Appraisal of Irrigation Projects in India,* published by the New Dehli Institute of Economic Growth (Sinha and Bathia 1982). As is well known, many large-scale irrigation projects in India cause loss of land and forced displacement of landed and landless families from reservoirs, canal areas, and adjacent road systems, and such displacement must be considered during project preparation and appraisal. Yet this volume, in its over 480 pages dedicated to "economic appraisal," found no place to analyze the economic consequences and remedies of displacement. The incomplete "guidance" that this, and similar textbooks, provide to practitioners leads to fallaciously incomplete appraisals of resettlement operations.

Perverse Effects of Insufficient Economic Analysis

This brief review of the economic literature is certainly not exhaustive. One can find now and then some studies on the economic aspects of resettlement (Paranjpye 1988, Goyal 1996); in China, the interest in the economic dimensions of recovery is stronger (Shi, Xun, and Yu 1996, Wu and Shi 1996, Shi 1996b). Overall, however, the contrast is sharp between the sociological and economic literatures.

Examining both literatures, I concluded that the least addressed in research and analysis, as well as in financial planning, are the *sources of economic recovery.*

This conclusion may be a bit puzzling to those who know well, as I do, that anthropologists and sociologists have certainly illuminated not only the cultural but also many of the economic aspects of resettlement. Social and cultural researchers (noneconomists) have substituted ad hoc for economists as well. They have often done a remarkable job generating insights into the economic implications of resettlement. Yet after studying hundreds of projects involving resettlement, I am convinced that the expertise of *professional* economists, using a solid *economic methodology* for resettlement projects, is indispensable. Therefore, forging a professional partnership between economists and sociologists in studying these issues is the next important step.

It should not be a surprise that insufficient economic research and knowledge result in inadequate methods for operational economic analysis at project level. Coercive mass expropriation of assets by the state causes losses not identified by the existing methodology for project economic analysis (Tamondong-Helin 1996). Current property acquisition procedures do not provide compensations sufficient to enable displacees to purchase replacement lands and other assets of comparable quality or size, because they either exclude or underpay many affected people. In this way, the current methodology externalizes part of the cost, instead of internalizing all costs within project budgets. This is not a minor issue, though I'd call it one of the best-kept "secrets" of resettlement misplanning and failure.

When resettlement costs are underestimated (whether deliberately or by error), allocations of financial resources for displacees fall short, often by large amounts. Thus displacees and hosts are forced to bear "out of pocket" a share of the cost, reducing the standard of living for all. Exacerbating the problems are budget constraints, often limited or absent political commitment, inflexible allocation procedures, and the fact that procedures are limited to instruments of *compensation* economics.

The fundamental financial issue, however, is investing in resettlement *with development*. Even if all material losses were compensated at their market value, the cash equivalent generally would fall far short of the amount needed to restart the economic and productive activities (new farms, small business, and so on) of resettlers in a new setting at levels that provide equal or improved income. To improve the livelihood of resettlers above their previous levels—which is the essence of *resettlement with development*—additional investments are needed to ensure recovery and development.

The only available economic methodology specially tailored for costing resettlement was published in 1988 by the World Bank. Following the Bank's first internal resettlement review (Cernea 1986), specific guidelines for the economic and financial analysis of resettlement components were prepared, discussed widely, and finally issued as an attempt to adapt the general logic of economic and financial analysis in Bank-assisted projects to the unique characteristics of dislocation and relocation (see Cernea 1988, annex 2). These innovative guidelines prepared by a group of Bank economists working together with sociologists, were—and probably remain—the best economic guidelines on resettlement available in the world literature.

But they may also rank among the most ignored. The inadequacy of economic analysis has been highlighted in some World Bank documents, including self-criticism targeting the Bank's practices, as well as criticism of the development economics field at large (World Bank

1994). Moreover, these 1988 guidelines have not been adopted in non-Bank–financed projects, which constitute the vast majority—over 95 percent—of interventions causing resettlement worldwide. The negative impacts are unmistakable, particularly in large countries with multiple infrastructure projects, such as India, Pakistan, and Brazil.

Several dilemmas in forced resettlement directly challenge conventional economic thinking and call for creative research and revised analytical methods. We will discuss some of them—about preventing underfinancing of resettlement, anticipating impoverishment risks, correcting cost-benefit analysis, and revising valuation techniques.

The Anatomy of Impoverishment: Risks, Safeguards, and Recovery

Economic research and operational economic analysis could vastly improve resettlement outcomes by focusing on how to overcome the risks of impoverishment inherent in displacementa fundamental issue still not included in routine economic project analyses.

Risk Analysis and Behavioral Risks

Risk analysis is one of the sophisticated instruments employed in economic analysis for designing and financing development interventions. But the primary questions are (a) which risks are considered and (b) whether the distribution of risks between project actors and stakeholders is taken into account. The "selection" of risks (Douglas and Wildawski 1982, Rosa 1998) that are seen to merit policy attention and economic-technical analysis in development projects is influenced by political and cultural factors. Conventional economic risk analysis selectively focuses only on the risks to capital investments, but not on various kinds of "post-normal risks" (Rosa 1998) that displacements impose upon affected people.

Conventional economic risk analysis evaluates the sources, magnitude, and effects of risks that may reduce the rate of return to capital investments in development projects. It estimates the switching values of key variables (such as duration of project implementation, cost overruns, and availability of local cofinancing). It also undertakes a sensitivity analysis for each key risk, testing the sensitivity of a project's net present value to possible changes in the variables. When necessary, sensitivity analyses are used to develop alternative investment scenarios, including contingency actions, to minimize risk and ensure best return on investment. But if good development practice calls for capital to be insured against political risk, currency exchange risk, implementation risk, and so on, so also should the local populations "be insured against the unintended, counter-development risks and consequences" (Downing 1998) of projects.

Among the types of project financial risks routinely analyzed at project outset, one category is defined in economics as "behavioral risks." In the phrase "behavioral risks," however, the notion of "behavior" does not refer to risks that the project imposed on people's normal behavior by compelling them to uproot. Again, the concept, refers to risks *to the project's capital investments* that can emerge from changes in people's unrelated and hard-to-anticipate behavior (for example, assumed consumption of project products, employment preferences, etc.).

Moreover, it is also common practice for governments to provide guarantees against various risks incurred by investors in infrastructure projects. The state takes responsibility for such risks in order to protect and encourage the private investors (see a detailed discussion of risk calculation methodology in infrastructural projects in Irwin and associates 1997). Yet when the same private investments *create* risks to such primary stakeholders as the residents of the project area, by expropriating and displacing them, the state does not provide comparable protection against risks to these affected people. Except compensation, most governments do not use any refined economic and legal methodology to institute risk insurance measures for such primary stakeholders.

In conclusion, we note that while economic analysis and sensitivity tests are generally designed to identify, measure, and counteract risks to the project and project investors, they are not conversely designed to measure the risks posed by the project to the other project actors, such as the displaced people. Obviously, this is a unidirectional consideration of the relations between stakeholders and projects. This conflicts with the objective of safeguarding people's interests and protecting them against major risks stemming from projects. Human perception and response to risks, risk aversion, and experience in dealing with risks are essential parameters. Therefore, risk analysis should be defined and practiced as an inherently interdisciplinary activity, a domain of cooperation between economics and sociology. The current methodology of risk analysis at project level must be broadened to recognize risk distribution among all project actors and address equitably the direct risks to area people as well. These major risks are defined next.

Impoverishment Risks to People

As stated at the outset, the key point for our risk discussion is that populations displaced by projects face a set of risks that are atypical for other categories of projects. These specific project risks must be pondered from both perspectives—economic and sociocultural.

What are these specific risks to people?

Understanding how impoverishment risks occur and how to counter them requires deconstructing the anatomy of impoverishment and defining the key determinants of income reconstruction. After synthesizing much empirical evidence, I have concluded that the onset of impoverishment can be represented through a model of eight interlinked potential risks intrinsic to displacement (Cernea 1990a, 1997, forthcoming). When not counteracted, these fundamental risks converge and combine into economic, social, and cultural impoverishment. Thus, the model captures the loss by displaced people *of all types of capital*—natural, manmade (physical), human, and social—as well as loss of opportunities and entitlements held at the prior location. The model is also a tool for risk management, suggesting strategies for countering the risks. The eight risks occur with varying intensity in different contents. Concisely, they are defined below:

LANDLESSNESS. Expropriation of land removes the main foundation upon which people's productive systems, commercial activities, and livelihoods are constructed. This is the principal form of decapitalization and pauperization for most rural and many urban displacees, who lose this way both natural and manmade capital.

JOBLESSNESS. Loss of employment and wages occurs more in urban areas, but it also affects rural people, depriving landless laborers, service workers, artisans, and small business owners of sources of income. Unemployment or underemployment resulting from resettlement tends to linger long after physical relocation.

HOMELESSNESS. Loss of housing and shelter is temporary for the majority of displacees, but threatens to become chronic for the most vulnerable. Considered in a broader cultural sense, homelessness is also *placelessness*, loss of a group's cultural space and identity (Downing 1994, 1995).

MARGINALIZATION. Marginalization occurs when families lose economic power and spiral downward; it sets in long before physical displacement, when new investments in the condemned areas are prohibited. Middle-income farm households become small landholders; small shopkeepers and craftsmen are downsized and slip below poverty thresholds. Economic marginalization is often accompanied by social and psychological marginalization, expressed in a drop in social status, oustees' loss of confidence in society and in themselves, and a feeling of injustice and increased vulnerability.

FOOD INSECURITY. Forced displacement increases the risk that people will fall into chronic food insecurity, defined as calorie-protein intake levels below the minimum necessary for normal growth and work. Sudden drops in food crop availability and income are endemic to physical relocation, and hunger or undernourishment lingers as a long-term effect.

INCREASED MORBIDITY AND MORTALITY. The health of oustees tends to deteriorate rapidly from the outbreak of relocation-related parasitic and vectorborne diseases (malaria, schistosomiasis), from malnutrition, and from increased stress and psychological traumas. Unsafe water supply and waste disposal tend to proliferate infectious diseases, and morbidity decreases capacity and incomes. This risk is highest for the weakest population segments—infants, children, and the elderly.

LOSS OF ACCESS TO COMMON PROPERTY. Loss of access to commonly owned assets (forested lands, bodies of water, grazing lands, and so on)—typically overlooked and uncompensated for in government schemes (with few exceptions, particularly China)—is another major cause of income deterioration for oustees, particularly for the assetless.

SOCIAL DISARTICULATION. Community dispersal means dismantling of structures of social organization and loss of mutual help networks. Although this loss of social capital is harder to quantify, it impoverishes and disempowers oustees in enduring ways, not recognized by project-level economic analysis. Other common risks are loss of access to some basic public services as well as the temporary or permanent loss of schooling for children (see Mahapatra in this volume and Mathur 1998).

These high-probability risks will certainly become realities if unheeded. However, like every risk forecast derived from past experience, this predictive model can become a "self-destroying prophecy" (Merton 1957). Impoverishment risks can be avoided or mitigated if they are anticipated, correctly identified, and counteracted. If the conventional forms of economic and financial risk analysis are broadened to include project-caused risks to people, as recommended earlier in this paper, the probability of this self-destroying effect is heightened.

When done jointly, project economic and social analysis can ascertain and quantify the presence of these basic risks during early project preparation, as their shape and intensity vary depending on project design and site circumstances. The combined tools of economists, sociologists, and technical specialists for designing safeguards—including compensatory allocations, benefit sharing, and growth-enhancing investments oriented toward resettlers' development—must become integral to a project's strategy and budget calculations.

The impoverishment risks and reconstruction model reveals not only the risks but also the ways to *positively reestablish* those displaced. Indeed, if we reverse this matrix of risks, the model shows what needs to be done to restore and improve livelihoods: the rehabilitation that must follow displacement. Specifically, for instance, landlessness risks should be eliminated through land reestablishment; homelessness, through sound shelter programs; joblessness, through employment creation; and social disarticulation, through community reconstruction and host-resettler inclusionary strategies. Furthermore, provisions to ensure that those displaced share in the *specific* benefits generated by the program that caused them to relocate should be included in projects. Practical modalities to do so include resettling reservoir outsees to the newly irrigated lands downstream (rather than around the reservoir), earmarking a share of the revenues from selling energy for resettlements or providing access to affordable housing in newly constructed urban areas (more options for benefit sharing are described by van Wicklin in this volume and Cernea 1988, 1991).

It is obvious from the above discussion of project-caused risks to people that these risks cannot be tamed solely through compensation for condemned assets. Yet the strategy of nearly all displacements worldwide is still centered on expropriation payments and not yet on income reestablishment. Expropriation laws provide for compensation for condemned assets, but they do not aim, nor do they promise, to reestablish prior levels of living. Therefore, in contrast with prevailing practice, our conclusion here is that the intrinsic socioeconomic risks of resettlement can and must be brought under control only through an *encompassing strategy* of safeguarding livelihoods and reestablishing income sources.

Limitations of the Cost-Benefit Method

The economic methodology employed to justify projects limited to compensation approaches is based solely on standard cost-benefit and role of return analyses, which do not address the mitigation of the consequences of displacement at the *individual* level. This is one of the most profound roots of failure of resettlement under such projects. If indeed the core risks are decapitalization and pushing the resettlers out of their prior economically productive positions, then to be adequate, the response strategy should be backed up by development investments tailored to the resettlers' capacities and based on growth-oriented economic analysis and financial provisioning.

Cost-benefit analysis (CBA) justifies a project economically when the sum of a project's benefits outweighs the sum of project costs. But CBA overlooks *distribution* patterns—distribution of both costs and benefits. It does not ask *who* is paying the costs, *who* specifically is getting the benefits, or *who* is losing. It only assesses the "total" effect of the project design to determine how it stacks up relative to other investment alternatives.

But harm caused to individual families—the displaced families—cannot be "outweighed" or explained away by benefits to other families, or by the aggregate of project benefits, independent of their allocation. Cost-benefit analysis does not answer the risks accruing to various subsets of individuals. Real impoverishment risks are distributed differently than project benefits (Cernea 1997). Aggregate benefits may be real, but they do not automatically offset each *individual's* costs.

Empirical research by anthropologists over decades has documented multiple types of "social costs." It has also revealed the commonly inadequate valuation of oustees' condemned assets. The concept of "social costs" ("social" is probably a misnomer here), is often misunderstood as referring only to the nonmeasurable costs. In fact, "social" costs define the project costs that are left to accrue to the society *outside* the project, as opposed to the project's direct *internal* costs (labor, materials, equipment, and so forth). But social costs are fully *project* costs in that they would not accrue without the project. Many of them *are* measurable. These "external" or "societal" costs include (but are not limited to) all that is lost by the forcibly displaced: land, houses, trees, crops, jobs, productive time, cultural assets, common property goods, shrines and places of prayer, burial grounds, and access to social services.

Internalizing these "external" costs into the project's overall costs should take the forms of (a) compensations to the displacees at replacement cost, plus (b) investments for facilitating recovery and accelerated takeoff for those uprooted. Unless all categories of losses, as well as the *costs of restarting comparable income-generating activities*, are budgeted fully into the project, externalization continues to occur. Sacrifices are imposed on resettlers, and the project transforms the displaced into net losers who have to bear many of the "hidden" social costs of projects.

It is true that some (not all) costs are not easy to quantify, but invoking "intangibles" is often used as an excuse for avoiding *any* valuation. "Unmeasurable" should not become "forgettable." Ignoring such costs, intentionally or not, "minimizes" the accounted costs of a project, without reducing real costs.

The cost-benefit method can be easily manipulated or influenced by (a) excluding costs caused by the project, (b) by the way in which costs and benefits are valued when direct market prices cannot be observed or are not conclusive, or (c) by the choice of the discount rate to estimate the present value of a condemned asset. But the point I want to emphasize is that *even at its best, without distortions,* the standard cost-benefit method is incapable of answering the economic and ethical questions involved in forced displacement.

Relying on cost-benefit analysis is methodologically questionable not only from a social perspective, but also from a market perspective. Market valuation is based on voluntary exchange between a willing seller and a willing buyer. Resettlement is involuntary: it imposes administrative acquisition of assets. Nor is resettlement a marginal market valuation decision for those affected: on the contrary, it imposes a total life change.

Involuntary resettlement components are included in certain development projects not by choice but by necessity. They are supposed to be included only after all possible alternatives to avoid and minimize displacement have been examined. Since the projects that involve displacement are a special subcategory of complex projects, they should undertake a *special economic and financial analysis for the displacement, relocation, and socioeconomic reestablishment component,* an analysis distinct from the routine cost-benefit analysis. Costs and benefits must be calculated distinctly for each vulnerable group and beneficiary group, not across all populations on the whole "project." The principle of recognizing differential impacts is, in fact, the reason for adopting safeguarding policies (such as resettlement policy). In fact, recent economic thinking (Londero 1996) is returning to the earlier pioneering interest in the social side of the cost-benefit analogy (as expressed in Squire and van der Tak 1975; see also other viewpoints discussed in Ray 1984) for introducing estimates of distributional effects into cost-benefit analysis.

Considerable thinking and research has been devoted in recent years in the World Bank to "reviving project appraisal" and improving the economic analysis of projects by shifting from rate of return calculations to a broader examination of the rationale and outcomes of public financial provisions for projects that result in private benefits (Devarajan, Squire, and Suthiwart-Narueput 1995). Such research demonstrated that projects assisted by the Bank in which costs are borne by the public sector while benefits are enjoyed by the private sector tend to *overestimate* net benefits (*ibid.,* 1995). The undesirable effects of such overestimating are aggravated by insufficient attention to issues of distributional weight. The efforts to improve the quality of economic work in the World Bank continue, particularly in areas like public spending programs, infrastructure financing (and entailed risks), microeconomics, public choice, principal-agent issues, safeguards and safety nets (Baird 1996), with expected gains also for the economic understanding of project-caused displacements.

Involuntary resettlement clearly complicates projects, so it should be equally clear that the project economic analysis would have to be modified to meet the requirements of such more demanding project contents. Differential calculation of project costs and benefits for the segment of population displaced is fully feasible. Other refined analytical procedures can be designed as well.

Of great concern also should be the fact that, in the absence of rigorous analytical demands, insufficient compensation can be easily camouflaged through nontransparent project budgets. I have seen many project budgets submitted by country agencies to the World Bank that, at first sight, appeared to have a sizable budget for the "R&R" component. But no breakdown of such budgets is provided. Upon closer examination, however, surprises emerge, showing that the nontransparent budgets create the *appearance* of high average expenditures per resettler family, by lumping all relocation expenses (infrastructure and human, public assets and family-owned assets) into one consolidated sum. Close examination soon reveals that the bulk of those budgets—up to 70 or 80 percent—represents the financing for condemned *public* assets (roads, bridges, government buildings, public utilities, military assets, and so on) that are to be relocated or expanded. Only a small percentage of the consolidated R&R budget goes to the affected families. Using such nontransparent budgets to avoid public inspection and debate is a bad practice. The point is that without requirements for an equitable structure of resettlement budgets, oblique accounting will continue to "forget" the "intangibles."

Finally, according to the World Bank's resettlement policy, resettlement components in development projects are not expected to pay for themselves. This is one more reason why they should undergo a separate analysis. This analysis would factor in the costs of recovery and the *investments* needed for resettlers to reach specified income levels.

Underfinancing of Recovery and Development

Whether or not the methodology of economic and financial analyses at project level is adequate is not just an academic matter. The operational consequences upon financing levels for resettlement are enormous.

Lack of a rigorous and generally accepted methodology leaves room for large degrees of imprecision and arbitrariness in allocations. The result is the *underfinancing of resettlement operations* in project after project. Such underfinancing directly deprives projects and resettlers of the material means needed for postdisplacement recovery and development.

In exploring the causes of success or failure in a subset of 30 projects included in the Bank's resettlement review (World Bank 1994), Guggenheim found an unexpectedly high degree of variance in per-family project allocations of financial resources for resettlement. The variations were not due to intrinsic site differences, but rather to haphazard project approaches. The effects were striking. Analysis showed that resettlement projects with high financial allocations were free of major difficulties, while virtually all of the projects with a low allocation rate experienced serious implementation difficulties.

The same wide variance in project expenditure per displaced family was revealed recently, once again, by OED's research of eight Bank-assisted projects in India, China, Thailand, Togo, and Brazil (World Bank 1998). It, too, showed a correlation between resettlement outcomes and level of financing. Yet, despite the general good quality of this OED study, it failed to point to the *methodological* weaknesses in the economic and financial analyses of resettlement in the evaluated projects.

The underfinancing of involuntary resettlement also appears alarmingly arbitrary in John Eriksen's study comparing voluntary settlement projects with involuntary (see Eriksen in this volume). By comparing pairs of projects in five countries, he demonstrates that in almost all cases the economic and financial analysis was performed better, with an orientation towards growth, in *voluntary* resettlement projects. Paradoxically, voluntary resettlers were more abundantly supplied, financially and technically, than the people compelled to resettle against their will. This comparative analysis demonstrates that, independent of the complexity of forced displacement, failures originate largely in subjective bias and errors in financing strategy. The study concluded that fixing the problem requires changes in the planning paradigm and in technical and financial support for involuntary resettlement.

Increasing financing for growth-oriented resettlement would benefit not only resettlers, but overall project outcomes as well. World Bank research found that 70 hydropower dams co-financed by the Bank registered average cost overruns of 30 percent (inflation adjusted). But cost overruns are often at least partially due to up-front underestimates of the real cost of resettlement. Furthermore, underfinancing of resettlement frequently leads to delays in the start of power generation and irrigation, which inflict losses to the project that are larger altogether than the amount needed up-front to adequately finance the resettlement and prevent delays. Our research found that a one-year delay in revenue will reduce the difference between benefits and costs by almost one-third; a two-year delay, by more than half (World Bank 1994). Therefore, it pays to finance resettlement correctly from the outset.

Relying on those research findings, World Bank management adopted the recommendations of the 1993–94 Resettlement Task Force to increase the Bank's share in co-financing resettlement operations, particularly for growth-enhancing investments directed to resettlers. "To prevent impoverishment, all future Bank-assisted projects will internalize the full cost of resettlement and of the investments required for income restoration within total project costs" (World Bank 1994). The Bank firmly recommends to its borrowing governments to increase resettlement financing from domestic resources as well.

The Promise of an Economics of Recovery

To sum up, the overall argument of this chapter is that resettlement components in projects would gain enormously from economic research on resettlement and new economic analytical tools. Numerous topics in the economics of resettlement area hold great promise: the task is to gain momentum in the necessary professional economic research.

Priority Economic Research Areas

A relevant precedent convincingly suggests the great contribution that economics can make. Until recently environmental economics was little researched. Environmental losses and mitigation costs were externalized out of project budgets and overlooked in planning. But when the civic and political recognition of environmental concerns grew to become a powerful force, mainstream economics could no longer afford to ignore environmental losses. The result: both economic theory and environmental practice gained substantially. The economics of the environment has leapt ahead during the past two to three decades, helping to better quantify losses, prescribe economic remedies, and ground environmental projects and policies in solid economic and financial analysis.

Clearly, similar steps are much needed to build up the economics of resettlement into an economics of recovery.

Such economics has fertile ground from which to grow: its basic premises lie in welfare economics, environmental economics, partly in public goods economics, and more generally in development economics and political economy.

Specific areas where the economic concepts and methods for addressing involuntary resettlement need better articulation are:

- Undervaluation of losses; the market's role versus administrative expropriations
- Risks of decapitalization to the displacees and risk-insurance options
- Impoverishment of resettlers, relative or absolute, and the design of effective safety nets
- Patterns of externalization and internalization of displacements and recovery costs (including transaction costs to displacees)
- Criteria for financing resettlement components in projects
- Distributional inequities in projects entailing relocation
- Reestablishment of the productivity of displacees through growth-enhancing financial investments, additional to compensation.

This substantive agenda offers economists a vast territory that holds generous promise for research and for consistent translation of knowledge into *analytical tools* for projects. Such research would also help reorient the current economics of resettlement from a compensation–centered economics confined to repaying losses toward an economics of recovery and growth enhancement. In such a reorientation the overall research priority is to study *the reestablishment segment* of the displacement-resettlement continuum, complementing the analysis of impoverishment with that of the financial support needed from governments.

The dramas of sudden displacement have understandably attracted more observers than the slow and arduous efforts of rebuilding livelihoods. However, if economic research is to illuminate people's way out of displacement dramas, studying coping strategies and the rebuilding of production systems could help accelerate the recovery of future resettlers—the key to successful resettlement. Longitudinal and comparative studies stand to discover what works and what fails to help dismantled societies and local cultures reassemble and function within new environments.

Additional Lines of Argument

Without going into great detail, there are several other arguments that support the call for deeper economic knowledge about resettlement. First, macroeconomic policy analyses for domains relevant to resettlement could introduce pricing limits on the demand for commodities whose production causes displacement. Pricing policies should support tariffs that reflect all external costs, social and environmental. This is bound to make demand management more effective and may significantly diminish the alleged "need" for displacement.

Second, full internalization of cost and correct financial analysis and risk consideration will reduce the number of projects causing displacement by weeding out those that prove the investment unprofitable. That weeding process also opens the way for alternative less disruptive and more profitable investments.

Third, the overall economics of projects will improve by avoiding cost overruns caused by delays and forgone utility. Further improvements could arise from budgeting for targeted investments that produce a new stream of long-term benefits from the resettlement *with development* components.

Fourth, by further researching the economic and social dynamics of reestablishment, other levers and resources (of a nonfinancial nature) that reduce costs and accelerate recovery will come to light. The process of income restoration is far from being just a money matter: it is a complex social readjustment process that largely depends on cultural factors, too, including resettlers' forms of social organization, degree of cohesion, local leadership, mobilization of resettlers' energy, entrepreneurship, participation, and motivation.

These arguments strengthen the overall case for better economic analysis of resettlement.

Strong political commitment from governments and development sponsors (including the private sector) is also critical because resource allocation is ultimately a political matter. As government agencies use the weight of the state and the force of the law to impose expropriation and displacement, *it is incumbent upon governments also to enable those displaced to get back on their feet and share in the benefits for which they are displaced.*

Social Contributions to Economic Analysis

The ball, however, is not passed only into the economists' court: it also remains in the court of anthropologists, sociologists, and political scientists, who must do much more to promote cross-disciplinary cooperation with economists. The historic priority of the noneconomic social sciences in this area remains an asset that should not be turned into the liability of disciplinary isolation or sectarianism.

In the past, to obtain recognition for resettlement issues in development, anthropologists have had to fight intellectually, and sometimes institutionally, against "externalizations" of various kinds, including their own. In the World Bank, for example, professional "jurisdiction" based on competence has been sought and successfully obtained by anthropologists, out of concern that without due understanding of sociocultural issues the nature of forced population displacement would not be grasped. But the involvement of economists is already long overdue. Economic research should be invited and integrated, so that resettlement difficulties can be better understood and resolved.

Inside the World Bank we have taken this road, with partial success to date. However, on a world scale, beyond the Bank, the task of bringing in economic research and analysis has a long way to go, but is imperative.

In addition to cross-disciplinary cooperation, anthropologists and sociologists must look for new insights in their own fields, addressing in more detail the multiple *economic* variables of displacement from the perspective of their own specialties. Poverty and impoverishment are the heart of the matter in displacement, and one of the tools for analyzing them is the impoverishment risks and reconstruction framework, outlined earlier in this chapter (see, for more detail, Cernea 1997). This conceptual model is increasingly being used for both in-depth socioeconomic analysis and improved planning (Thangaraj 1996; Ota 1996; Spiegel 1997; Pandey and others 1998; Mathur and Marsden 1998; Mohapatra, Ota, and Mohanti 1998; Mahapatra 1999).

Modeling impoverishment risks has led to further explorations about economic counteractions to risks, such as searching for a system of risk insurance, outlining new kinds of "insurance products" and safety net policy provisions (Downing 1998), or linking the risks and reconstruction model with the "basic needs" framework in conceptualizing recovery (Basu 1996; see also on broader safety net experiences, Subbarao and others 1996).

Anthropological fieldwork should also generate long series of empirical data—using the displaced household as unit of analysis and household budgets as the measuring tool—recording incomes and expenditures, before and after displacement.

Such data are surprisingly scarce. Gender-based economic comparisons are another angle for innovative research, as some good studies (Köenig and Diarra 1999, Feeney 1995) have demonstrated. Sociological research in Spain has found that when the would-be resettlers themselves "shifted" their arguments about the risks caused by an impending dam from the "cultural" arguments to the economic and technical risks, their case became much more convincing to the government authorities—what Mairal and Bergna (1996) called a successful "argumental detour." Longitudinal studies on resettled populations, like those advocated by Scudder and Colson, can be powerful in measuring economic variables over time, particularly along the various stages of the Scudder-Colson model (Scudder and Colson 1982; Scudder 1985, 1993). And, of course, we shouldn't forget anthropology's specialized branch—economic anthropology—which is well positioned to integrate the cultural and the economic in resettlement inquiry.

The sober analysis of global trends tells us that involuntary resettlement will not disappear. It is actually likely to increase because of urban growth, demographic trends, infrastructural investments, irrigation needs, and policy-induced (as distinct from project-induced) population displacements. But if a certain degree of displacement cannot be avoided, then the standing challenge is to improve its standards and the overall body of knowledge—both economic and social—apt to guide it.

APPENDIX
Brief Overview of the State of the Art
in Social Research on Involuntary Resettlement

Historically, the study of involuntary population resettlements as a consequence of purposive development programs began about six or seven decades ago, but only during the 1960s did it start to expand in earnest. Anthropologists and sociologists took the lead in this research from the outset, initiating resettlement research long before the issue became subject to public policy and analysis by other disciplines.

Empirical sociological studies on involuntary resettlement have been carried out in both developed and developing countries. In developed countries, one of the first seminal contributions was Herbert Gans' research in the 1960s in the United States on urban involuntary relocation in the Boston area (Gans 1968). Laying the early foundations of research and knowledge about involuntary resettlement in developing countries are anthropologists Roy-Burman (1961) in India, Colson and Scudder's field studies in the 1960s on the Gwembe Tonga (see Colson 1971; Scudder 1962, 1973), Brokensha and Scudder (1968), Butcher (1971), sociologist Juan Fernando Mesa in Colombia (1969), political scientist Chambers (1970) in Africa, and others.

Yet officials—including governments and international agencies, policymakers, and economic planners alike—have overlooked this scholarly knowledge and its implications for general development policymaking, as well as for the practice of project design. Only two decades ago, around 1979, was this general official indifference finally broken by the World Bank. At that time the Bank took the initiative to adopt an operational policy on resettlement (see beginning of chapter 1 and Cernea 1986, 1988). This was the first time that a major international

development agency turned to social research on resettlement and to social scientists for crafting a policy approach to the thorny, layered problems of involuntary displacement. Based on in-house proposals, Bank
management issued explicit guidelines on how staff should treat involuntary resettlement under Bank-financed projects and on the Bank's expectations from borrowing governments (World Bank 1980; Cernea
1986, 1993–94).

This major policy breakthrough also institutionally and intellectually affirmed the contribution of social knowledge to policymaking.

From then on, operational social research on resettlement has been
strongly promoted for Bank-assisted projects, at headquarters, and in
many developing countries. Some of the world's best resettlement social
specialists were invited to contribute (as regular staff or as consultants),
and since then, the World Bank has become the world's most important
hub of social research on resettlement. The social scientists associated
with it have produced a vast number of policy and applied studies, theoretical publications, field surveys, and impact evaluation analyses, while
incorporating their knowledge into development processes through
"hands on" work. Relying on the expanding contributions of its social scientists, resettlement institutionally became recognized as a "topic which
touches upon the central aspects of the Bank's work" (Qureshi 1989).

Interestingly enough, legal minds inside the Bank responded much
faster to these social issues than its economic theoreticians. Issues of legal philosophy and the Bank's position were analyzed for the first time
and were conceptually defined (Shihata 1991, 1993) in terms that were
novel to the existing legal literature worldwide. Accordingly, legal procedures regarding resettlement were patterned for the "legal agreements" concluded between the Bank and governments for loans and
credits (Escudero 1989).

More recently, the Bank's Legal Department issued explicit and detailed "Guidelines for Lawyers" (LEGOP 1996) to address legal and policy issues in projects involving resettlement, guidelines derived from
the Bank's resettlement policy document. Notably, the attention of
many governments was forcefully drawn to the resettlement issues
through policy and legal dialogues initiated by the Bank.

Operational needs often stimulate new intellectual inquiry. Social
science research on involuntary resettlement is a case in point. Its
growth has been explosive—in dissertations and books, major studies in
journals, national and international conferences, policy documents and
evaluation reports, university syllabi, training courses, and briefs for
parliamentary hearings or courts of law. Over the past 15 years this
growth has practically established a topical resettlement subfield in
development anthropology and sociology, causing the intellectual

resettlement-development nexus to swell. The first annotated bibliography of the global resettlement literature, published by Scott Guggenheim (1994), impressively documents this growth.

The public perception of involuntary displacement as a problem of global dimension owes much to this surge in research and publications. In turn, the growing resistance of many affected populations against displacement and the militancy of nongovernmental organizations have endeavored to recast forced displacement as a key political and economic issue in development.

What then defines the major advances over the past 15 to 20 years of social research on involuntary resettlement? I characterize this gain in research and knowledge as follows.

Intensive, "Thick" Knowledge

Today, social knowledge about displacement is shrinking the gaps, going deeper than ever before. To use a common concept in anthropology, it is "thick knowledge." Cognitive gains have been made through refining the understanding of how displacement occurs, in content and in consequences, though our knowledge of the meandering processes of recovery (or lack thereof) that follow remains less advanced.

This remarkable deepening of knowledge is primarily the product of an unprecedented hands-on involvement of scores of social scientists during the past 15 years in actual development programs that entail displacement. Groups of sociologists and anthropologists left behind their roles as "observers" of such processes and became "participant actors," using their expertise to prevent or minimize displacement. They also help to correct its adverse consequences on the ground by improving the planning, supervision, ongoing analysis, and *ex post* evaluation of operations.

Although this type of *operational action research* is still little heralded, from my vantage point in overseeing the implementation of the World Bank resettlement policy for over 20 years I can stand witness to the good analytical quality, detailed action-oriented prescriptions, and sharpened operational expertise achieved by scores of resettlement social scientists (Bank staff and consultants). They are making a tangible contribution to protecting the welfare of people caught in involuntary displacement processes.

More Extensive Knowledge

Basic social knowledge about population resettlement has also grown extensively by expanding geographic coverage, which increases opportunities for comparative analysis among countries, and by including previously unstudied sectors of the economy that also trigger involuntary resettlement.

During the 1960s and 1970s, most of the knowledge about resettlement resulted from research on urban displacements (done mainly by sociologists in industrial countries) and research on dam-caused displacements (done mainly by anthropologists in developing countries). Over the past 15 years, however, considerable empirical research has been devoted to displacements occurring in other sectors, affecting different population groups. Forced relocations unrelated to development projects have also been more systematically studied.

Among the sectors of the economy encompassed in recent social research are *forestry* (Turnbull 1987; Fernandes, Das, and Rao 1989); *mining*, especially open-pit mining and the construction of thermal power plants (Ray 1994a, 1994b; Hall 1991; and the large literature on Singrauli); *biosphere reserves and parks* established for environmental reasons (West and Brechin 1991, Brandon and Wells 1992); *conversions in land use* from pasture to agriculture (Lane 1996); *transportation corridors* (roads, highways, power transmission lines, canals); *urban* and *environmental infrastructure* in developing countries (Cernea 1989; Jellinek 1991; Davidson and others 1993; Reddi 1992, 1994); *politically mandated* mass relocation (Clay 1988, Pankhurst 1992, Dieci and Viezolli 1992, de Wet 1993); or resettlement caused by structural adjustment reforms.

Research on resettlement has also expanded geographically, to include all continents. Much of this expansion has been to countries where no such inquiry has been carried out before. And in countries with a tradition in such research, the expansion has been to new topics. In Africa, for example, experiences with high dams on the Volta, Zambezi, and Nile rivers have been the basis of classic anthropological writings on displacement. But a second generation of studies has produced empirical information from new countries that illuminates new facets of resettlement (see the 1994 volume on resettlement in Africa by Cook 1994, Cook and Ivarsdotter 1994, Adams 1991, Mburugu 1994, McMillan 1995, Oyedipe 1987, Scudder 1993, Salem-Murdock 1989, Hansen 1990, Roder 1994, Cernea 1997, and many others).

In Latin America, the pioneering studies of Alfonso Villa Rojas and Fernando Camaro Barbachano on the Mazatec resettlement have been followed by significant research on dam-related and urban resettlement (Partridge 1993; Partridge, Brown, and Nugent 1982; Bartolome and Barabas 1973, 1990; Wali 1989; de Santos and de Andrade 1990; Bartolome 1992; Serra 1993; Hall 1987; Guggenheim 1994; Mejía 1996; see also Mejía in this volume; Ribeiro 1994; Posey 1996).

In Europe, recent writings on resettlement address more the political and moral issues involved in development aid given by European donors to developing countries (Usher 1997, Lassailly-Jacob 1998, Conac 1995) than the displacement process taking place in European countries (except for Turkey, see Kudat, Bayram, and Hajai 1996, 1997). In fact, involuntary resettlements continue to take place in some largely industrialized, densely populated countries (to build railways for the new high-speed train, in France; for airports, in Japan and in France). But research on such processes, to my knowledge, is still too limited.

In Asia, the resettlement literature has registered the largest and undoubtedly the fastest growth in India. India's social scientists have devoted much research to the impact of displacement on tribal groups and scheduled castes (Fernandes, Das, and Rao 1989; Mahapatra 1994; Pandey 1998a). The growing literature on dam-related displacements, particularly on Narmada Sardar Sarovar dam, enriched the debate with new topics—from the role of the state to resettlers' resistance (Thukral 1992; Fernandes and Thukral 1989; Joshi 1987, 1991; Singh 1992; Baboo 1992; Mathur 1994; Baviskar 1995; Fisher 1995; Gill 1995; Drèze, Samson, and Singh 1997; Mathur and Marsden 1998; Mohapatra, Ota, and Mohanty 1998; see also Mahapatra, in this volume, for a discussion of resettlement research in India).

Also a series of statistical syntheses, state by state , was started with a volume on resettlement in Orissa State (Fernandes and Asif 1997). Increasing specialization in resettlement research is illustrated by the landmark volume on legal frameworks governing resettlement practice published by Fernandes and Paranjpye (1997) and other legal studies (Ramanathan 1995, 1996), by books and studies on displacement in the mining sector (Ray 1994a, Pandey 1998b, Areeparampil 1996), and by studies in other industries (Reddi 1994).

China's creation of a National Research Center on Resettlement (NRCR) has multiplied exponentially the studies of Chinese experiences in resettlement (NRCR 1995, 1996; Huang 1984; Wangxiang 1993; Shi 1996a, 1996b), proving that country's continuous interest in measuring the economic impacts of displacements and their remedies. Expanding resettlement research carried out in China by outside scholars complements the work of Chinese researchers (Barth and Williams 1994; Meikle and Zhu 1999).

Altogether, the broadened empirical base creates favorable circumstances for new theorizing and generalization in resettlement.

From Description to Prescription

Resettlement research has made considerable strides in advancing from descriptions to prescriptions and from academic study to operational research and applied work—a profound change in the state of the art.

Early writings on resettlement did not venture far into the territory of recommendations. One exception was the early "handbook" written by Butcher (1971) for the Food and Agricultural Organization (FAO), which, despite its high quality, was in practice totally ignored (Butcher 1979) by FAO and by other development agencies. Over the past 15 years, however, the anthropologists and sociologists from the World Bank, at work on hundreds and hundreds of projects, have studied not only how displacement affects resettlers but also how countless agencies around the world plan, finance, manage, and execute resettlement processes (Butcher 1990; Cernea 1986, 1997; Cook 1994; Guggenheim 1989, 1994; Mejía 1996; Partridge 1989; Rew and Driver 1986; World Bank 1994; and other writings, most of which are not yet published). This latter research has led to new knowledge about the administrative, institutional, and legal mechanics of resettlement operations, including the roots of failure and of success.

This firmer prescriptive posture taken by social scientists shows their growing confidence and the maturing of resettlement as a field of study. The group of resettlement specialists at the World Bank has synthesized much of these experiences in a first electronic "guidebook" on resettlement work (Gill, Gibson, Field, and Schaengold 1998), which makes available a rich inventory of approaches and methods. In turn, the Asian Development Bank (ADB) has sponsored the elaboration of several training manuals for practitioners on project resettlement issues (ADB 1995, 1998a, 1998b), which help to disseminate policy ideas and to improve procedures. Practitioners of applied anthropology and sociology are making some of their finest contributions ever, triggering landmark changes in how resettlement processes take place.

Policy Formulation

Social research on involuntary resettlement has come of age by crossing the difficult threshold from micro to macro, moving from writing piecemeal ethnographies on localized resettlement to crafting general policy frameworks.

Case-focused ethnographies describe past processes. Policies guide forthcoming activities. Of course, case studies remain a staple of today's research, but there is much to gain from articulating credible policy frameworks. The technical and conceptual work of professional social scientists has been decisive, not only in advancing the World Bank's resettlement policy, but also the policy of all donor agencies representing the 25 countries in the Organisation for Economic Cooperation and Development (OECD 1992), the resettlement policy of the Asian Development Bank (ADB 1995), and other agencies.

Social science has played a similar role in formulating national or sectoral resettlement policies in Brazil, Central African Republic, Colombia, Guyana, Indonesia, Jamaica, Uganda, Vietnam, and other countries. Most significant is the current growing debate in India over the adoption of a national resettlement policy and of related state policies (see Fernandes and Paranjpye 1997).

But we should not overstate the achievements. While social science has helped to articulate resettlement policies in several countries, policy adoption has yet to occur routinely everywhere. Political and bureaucratic obstacles continue to impede the incorporation of social science research into policy and law. In scores of developing countries, resettlement policies and laws do not exist and are far from being adopted—or even contemplated (Cernea 1996).

Measurements and Quantification

Much of the past "softness" in social science fieldwork has been replaced by statistics building. More precise measurements of displacement and relocation processes and their empirically observable impacts have succeeded in estimating the magnitudes of national and global development–induced displacements, producing a comprehensive image of the process.

Through collecting, verifying, and combining a vast body of data, our group at the World Bank has generated the most significant worldwide estimate. Though conservative, it is nothing less than stunning: we found that about *10 million people annually* enter the cycle of forced displacement and relocation just in the sectors of dam construction and urban and transportation development (World Bank 1994). That means that in the past decade about 100 million people have been displaced.

This magnitude is comparable to the refugee crisis, long recognized as a major international problem. Development-caused displacements—which appear piecemeal and to total far less than the number of war and natural disaster refugees (estimated by UNHCR at 15 to 20 million worldwide)—turn out to involve more people than all the world's refugee flows. Of course, refugees and development displacees are not "numbers" that compete with each other: they are global parallel dramas, sometimes intertwined. But the quantifications are part of the "social construction" of forced resettlement as a worldwide issue, and the comparison increases public attention to resettlement issues.

We must also note that the estimate of 100 million people displaced over 10 years does not include displacements from forests and reserve parks, mining and thermal power plants, and other comparable situations. Reliable aggregate data for all sectors worldwide are needed to capture more fully the magnitude of the process.

New Theory and Models

The Scudder-Colson framework has informed and inspired the field-work of numerous resettlement researchers since its publication in the early 1980s (Scudder and Colson 1982, Scudder 1985). This diachronic model identifies four stages of a *successful* resettlement operation—recruitment, transition, potential development, and incorporation—with each stage tracking resettlers' behavioral response patterns to the disruptions and stress caused by relocation. When resettlements are not successful, the stage framework does not apply.

In the 1990s, theoretical work on resettlement evolved further, and the impoverishment risks and livelihood reconstruction model was formulated (Cernea 1990a, 1991, 1995, 1996, 1997, and 1998b). This model is synchronic, yet it also captures the process of moving from displacement to relocation and recovery. It conceptualizes the *economic and social content* of both displacement and reestablishment processes. In this model, the behavior of displaced populations is explained as a response to a range of potential impoverishment risks (or realities)—*economic, cultural, and social*—and it incorporates the risks of decapitalization and community unraveling. This theoretical framework can be used as a tool for predicting, diagnosis and planning, problem solving, and research on resettlement. Most important, the model suggests *action strategies* and focuses on the heart of the matter in resettlement: *preventing* pauperization and *reconstructing* livelihoods.

This conceptual model has been widely discussed and adopted as a guide for preparing resettlement and recovery components in projects. It is currently at work in numerous field studies and in strategies to counter impoverishment in India, Vietnam, the Philippines, and China (see Agnihotri 1996; Basu 1996; Downing 1996; Joseph 1998; Pandey 1998; Mathur and Marsden 1998; Mohapatra, Ota, and Mohanty 1998; Ota 1996; Thangaraj 1996; Spiegel 1997; Nayak 1999; see also Mahapatra, in this volume). Some researchers have also explored its application to the study of refugee populations (Kibreab 1999).

Resistance to Displacement

Resistance to development has heightened in many countries, and opposition led by nongovernmental organizations (NGOs) has become more politically oriented during the past decade. But it was not until this decade that anthropological research "discovered" this resistance as a big theme and started to focus its analytical lens upon its structure, growth, composition, and impacts (Oliver-Smith 1991b, 1996; Good 1992; Gray 1996; Kothari 1995; Posey 1996; Dhagamwar, Thukral, and

Singh 1995). Such opposition has been encouraged by an expanding and powerful international critique of dam building, solidly documented in studies generated by environmental NGOs (McCully 1996, Udall 1995). This expanding segment of the resettlement literature is increasingly influential and has contributed directly to the establishment of the World Commission of Dams in 1998, among other outcomes.

The several characteristics of knowledge progress I have defined here summarize the current state of the art in social research on resettlement. The anthropological and sociological communities can be proud to have collectively expanded in depth and breadth, "intensive" and "extensive" knowledge expansion; to have shifted from academic analysis alone to operational research on a vast scale, from description to prediction and prescription, from deploring ill effects to also charting ways to overcome them; to have moved up from case micro-ethnographies to macro policy formulation; from narrating discrete resettlement instances to measuring and quantifying aggregates and worldwide trends; to have renewed its theory with poverty-center frameworks and analysis; and to have expanded its topics and perspective by including the study of resettlers' resistance to displacement, social opposition, and NGO-led movements. The "on the ground" positive effects are embodied in many tangible improvements accomplished in resettlement programs and policies worldwide.

Acknowledgements

From my many economist colleagues, I drew considerable wisdom and realism about the economic anatomy of development. From my own experience, I realized that the highest benefits are obtained when sociologists and economists reinforce each other in linking the economic and social analyses of development interventions.

Enriched with these lessons, I want to thank specifically those economists who, in preparing studies for this volume or in discussing resettlement issues throughout the years, as well as in other circumstances of my own development work, have contributed their advice, guidance, suggestions, or criticisms. Many of their comments have been taken directly into account in articulating the argument of this chapter. My debt is substantial to Irma Adelman, Leif Christoffersen, Herman Daly, John Page, Michel Petit, Robert Picciotto, Joanne Salop, G. Edward Schuh, Andrew Steer, Paul Streeten, Herman van der Tak, Vijay Vyas, Montague Yudelman, and, in fact, to a much larger number of economist colleagues than I can name here.

Suggestions and feedback from many resettlement specialists, particularly my late friend David Butcher, Ashraf Ghani, Scott Guggenheim, William Partridge, Ted Scudder, and, not in little measure, Ruth Cernea, have strengthened my argument for the need to develop not only social but also economic knowledge about resettlement. My thanks go to all of them.

Part of this paper was included in the Honorary Elizabeth Colson Lecture that I was invited to present at the University of Oxford, RSP, in May 1998. I thank also those whose questions and comments on that lecture helped to sharpen my argument.

Notes

1. This point was also developed and documented by Robert Picciotto with OED-generated evidence in a lecture given in June 1998 on the findings of OED's 1998 study on resettlement experiences.

2. This economic book was published three years *after* the famous Morse report (Morse, Berger, Brody, and Gamble 1992) was made public. That independent report severely criticized the socioeconomics of the Narmada Sardar Sarovar project, particularly on resettlement issues. Yet the book by Alagh and others and their economic reappraisal didn't give any response to the critique of Sardar Sarovar's economics by the Morse report.

3. Most governments use the might of the law and their institutional instruments to forcibly displace people, but they do not sufficiently use their institutional capacities to facilitate "land for land" alternatives. They rely instead on cash compensation.

4. See Guidelines for the Economic and Financial analysis of Project Components Addressing Involuntary Resettlement. Annex 2 in Cernea, Michael, *Involuntary Resettlement in Development Projects: Policy Guidelines in World Bank-Financed Projects*, World Bank Technical Paper No. 80, 1988, Washington, D.C.

5. The only significant country exception is China, where internal guidelines require planners to do a meticulous inventory of all displacement costs and an equally meticulous projection of the economic components of livelihood recovery.

6. The authors of that study recommended, among other measures, the "reinstatement of a Central Projects Unit (in the World Bank) to both provide assistance to project analysts and exert a degree of quality control" in the interest of the Bank's "development impact and the quality of its portfolio" (Devarajan, Squire, and Suthiwart-Narueput 1995, p. 27).

7. We have moved since to a more encompassing concept in the World Bank, that of "resettlement specialist," who is not always and necessarily an anthropologist; in some cases she or he is an economist or technical expert.

8. We also know that sociocultural variables have been frequently overlooked in economic analyses in many other areas as well. Since the early 1980s an increasing number of anthropologists and sociologists have argued that traditional economic analysis misrepresents reality by failing to acknowledge essential social factors (Swedberg 1993, Granovetter 1988, Smelser and Swedberg 1994). Such concerns have propelled exciting developments in the field of economic sociology, illuminating essential economic variables and processes through social analysis.

9. The Bank's resettlement policy describes the advisory role of the Legal Department with respect to policy and legal issues arising from the involuntary resettlement of people. It requires that the Bank's legal experts review the domestic laws and regulations of the borrowing country and the legal aspects of project resettlement plans. Further, the participation of the Legal Department is required throughout the project cycle. Along with these policy provisions, the Legal Department has defined the lawyers' responsibilities and the kind of advice and inputs they must provide, as their professional obligation, during the identification, appraisal, negotiation, and implementation of projects involving resettlement operations. The guidelines for lawyers refer to such important aspects as defining the project concept, land acquisition, valuation and compensation for assets, the rights of the project-affected people, eligibility criteria; provision of rehabilitation measures; monitoring and impact evaluation arrangements, and so forth. The guidelines also define what must be included, as a minimum, in the legal agreements between the Bank and the loan- or credit-receiving country, so as to establish the obligations of the borrower and the implementing agency as a legal contract between the Bank and the borrowing country (see LEGOP 1996, Sherif Omar Hasan "OD 4.30—Involuntary Resettlement: Guidelines for Lawyers," prepared by Carlos Escudero).

10. The bibliographic references provided for these domains, and for the burgeoning research in various countries, are intended as examples rather than as a comprehensive listing of all relevant publications. Certainly, an updated international bibliography, to following up on Guggenheim (1994), would be a useful tool for further comparative research and analysis.

11. Comparable examples can be provided from the work of other practicing social scientists in various national and international agencies or research centers, such as the Indian Social Institute, New Delhi; the Institute of Development Anthropology, Binghamton, New York; the Refugee Studies Programme of the University of Oxford, England; the National Research Center on Resettlement in China; and others.

References

The word "processed" describes informally reproduced works that may not be commonly available through libraries.

Adams, W. M. 1991. *Wasting the Rain: Rivers, People, and Planning in Africa*. London: Earthscan Publications.

ADB (Asian Development Bank). 1995. *Indonesia: Operational Guidelines for Resettlement Management in Road Projects: A Handbook*. Manila: ADB and Government of Indonesia, Directorate General of Highways.

_____. 1998a. *Handbook on Resettlement: A Guide to Good Practice*. Manila: ADB, Office of Environment and Social Development, processed. Prepared by M. Zaman.

_____. 1998b. *Manual for Land Acquisition and Resettlement Management in Water Resources Development Projects*. (draft) Manila: ADB and Government of Indonesia, Directorate General of Water Resources Development. Prepared by M. Zaman and Sheladia Associates, Inc.

Agnihotri, Anita. 1996. "The Orissa Resettlement and Rehabilitation of Project-Affected Persons Policy, 1994: An Analysis of its Robustness with Reference to the Impoverishment Risk Model." In A. B. Ota and A. Agnihotri, eds., *Involuntary Displacement in Dam Projects*. New Delhi: Prachi Prakashan.

Alagh, Y. K., R. D. Desai, G. S. Guha, and S. P. Kashyap. 1995. *Economic Dimensions of the Sardar Sarovar Project*. Delhi: Har-Anand Publications.

Areeparampil, Mathew. 1996. "Displacement due to Mining in Kharkhand." *Economic and Political Weekly*, 31:24.

Baboo, Balgovind. 1992. *Technology and Social Transformation: The Case of the Hirakud Multi-Purpose Dam Project in Orissa*. Delhi: Concept Publishing.

Baird, Mark. 1996. "Economists and Economic Work in the World Bank," DEC Notes, Policy directions, nr. 24. World Bank, Washington, D.C. Processed.

Bardhan, Pranab, ed. 1989. *Conversations between Economists and Anthropologists: Methodological Issues in Measuring Economic Change in Rural India*. New Delhi: Oxford University Press.

Barth, Fredrik, and T. R. Williams. 1994. "Initial Resettlement Planning and Activity (1992–1994) in a Large Scale Hydropower Process: The Ertan Dam in Southwest China." World Bank, Washington, D.C. Processed.

Bartolome, Miguel, and Alicia Barabas. 1973. "Hydraulic Development and Ethnocide: The Mazatec and Chinantec People of Oaxaca, Mexico," Copenhagen: IWGIA.

_____. 1990. *La presa Cerro de Oro y el ingeniero El Gran Dios*, Mexico DF: Instituto Nacional Indigenista.

Basu, Malika. 1996. "Basic Needs Approach in Displacement Situations." *Mainstream*, 24, July-August.

Baviskar, Anita. 1995. *In the Belly of the Beast*. New Delhi: Oxford University Press.

Brandon, Katrina, and Michael Wells. 1992. *People and Parks: Linking Protected Area Management with Local Communities*. Washington, D.C.: World Bank.

Brokensha, David, and Thayer Scudder. 1968. "Resettlement." In N. Rubin and W. M. Warren, eds. *Dams in Africa: An Interdisciplinary Study of Man-Made Lakes in Africa*. London: Frank Cass.

Butcher, David. 1971. *An Operational Manual for Resettlement: A Systematic Approach to the Resettlement Problem Created by Man-Made Lakes, with Special Relevance for West Africa.* Rome: FAO.

_____. 1979. Personal communication.

_____. 1990. "Review of the Treatment of Environmental Aspects of Bank Energy Projects." PRE Working Paper. Industry and Energy Department, World Bank, Washington, D.C. Processed.

Cernea, Michael M. 1986. "Involuntary Resettlement in Bank-Assisted Projects: A Review of the Application of Bank Policies and Procedures in FY97-85 Projects." World Bank, Agriculture and Rural Development Department, Washington, D.C. Processed.

_____. 1988. *Involuntary Resettlement in Development Projects: Policy Guidelines in World Bank–Financed Projects.* World Bank Technical Paper 80. Washington, D.C.: World Bank.

_____. 1989. "Metropolitan Development and Compulsory Population Relocation: Policy Issues and Project Experiences." *Regional Development Dialogue,* 10(4).

_____. 1990a. *Poverty Risks from Population Displacement in Water Resource Projects.* DDP 355. Cambridge, Mass.: Harvard University, HIID.

_____. 1991. "Involuntary Resettlement: Social Research, Policy, and Planning." In Michael M. Cernea, ed., *Putting People First: Sociological Variables in Development.* 2nd ed. New York: Oxford University Press.

_____. 1993. "Social Science Research and the Crafting of Policy on Population Resettlement." *Knowledge and Policy: The International Journal of Knowledge Transfer and Utilization.* Fall/winter 1993/94, 6:3–4, 176–200.

_____. 1995. "Understanding and Preventing Impoverishment: The State of Knowledge in Resettlement." *Journal of Refugee Studies.* December.

_____. 1996a. "Public Policy Responses to Development-Induced Population Displacement." *Economic and Political Weekly.* (India) 31 (June 15): 1515–23.

_____. 1996b. "Bridging the Research Divide: Studying Refugees and Development Oustees." In Tim Allen, ed., *In Search of Cool Ground: Displacement and Homecoming in Northeast Africa.* London: James Currey.

_____. 1997. "The Risks and Reconstruction Model for Resettling Displaced Populations." *World Development* 25 (October): 1569–87.

_____. 1998a. "La sociologie des déplacements forcés: un modèle théorique." In V. Laissailly-Jacobs, ed., *Communautées deracinées dans les pays du Sud.* Paris: Autrepart, ORSTOM.

_____. 1998b. "Economics and the Private Sector: Open Issues in Resettlement Research." The 1998 Colson Lecture, University of Oxford, RSP, May 13. Processed.

_____. Forthcoming. "A Theoretical Model for Population Displacement and Resettlement." In Michael M. Cernea and Chris McDowell, eds., *Reconstructing Livelihoods: Theory and Practice—Resettlers' and Refugees' Experiences.* Washington, D.C.: World Bank.

Chambers, Robert, ed. 1970. *The Volta Resettlement Experience*. London: Pall Mall Press.

Clay, Jason W. 1988. "Villagization in Ethiopia." In J. Clay, S. Steingraber, and P. Niggli, eds., *The Spoils of Famine*. Cambridge, Mass.: Cultural Survival.

Colson, Elizabeth. 1971. *The Social Consequences of Resettlement: The Impact of the Kariba Resettlement on the Gwembe Tonga*. Manchester, U.K.: Manchester University Press.

Cook, Cynthia C., ed., 1994. *Involuntary Resettlement in Africa*. Washington, D.C.: World Bank.

Cook, Cynthia C., and Kristine Ivarsdotter. 1994. "Development and Displacement: Resettlement Review for the Africa Region." World Bank, Africa Technical Department, Washington, D.C. Processed.

Conac, Françoise, ed. 1995. *Barrages internationaux et coopération*, Paris: Karthala.

Cornia, Giovanni Andrea, Richard Jolly, and Frances Stewart, eds. 1987. *Adjustment with a Human Face*. New York: Oxford University Press.

Davidson, Forbes, and others. 1993. *Relocation and Resettlement Manual: A Guide to Managing and Planning Relocation*. Rotterdam: IHS.

de Santos, Leinad, and Lucia M. M. de Andrade, eds. 1990. *Hydroelectric Dams on Brazil's Xingu River and Indigenous People*. London: Cambridge University Press.

Devarajan, S., L. Squire, and S. Suthiwart. 1995. "Reviving Project Appraisal at the World Bank." World Bank, Policy Research Department, Washington, D.C. Processed.

de Wet, C. 1993. "A Spatial Analysis of Involuntary Community Relocation: A South African Case Study." In M. Cernea and S. Guggenheim, eds., *Anthropological Approaches to Resettlement: Policy, Practice, and Theory*. Boulder, Colo.: Westview Press.

Dhagamwar, Vasuda, E. Ganguly Thukral, and M. Singh.1995. "The Sardar Sarovar Project: A Study in Sustainable Development." In W. Fisher, ed., *Toward Sustainable Development: Struggling over India's Narmada River*. Armonk, N.Y.: M. E. Sharpe.

Diara, T., D. Koenig, Y. F. Kone, and M. F. Maiga. 1995. "Reinstallation et development dans la zone du barrage de Manantali." Bamako. Processed.

Dieci, Paolo, and Claudia Viezolli, eds. 1992. *Resettlement and Rural Development in Ethiopia*. Milano: Franco Angeli.

Douglas, Mary, and Aaron Wildawski. 1982. *Risk and Culture: The Selections of Technological and Environmental Dangers*. Berkeley, CA: University of California Press.

Downing, Theodore E. 1994. "Social Geometrics: A Theory of Social Displacement in Resettlement." Paper presented at the International Congress of the Americanists. Stockholm/Uppsala, Sweden. Processed.

_____. 1996. "Mitigating Social Impoverishment When People Are Involuntarily Displaced." In C. McDowell, ed., *Understanding Impoverishment*. Oxford and Providence: Berghahn.

_____. 1998. "Protecting the Widow's Mite: Designing Local Environmental Risk Insurance." Paper presented at the Annual SRAA Meetings, San Jose, Puerto Rico. Processed.

Drèze, J., M. Samson, and S. Singh, eds. 1997. *The Dam and the Nation: Displacement and Resettlement in the Narmada Valley*. Delhi: Oxford University Press.

Escudero, Carlos R. 1988. "Involuntary Resettlement in Bank-Assisted Projects: An Introduction to Legal Issues." World Bank, Legal Department, Washington, D.C. Processed.

Fabre, Pierre. 1997. *Financial and Economic Analysis of Development Projects: Manual*. Luxembourg: European Commission, Methods and Instruments for Project Cycle Management.

Feeney, Patricia. 1995. *Displacement and the Rights of Women*. Oxford: Oxfam.

Fernandes, Walter. Forthcoming 1999. "From Marginalization to Sharing the Project Benefits." In Michael M. Cernea and Chris McDowell, eds., *Reconstructing Livelihoods*. Washington, D.C.: World Bank.

Fernandes, Walter, and Mohammed Asif. 1997. *Development-Induced Displacement and Rehabilitation in Orissa 1951 to 1995: A Database on its Extent and Nature*. New Delhi: ISI.

Fernandes, Walter, J. C. Das, and Sam Rao. 1989. "Displacement and Rehabilitation: An Estimate of Extent and Prospects." In W. Fernandes and E. Ganguly Thukral, eds., *Development, Displacement and Rehabilitation*. New Delhi: ISI.

Fernandes, Walter, and Vijay Paranjpye, eds. 1997. *Rehabilitation Policy and Law in India: A Right to Livelihood*. Delhi: ISI and Pune: Econet.

Fernandes, Walter, and Enakshi Ganguly Thukral, eds. 1989. *Development, Displacement and Rehabilitation*. New Delhi: ISI.

Fisher, William F., ed. 1995. *Towards Sustainable Development? Struggling Over India's Narmada River*. Armonk, N.Y.: M. E. Sharpe.

Gans, Herbert J. 1968. *People and Plans: Essays on Urban Problems and Solutions*. New York: Basic Books.

Gibson, Daniel R. 1993. "The Politics of Involuntary Resettlement: World Bank–Supported Projects in Asia." Ph.D. dissertation, Department of Political Science, Duke University. Processed.

Gill, Maninder S. 1995. "Resettlement and Rehabilitation in Maharashtra for the Sardar Sarovar Project." In W. F. Fisher, ed. *Towards Sustainable Development? Struggling Over India's Narmada River*. Armonk, N.Y.: M. E. Sharpe.

Gill, M., D. Gibson, A. Fields, and E. Schaengold. 1998. "Resettlement Guidebook." World Bank, Washington, D.C. Processed.

Goyal, Sangeeta. 1996. "Economic Perspectives on Resettlement and Rehabilitation." *Economic and Political Weekly*, June 15.

Gray, Andrew. 1996. "Indigenous Resistance to Involuntary Relocation." In Christopher McDowell, ed., *Understanding Impoverishment: The Consequences of Development-Induced Displacement*. Providence: Berghahn.

Guggenheim, Scott E. 1989. "Development and the Dynamics of Displacement." In Al Fernandes, ed., *Workshop on Rehabilitation of Persons Displaced by Development Projects*. Bangalore: Myrada.

_____. 1994. "Involuntary Resettlement: An Annotated Reference Bibliography for Development Research." Environment Working Paper 64, World Bank, Washington, D.C. Processed.

Hall, Anthony. 1987. "Agrarian Crisis in Brazilian Amazonia: The Grande Carajas Programme." *Journal of Development Studies*. 23(4, July): 522–552.

_____. 1991. "O Programa Grande Caragas genese e evoluçao." In Jean Hebette, ed., *O Cerco Esta be Fechand*. Vozes FASE NAEA: Petropolis-Rio-Belem.

_____. 1992. "From Victims to Victors: NGOs and the Politics of Employment at Itaparica." In David Hulme and Mike Edwards, eds., *Making A Difference*. London: Earthscan.

Hansen, Art. 1990. "Long-term Consequences of Two African Refugee Settlement Strategies." Paper presented at the meetings of the Society for Applied Anthropology. York, U.K. Processed.

Huang, Yao Fei. 1984. "On the Reform of Resettlement Policies in China." *Chinese Journal of Water Conservation 6*.

Irwin, Timothy and associates. 1997. *Dealing with Public Risk in Private Infrastructure*, Washington, D.C.: World Bank.

Jellinek, Lea. 1991. *The Wheel of Fortune. The History of a Poor Community in Jakarta*. London: Allen and Unwin.

Joseph, J. 1998. "Evolving a Retrofit Economic Rehabilitation Policy Model Using Impoverishment Risks Analysis—Experience of Maharashtra Composite Irrigation Project III." In H. M. Mathur and D. Marsden, eds., *Development Projects and Impoverishment Risks in Resettlement*. New Delhi: Sage Publications.

Joshi, Vidyut. 1987. *Submerging Villages: Problems and Prospects*. New Delhi: Ajanta Publications.

_____. 1991. *Rehabilitation—A Promise to Keep: The Case of the Sardar Sarovar Project*. Ahmedabad: Tax Publication.

Joy, J. L. 1968. "What an Economist Wants to Know about Dams?" In Rubin Neville and William M. Warren, eds. *Dams in Africa. An Interdisciplinary Study of Man-Made Lakes In Africa*. New York: Augustus Kelley Publishers.

Kibreab, Gaim. Forthcoming 1999. "Common Property Resources and Involuntary Resettlement." In Michael M. Cernea and Chris McDowell, eds., *Reconstructing Livelihoods*. Washington, D.C.: World Bank..

Koenig, Dolores, and Tieman Diara. Forthcoming 1999. "The Effects of Resettlement on Assets and Common Property Resources." In Michael M. Cernea and Chris McDowell, eds., *Reconstructing Livelihoods*. Washington, D.C.: World Bank.

Kothari, Smithu. 1995. "Damning the Narmada and the Politics of Development." In William F. Fisher, ed., *Towards Sustainable Development? Struggling Over India's Narmada River*. Armonk, N.Y.: M. E. Sharpe.

Kudat, Ayse, Mumtaz Bayram, and T. Hazar, eds. 1996. *Rural Resettlement in Theory and Practice* (in Turkish). Ankara: Anatolian Development Foundation.

_____. 1997. *Urban Resettlement* (in Turkish). Ankara: Turkish Rural and Urban Development Foundation.

Lane, Charles. 1996. *Pastures Lost.* Nairobi, Kenya: Initiative Publishers.

Laissailly-Jacobs, V., ed. 1998 *Communautées deracinées dans les pays du Sud.* Paris: Autrepart, OSTROM.

LEGOP (Legal Department – Operations). 1996. *OD 4.30 — Involuntary Resettlement: Guidelines for Lawyers.* Prepared by Carlos Escudero.

Lipton, Michael. 1992. "Economics and Anthropology: Grounding Models in Relationships." *World Development* 20 (10): 1541–46.

Little, I. M. D., and J. A. Mirrlees. 1974. *Project Appraisal and Planning for Developing Countries.* New York: Basic Books.

Londero, Elio. 1996. *Benefits and Beneficiaries: An Introduction to Estimating Distributional Effects in Cost-Benefit Analysis.* IDB. Washington, D.C.: Johns Hopkins University Press.

Mahapatra, L. K. 1994. *Tribal Development in India. Myth and Reality.* New Delhi: Vikas Publishing House.

Mairal, Gaspar and J. A. Bergua. 1996. "From Economicism to Culturalism: The Social Impact of Dam Projects in the River Esera." Paper presented at the Biennial Conference of the European Association of Social Anthropologists, Barcelona. Processed.

Mathur, Hari M., in collaboration with M. Cernea, eds. 1994. *Development, Displacement and Resettlement: Focus on Asian Experiences.* Delhi: Vikas Publishing House.

_____. 1998. "Loss of Access to Basic Public Services." In H. M. Mathur and David Marsden, eds., *Development Projects and Impoverishment Risks.* New Delhi: Oxford University Press.

Mathur, Hari Mohan, and David Marsden, eds. 1998. *Development Projects and Impoverishment Risks.* New Delhi: Oxford University Press.

Mburugu, E. K. 1993. "Dislocation of Settled Communities in the Development Process: The Case of Kiambere Hydroelectric Project." In Cynthia C. Cook, ed., *Involuntary Resettlement in Africa.* World Bank Technical Paper 227, Washington, D.C.: World Bank.

McCully, Patrick. 1996. *Silenced Rivers.* London: Zed Books.

McDowell, Christopher, ed. 1997. *Understanding Impoverishment: The Consequences of Development-Induced Displacement.* Providence: Berghahn.

McMillan, Della E., 1995. *Sahel Visions: Planned Settlement and River Blindness Control in Burkina Faso.* Tucson : University of Arizona Press.

Meikle, Sheilah, and Youxuan Zhu. Forthcoming 1999. "Employment for Displacees in the Socialist Market Economy of China." In Michael M. Cernea and Chris McDowell, eds., *Reconstructing Livelihoods.* Washington, D.C.: World Bank.

Mejía, Maria Clara. Forthcoming 1999. "Involuntary Resettlement and Economic Recovery: The Case of the Brickmakers Displaced by the Yacyreta Hydroelectric Project Argentina-Paraguay." In Michael M. Cernea and Chris McDowell, eds., *Reconstructuring Livelihoods*. Washington, D.C.: World Bank.

Merton, Robert K. 1957. *Social Theory and Social Structure*. New York: Free Press.

Mesa, Juan Fernando. 1969. "Emergencia Social de El Penol." Medellin. Processed.

Mohapatra, P., A. B. Ota, and R. N. Mohanty, eds. 1998. *Development-Induced Displacement and Rehabilitation*. New Delhi/Bhubaneswar: Prachi Prakashan.

Morse, Bradford, T. Berger, H. Brody, and T. Gamble. 1992. *Sardar Sarovar: Report of the Independent Review*. Ottawa: Resource Futures International, Inc.

Nayak, Ranjit. Forthcoming. "Risks Associated with Landlessness: Exploration towards Socially Friendly Resettlement." In Michael M. Cernea and Chris McDowell, eds., *Reconstructing Livelihoods*. Washington, D.C.: World Bank.

NRCR (National Research Center for Resettlement). 1995. *Resettlement and Rehabilitation*. Nanjing, China: Hohai University Press.

_____. 1996. *Papers on Resettlement and Development*. Nanjing, China.

OECD. 1992. *Guidelines for Aid Agencies on Involuntary Displacement and Resettlement in Development Projects*. Paris: DAC.

Oliver-Smith, Anthony. 1991a. "Successes and Failures in Post-Disaster Resettlement." *Disaster*, 15(1, March): 12–23.

_____. 1991b. "Involuntary Resettlement, Resistance and Political Empowerment." *Journal of Refugee Studies* 4 (2): 132–149.

_____. 1996. "Fighting for a Place: The Policy Implications of Resistence to Development-Induced Resettlement." In Chris McDowell, ed., *Understanding Impoverishment*. Providence: Berghahn.

Ota, A. B. 1996. "Countering the Impoverishment Risk: The Case of the Rengali Dam Project." In A. B. Ota and A. Agnihotri, eds., *Involuntary Displacement in Dam Projects*. New Delhi: Prachi Prakashan.

Oyedipe, F. P. A. 1987. "The Relative Success of the Kainji Resettlement Scheme as Compared with that of Volta." *Research for Development* (Nigeria) 3: 41–54.

Pandey, Balaji. 1998. *Displaced Development: Impact of Open-Cast Mining on Women*. Delhi: Friederich, Ebert, and Stiftung.

Pandey, Balaji, and others. 1998. *Depriving the Underprivileged for Development*. Bhubaneswar, Orissa: Institute for Socio-Economic Development.

Pankhurst, Alula. 1992. *Resettlement and Famine in Ethiopia: The Villagers' Experience*. Manchester: Manchester University Press.

Paranjpye, Vijay. 1988. *Evaluating The Tehri Dam: An Extended Cost Benefit Appraisal*. New Delhi: Indian National Trust for Art and Cultural Heritage.

_____. 1990. *High Dams on the Narmada: A Holistic Analysis of the River Valley Projects*. New Delhi: Indian National Trust for Art and Cultural Heritage.

Parasuranam, S., and N. Purendra Prasad. 1997. "Differential Distribution of Social Cost." *Economic and Political Weekly* (August): 2218–22.

Partridge, William. 1989. "Population Displacement Due to Development Projects." *Journal of Refugee Studies* 2 (3).

_____. 1993. "Successful Involuntary Resettlement: Lessons from the Costa Ri-
can Arenal Hydroelectric Project." In Michael M. Cernea and Scott E.
Guggenheim, eds., *Anthropological Approaches to Resettlement: Policy, Practice,
Theory*. Boulder, Colo.: Westview Press.

Partridge, William L., A. B. Brown, and J. B. Nugent. 1982. "The Papaloapan
Dam and Resettlement Project: Human Ecology and Health Impacts." In Art
Hansen and Anthony Oliver-Smith, eds., *Involuntary Migration and Resettle-
ment*, Boulder, Colo.: Westview Press.

Paul, James C. N. 1988. "International Development Agencies, Human Rights
and Human Development Projects." *Denver Journal of International Law and
Policy* 17 (1): 67.

Posey, Darrell A. 1996. "The Kayapó Indian Protests against Amazonian Dams:
Successes, Alliances, and Unending Battles." In C. McDowell, ed., *Understanding Impoverishment*. Providence: Berghahn.

Qureshi, Moeen. 1989. "Resettlement, Development, and the World Bank." In
The Bank's World (May): 12–13.

Ramanathan, Usha. 1995. "Displacement and Rehabilitation: Towards a National Policy." *Lokayan Bulletin*, 11(5): 41–56.

_____. 1996. "Displacement and the Law." *Economic and Political Weekly* 31 (24):
1486–92.

Ray, Anandrup. 1984. *Cost-Benefit Analysis: Issues and Methodologies*. Baltimore:
Johns Hopkins University Press.

Ray, Rita. 1994a. *Underground Drama: The Social Ecology of Two Chromite Mines in
Orissa*. Delhi: Ajanta Publications.

_____. 1994b. "Demographic and Socio-Economic Study of the Proposed
Naraj Thermal Power Project." Utkal University, Bhubaneswar, India. Processed.

_____. 1995. "Evaluation of Rehabilitation and Resettlement of Talcher
Super Thermal Power Project." A study conducted for NTPC, New Delhi.
Processed.

Reddi, I. U. B. 1992. *Displacement and Rehabilitation*. New Delhi: Mittal Publications.

_____. 1994. *Industrial Development and Problems of the Uprooted*. New Delhi:
Rawat Publications.

Rew, Alan W., and P. A. Driver. 1986. "Evaluation of the Victoria Dam Project in
Sri Lanka." Vol. III. Initial Evaluation of the Social and Environmental Impacts of the Victoria Dam Project, Annexes J and K. Processed.

Riberio, Gustavo Lins. 1994. *Transnational Capitalism and Hydropolitics in Argentina: The Yacyretá High Dam*. Gainesville: University Press of Florida.

Roder, W. 1994. *Human Adjustment to Kainji Reservoir in Nigeria: An Assessment of the Economics and Environmental Consequences of a Major Man-Made Lake in Africa.* Lanham: University Press of America.

Rosa, Eugene A. 1998. "Metatheoretical Foundations for Post-Normal Risk." *Journal of Risk Research* 1 (1).

Roy-Burman, B. K. 1961. *Social Processes in the Industrialization of Rourkhela.* New Delhi: Census of India.

Ruttan, Vernon W. 1988. "Cultural Endowments and Economic Development: What Can We Learn from Anthropology?" *Economic Development and Cultural Change* 36 (3, April): S248–S271.

Salem-Murdock, Muneera. 1989. *Arabs and Nubians in New Halfa.* Salt Lake City: University of Utah Press.

Schuh, G. Edward. 1993. "Involuntary Resettlement, Human Capital, and Economic Development" In Michael M. Cernea. and Scott Guggenheim, eds. *Anthropological Approaches to Resettlement: Policy, Practice, Theory.* Boulder, Colo.: Westview Press.

Scott, R. Parry. 1992. "Dams, Forced Resettlement, and the Transformation of the Peasant Economy in the São Francisco River Valley, Brazil." Paper presented at the XVII International Congress of the Latin American Studies Association (LASA), Los Angeles. Processed.

Scudder, Thayer. 1962. *The Ecology of the Gwembe Tonga.* Manchester, U.K.: Manchester University Press.

_____. 1973. "The Human Ecology of Big Projects: River Basin Development and Resettlement." In B. Siegel, ed., *Annual Review of Anthropology.* Palo Alto: Annual Review.

_____. 1985. "A Sociological Framework for the Analysis of New Land Settlements." In Michael M. Cernea, ed. *Putting People First: Sociological Variables in Rural Development.* New York: Oxford University Press.

_____. 1993. "Development-Induced Relocation and Refugee Studies: 37 Years of Change and Continuity among Zambia's Gwembe Tonga." *Journal of Refugee Studies* 6 (2): 123–52.

_____. 1996. "Development-Induced Impoverishment, Resistance, and River-Basin Development." In Chris McDowell, ed. *Understanding Impoverishment: The Consequences of Development-Induced Displacement.* Providence: Berghahn.

Scudder, Thayer, and Elizabeth Colson. 1982. "From Welfare to Development: A Conceptual Framework for Analysis of Dislocated People." In Art Hansen and Anthony Oliver-Smith, eds., *Involuntary Migration and Resettlement.* Boulder, Colo.: Westview Press.

Serra, Maria Teresa Fernandes. 1993. "Resettlement Planning in the Brazilian Power Sector: Recent Changes in Approach." In Michael M. Cernea and Scott E. Guggenheim, eds., *Anthropological Approaches to Resettlement: Policy, Practice, Theory.* Boulder, Colo.: Westview Press.

Shi, Guoqing. 1996a. "Comprehensive Evaluation on Resettlers' Production and Living Level in Gaojiajing of Dongfeng Hydroelectric Stations." In NRCR, *Papers on Resettlement and Development*. Nanjing.

_____. 1996b. "The Comprehensive Evaluation Method and Its Application of Production and Living Standard for Rural Resettlers in Reservoir Area." In NRCR, *Papers on Resettlement and Development*. Nanjing.

Shi, Guoqing, and Hu Weison. 1994. *Comprehensive Evaluation and Monitoring of Displaced Persons: Standards of Living and Production*. Nanjing: NRCR.

Shi, Guoqing, Huoping Xun, and Wenxue Yu. 1996. "Research on Economic Evaluation of Reservoir Protection." In NRCR, *Papers on Resettlement and Development*. Nanjing.

Shihata, Ibrahim F. I., 1988. "The World Bank and Human Rights: An Analysis of the Legal Issues and the Record of Achievements." *Denver Journal of International Law & Politics* 17 (1).

_____. 1991. "Involuntary Resettlement in World Bank-Financed Projects." In Ibrahim Shihata, ed., *The World Bank in a Changing World*. The Netherlands: Martinus Njhoff Publishers.

_____. 1993. "Legal Aspects of Involuntary Population Resettlement." In Michael M Cernea and Scott E. Guggenheim, eds., *Anthropological Approaches to Resettlement: Policy, Practice, Theory*. Boulder, Colo.: Westview Press.

Singh, Mridula, and Associates. 1992. *Displacement by Sardar Sarovar and Theri: A Comparative Study of Two Dams*. Delhi: MARG.

Sinha, Basawan, and Ramesh Bhatia. 1982. *Economic Appraisal of Irrigation Project in India*. New Delhi: Agricole Publishing Academy.

Smelser, Neil J., and Richard Swedberg, eds. 1994. *The Handbook of Economic Sociology*. New Jersey: Princeton University Press.

Spiegel, H. 1997. Personal communication.

Squire, Lyn, and Herman van der Tak. 1975. *Economic Analysis of Projects*. Baltimore, MD: Johns Hopkins University Press.

Stiglitz, Joseph E. 1998. "Towards a New Paradigm for Development: Strategies, Policies, and Processes." Presented as the Prebisch Lecture at UNCTAD, Geneva, October 19, 1998. Processed.

Subbarao, Kalanidhi, and others. 1996. *Safety Net Programs and Poverty Reductions: Lessons from Cross-Country Experience*. Washington, D.C.: World Bank.

Swedberg, Richard, ed. 1993. *Explorations in Economic Sociology*. New York: Russell Sage Foundation.

Tamondong-Helin, Susan D. 1996. "State Power as a Medium of Impoverishment: The Case of Pantabangan Dam Resettlement in the Philippines." In Chris McDowell, ed., *Understanding Impoverishment: The Consequences of Development-Induced Displacement*. Providence: Berghahn.

Thangaraj, Sam. 1996. "Impoverishment Risk Analysis: A Methodological Tool for Participatory Resettlement Planning." In Chris McDowell, ed., *Under-*

standing Displacement: The Consequences of Development-Induced Displacement. Providence: Berghahn.

———. 1998. "Impoverishment Risks in Involuntary Resettlement: An Overview." In Hari Mohan Mathur and David Marsden, eds., *Development Projects and Impoverishment Risks in Resettlement.* New Delhi: Oxford University Press.

Thukral, Enakshi Ganguly, ed. 1992. *Big Dams, Displaced People: Rivers of Sorrow, Rivers of Change.* New Delhi: Sage Publications.

Torado, Michael P. 1989. *Economic Development in the Third World.* Fourth Edition. New York: Longman.

Turnbull, Colin M. 1987. *The Mountain People.* Touchstone Books.

Udall, Lori. 1995. "The International Narmada Campaign: A Case of Sustained Advocacy." In William F. Fisher, ed., *Towards Sustainable Development? Struggling over India's Narmada River.* Armonk, N.Y.: M. E. Sharpe.

Usher, Ann Danaiya. 1997. *Dams as Aid: A Political Anatomy of Nordic Development Thinking.* London: Routledge.

Wali, Alaka. 1989. *Kilowatts and Crisis: Hydroelectric Power and Social Dislocation in Eastern Panama.* Boulder, Colo.: Westview Press.

West, Patrick, and Stephen Brechin, eds. 1991. *Resident Peoples and National Parks.* Tucson: University of Arizona Press.

Wangxiang, Chen. 1993. "Resettlement Associated with Hydro Projects in China." *International Water Power & Dam.* 45 (2):19–20.

World Bank. 1980. Operational Manual Statement 2.33. "Social Issues Associated with Involuntary Resettlement in Bank-Financed Projects." Washington, D.C. Processed.

———. 1990. Operational Directive 4.30: "Involuntary Resettlement." Washington, D.C. Processed.

———. 1994. "Resettlement and Development: The Bankwide Review of Projects Involving Involuntary Resettlement 1986–1993." (2nd ed. 1996.) Environment Department, Washington, D.C. Processed.

———. 1998. "Recent Experience with Involuntary Resettlement. Overview." Operations Evaluation Department, Washington, D.C.

Wu, Zougfe, and Shi Guoqing. 1996. "Study on the Planning Theory of Production Development in Reservoir Resettlement." In NRCR, *Papers on Resettlement and Development.* Nanjing.

2

Methodological Issues in the Economic Analysis for Involuntary Resettlement Operations

David W. Pearce

Editor's Note   Environmental economics has evolved in recent decades into a powerful field that has helped to quantify the losses caused by environmental degradation and to ground environmental protection policies in rigorous analysis. In this chapter David Pearce, a founder of environmental economics, discusses the methodological issues involved in applying basic economic analysis to involuntary population resettlements—an area that has yet to be solidly researched.

Resettlement issues, he notes, have been "something of a Cinderella issue" in the economic literature; even the leading manuals of development economics and project work have "virtually ignored the subject." Pearce's study is revealing in its critique of the lack of economic reflection on resettlement and in its positive methodological suggestions for improving that situation. The author draws on recent experiences in using environmental valuation techniques to identify and reduce resettlement costs.

The author finds that compulsory resettlement does not differ essentially from other project externalities; thus losses should be internalized in project budgets, not externalized to those displaced. The first step: accurate valuation of assets and incomes lost, both public and private. Pearce makes several recommendations for improving the routine economic analysis of resettlement operations, including standard full cost minimization in project design, where full cost refers to the sum of economic, social, and environmental costs; trade-off analysis, where resettlement minimization is at the expense of project benefits; and recognition that a $1 loss for project "losers" (displaced people) has a higher social value than $1 gains to project "beneficiaries."

In support of the anthropological findings about typically inadequate compensations, Pearce also unveils the cognitive and methodological fallacies that account for the persistent undercompensation of dislocated people in many developing countries. His analysis concludes with a discussion of the income curve of displaced families, where he demonstrates that, contrary to widespread but erroneous assumptions, asset replacement through compensation will not prevent resettlers from becoming "worse off." To make the "catching up" process possible, new assets must be created through investment.

The involuntary resettlement of large numbers of people because of major water resource development projects has been described as "the single most serious counterdevelopmental social consequence of water resource development" (Cernea 1990). What is true of water resources projects is also true of many other types of development projects in the urban, energy, and transportation sectors.

Self-evidently, if the means of compensation such "losers" receive from major projects is inadequate, significant loss of well-being must ensue simply because of the numbers affected. Because baseline surveys have been inadequate in the past, the asset and income base of the populations affected is not known with certainty. By and large, however, those affected are the poor. Thus, an additional concern about the effects of displacement is based on equity grounds.

The well-being lost by those who are displaced by a project, such as a dam, is an example of an *externality*, or more strictly, of an *external cost*. Project evaluators must account for this externality and add it to the project's internal costs (the costs of materials, labor, and so on), otherwise investment and policy choices will be economically inefficient. World Bank guidelines go beyond this accounting requirement and call for the externality to be internalized by requiring that the costs of resettlement be calculated as part of the project's cost and that affected people be compensated. This distinction between accounting for externalities and actual compensation for externalities is important.

Conclusions from Past Resettlement Experiences

In 1993–94 the World Bank reviewed its portfolio of projects entailing involuntary resettlement and the performance of governments and the Bank itself in those projects (World Bank 1994). Earlier reviews (Butcher 1987; Cernea 1986, 1988, 1990) had already led to substantial modifications of the Bank's initial (1980) policy and procedures, which are codified in the Bank's June 1990 Operational Directive (OD) 4.30 on involuntary resettlement. Nonetheless, many still view the Bank's operational treatment of resettlement in the context of development projects as unsatisfactory. This study, which was initially started as part of the Bank's (1994) review, focuses on the relationship between economic methodology and resettlement, specifically, the Bank's guidelines on the economic and financial analysis of resettlement projects as set out in Cernea (1988, annex 2).

Based on the large volume of material examined, my main conclusions are:

- That the methodological arguments that underlie some of the reluctance to elevate the problems of resettlement in project appraisal are without foundation and that routine project design based on social cost minimization might help reduce the scale of the resettlement problem.
- That full and proper compensation, consistent with the Bank's OD 4.30 and the concept of resettlement as a development opportunity, can be thought of in terms of some recent literature on the economics of sustainable development. This reinforces the requirement that involuntary resettlement be treated as a development activity in itself, rather than as a relief or salvage operation.
- That additional means of determining full and proper compensation are available to governments, over and above the Bank's emphasis on valuing private and public assets and income. These methods draw on recent experience with environmental valuation techniques in developing countries; government agencies dealing with resettlement and Bank staff should experiment with them to ensure that underestimation of resettlement costs is minimized. Such underestimation arises often because (a) country planners do not follow the existing guidelines properly (World Bank 1994; see also chapters by Cernea and Eriksen in this volume), and (b) the existing guidelines for economic analysis fail to capture the full social costs of dislocation. These full social costs include the loss of nonpriced environmental and cultural assets, the loss of social

cohesion, the loss of market access, and psychological damage from dislocation.

- That governmental procedures and Bank guidelines need to give more emphasis to the role of nonmarket assets in the "before development" incomes of displaced people and to the process of asset growth in preproject communities.
- That the focus on resettlers should not overshadow the needs of host communities. Some evidence indicates that inadequate host community assistance can result in unsatisfactory resettlement.
- That unwarranted displacement of families may also result from the domestic policy context in which projects are formulated. While projects are blamed for the human costs associated with development, responsibility also lies with the policies in the country in question.

More generally, environmental economics and the welfare economics that underlies most Bank development practice at the microeconomic level emphatically reinforce the importance sociologists and anthropologists attach to the design of socially acceptable resettlement programs.

Many inadequacies of resettlement operations arise from failure to implement the existing guidelines formulated by the Bank. Quite often, government agencies that agree with the Bank's resettlement policy guidelines at project outset fall back on their old routines during implementation and do not carry out the policy agreements made at project inception. In other words, as several reviews indicate (Cernea 1990; Eriksen in this volume; Gutman 1993; World Bank 1993b, 1994), resettlement inadequacies derive from bad practice, not from bad policy.

In particular, many projects tend to systematically underestimate the costs of resettlement (World Bank 1993b, 1994). We know that cost underestimation tends to be a feature of public projects generally. Resettlement projects are unlikely to be an exception. However, better and clearer guidelines could address some of the sources of these underestimates. More important, better guidelines might raise the probability of resettlement projects being successful. Ultimately, bad practice is a matter of political will in the countries in question and of the determination of funding agencies, such as the Bank, to enforce covenants and agreements. Where that domestic political will is lacking, it is important that it is not given any support from weakness in the guidelines.

In terms of the priority given to it, resettlement has been something of a Cinderella issue as concerns project appraisal. Remarkably, until recently, the economic literature virtually ignored the subject, the main exception being the discussion in Cernea (1988, particularly annex 2). Thus, the main economic manuals used for project appraisal in developing countries—for example, Curry and Weiss (1993), Gittinger (1982), Squire and van der Tak (1975), UNIDO (1972), and Ward and Deren (1991)—do not address issues of compensation for displacement.

Although the World Bank's policy guidelines focus, explicitly and primarily, on the social issues involved in displacement and relocation, they also directly address some basic economic issues of income recovery and contain many economic implications. The following are relevant to this study and will be discussed in more detail later:

- Projects should avoid or minimize involuntary resettlement (OD 4.30, paragraph 3a).
- Project designers should regard both customary and formal property rights as criteria for eligibility for compensation (OD 4.30, paragraphs 3e and 17).
- Resettled people should be better off, or at least no worse off, after resettlement (OD 4.30, paragraph 4), and project designers should focus on resettlement as a development opportunity.
- For the above point to hold, full and proper assessment of compensation must be carried out through the valuation of private and public assets and income (OD 4.30, paragraph 3b).

Does Resettlement Differ from Other Project Externalities?

The Bank's policy guidelines require that actual compensation be paid for displacement and lost assets. However, cost-benefit analysis theory, whose principles underlie Bank project and policy appraisal methodology, does not prescribe the payment of actual compensation to "losers." In theoretical terms, it is only necessary for the project's benefits to be able to compensate for the losses and still have some gains left over. No actual transfers from gainers to losers are required. This is the accounting procedure referred to at the beginning of this chapter. If the Bank accepts this hypothetical compensation principle, why should resettlement costs be special? Or to put it another way, if OD 4.30 mandates actual compensation for resettlement, why not mandate compensation for other externalities, such as environmental impacts?[1]

This question has several answers as follows:

- Resettlement involves the loss of property rights to land and resources, although these rights may range on a broad spectrum, from secure and well-articulated rights to customary rights not enshrined in any formal law or registration. In contrast, environmental impacts are not usually the subject of such rights.

- Involuntary displacements may differ from other impacts because of the large numbers of people affected.
- Displacement often affects the very poor, providing a strong equity argument for special attention.

As Bank policy already mandates actual compensation, these considerations may seem academic, but they do raise the issue of why other impacts, notably environmental impacts, are not subject to actual compensation. One answer is that perhaps they should be where they are significant, for example, where they affect large numbers of people or the group in question is poor. This could be the case for downstream effects of hydroelectric dams.

In industrial countries, domestic compensation practices vary widely. Many countries operate compensation policies based on property values and removal costs only. For environmental impacts, their usual practice is not to compensate at all, except perhaps through noise insulation grants for houses near airports, but generally not for roads. An interesting departure from this practice is Germany's Nature Protection Law, which requires that environmental impacts be offset through the creation of equivalent environmental assets elsewhere. Thus, arguing that all significant externalities be compensated is not absurd, although one does have to acknowledge the complexities of implementing such a policy.

Issues in the Economics of Resettlement

Avoiding Involuntary Resettlement

Economics lends support to the idea that projects should first be screened to ensure that resettlement is minimized. Thus, Bank projects should attempt to avoid involuntary resettlements where possible. In avoiding involuntary resettlement, two contexts need to be distinguished. The first is where resettlement is minimized for a given project benefit. For example, if a project to produce 100 units of electricity has two possible designs, one of which involves moving 100 people while the other involves moving 120 people, then the screening process should select the project that involves displacing fewer people. This usually amounts to ensuring that the concept of an efficient project design is extended to incorporate resettlement as a cost. Typically, efficient design is taken to mean minimizing the private costs of construction and operation for a given level of project benefit; that is, minimizing the costs of capital, raw materials, labor, and energy. However, this fundamental feature of good project appraisal must be extended to become the principle of minimizing all costs, economic, social, and environmental, of producing benefits from a development project.

Typically, cost-benefit guidelines emphasize maximizing the net benefits from a project, or at least ensuring that its benefits are greater than its costs.[2] Implicit in these requirements is the idea that costs are no higher than they need be, but in practice, project designers often overlook this requirement. Project design often emerges without detailed scrutiny of the cost dimension, and even when such scrutiny is carried out, it tends to relate to private costs, not to the wider concept of costs, that is, economic plus social plus environmental costs. Thus, one of the major social costs, resettlement, can easily be overlooked when project designers are trying to minimize costs. Failure to minimize these costs means that some resettlement occurs needlessly.[3]

The second context differs from the first in that a tradeoff is involved between minimizing resettlement costs and the benefits of the project. In the first context, no tradeoff is involved: wasteful expenditures are being avoided. Tradeoffs can occur when, for example, in a hydroelectric project the height of the dam is lowered to reduce the area of inundation, and hence the number of people displaced. While lowering the dam's height need not sacrifice electricity output, it may do so. The situation then is that project designers must compare displacement costs, the human costs associated with resettlement, with project benefits. If the affected parties are equally "deserving," for example, electricity consumers are as poor as displaced families, then project designers can carry out a direct comparison of costs. If full compensation for displaced families is less than the value of the electricity, then maintaining the dam's height and moving the families will be beneficial. If the compensation costs are higher than the added value of the electricity, then the designers should lower the dam. Some projects have gone through this kind of analysis, but inspection of many projects involving human displacement does not reveal evidence of project designers routinely calculating these tradeoffs.

Although this form of tradeoff analysis assumes that all parties are equally deserving, one can make a strong case for applying greater weight to the loss of well-being of the displaced than to the gain of the electricity consumers. In the first place, electricity beneficiaries may often be better off to begin with than those displaced. Second, and perhaps more important, a fundamental asymmetry exists between the value of a loss of well-being (displaced people) and the value of a gain in well-being (electricity consumers). This basic asymmetry is dealt with in more detail later. For now, note simply that a $1 loss may be far more important in social terms than a $1 gain, even where the gains and losses accrue to people with the same incomes or wealth.[4]

This discussion suggests several recommendations for routine economic analysis of resettlement operations in developing (as well as developed) country projects. Thus, any set of guidelines on resettlement should emphasize the following:

- The fundamental need to engage in standard full cost minimization in project design, where full cost refers to the sum of economic, social, and environmental costs
- The need to engage in tradeoff analysis where resettlement minimization is at the expense of project benefits
- The need to recognize that a $1 loss for project losers (displaced people in this case) has a higher social value than the $1 gain to project beneficiaries.

None of these recommendations is inconsistent with the economics of project appraisal as prescribed by the Bank. They are, in fact, logical outcomes of that economics.

Property Rights

The emphasis in OD 4.30 on treating people with customary property rights in the same way, as far as is feasible, as people with full legal rights is important. It is also consistent with the Bank's policy guidelines on indigenous people (World Bank 1991). Clearly, however, when issues of actual compensation for displaced people arise, those with less well defined tenure and resource rights are often treated less well than those with secure rights (Cernea 1990). This asymmetry of treatment is often conveniently justified by the absence of legal registration documents and so on, but has more to do with minimizing the monetary, rather than the human, cost of resettlement.

There are two strong reasons for treating customary rights in the same way as legal rights. First, project analysis is concerned with the aggregate well-being of people. Gains and losses in well-being are no different if customary rights are involved than if full legal rights are involved. Second, by conferring full recognition on holders of customary rights, the resettlement project is likely to generate better protection of land and natural resources. While social analysts have shown that the traditional distinction between common property and private ownership in terms of sustainable land and resource use is false (Bromley 1991, Bromley and Cernea 1989, Stevenson 1991), a better definition of land

and resource rights generally acts as a means of ensuring sustainable agricultural practices.[5]

Thus, recognizing customary rights is not just a matter of fairness (in itself a powerful enough argument) but also an issue of economic efficiency and sustainability. The recommendation that follows from this is that in developing countries guidelines for resettlement could find strong economic justifications for the need to recognize customary rights as being on a par with legal rights. Such treatment is consistent with the concepts of economic efficiency and sustainable development.

Of course, determining what the structure of rights actually is in a particular local context is immensely complex. There is always the risk that outsiders will seek to exploit the availability of compensation funding by claiming customary rights where none exist. This is a hazard of any situation in which compensation for harm is paid and is an example of a much wider phenomenon that economists call rent seeking. It is not peculiar to resettlement.

The No-Worse-Off Criterion

The exact meaning of being no worse off as a result of resettlement requires some clarification. Two considerations are involved: the correct application of the welfare economics underlying cost-benefit analysis and the implications of the philosophy of sustainable development.

It is tempting to compare incomes and assets before and after the project and use that as a test of whether or not resettlers (and hosts) are better or worse off. This is inadequate for two reasons. The first is that we need to know how much better off resettlers would have been had the development not occurred. An estimate of their incomes in the project's absence is at best only a minimum estimate, because it is necessary to project what the situation would have been without the project. This is not necessarily the same as the situation before the project. The second reason is that the methods for valuing assets and income do not allow for the displaced people's own valuations of assets and access to employment. Moreover, practice in domestic projects in many countries seldom relies on genuine consultation of affected groups.

The World Bank's policy requirement that those resettled, at the very least, not become any worse off and its focus on resettlement as a development package receives strong support from the recent literature on sustainable development. The essence of sustainable development is (a) that future generations should be no worse off than those currently living, and (b) that the currently least advantaged in society should be given special attention and, at the very least, should be no worse off because of development. That is, both intragenerational and intergenerational equity are of paramount importance (Pearce, Barbier, and Markandya 1990; World Commission on Environment and Development 1987). The implications of sustainable development for cost-benefit analysis are still being worked out in the literature (Pearce, Markandya, and Barbier 1990; von Amsberg 1993), but conventional interpretations of cost-benefit analysis are inconsistent with these precepts of sustainable development. Essentially, these equity considerations require procedures for actually compensating future generations and the poor now.

The idea that resettled people should be no worse off as a result of being displaced is thus consistent with the basic philosophy of sustainable development. This consistency is reinforced by considering the other feature of OD 4.30, namely, the emphasis on transforming resettlement into a development opportunity. The literature on sustainable development shows that one of the conditions for intergenerational equity is that stocks of capital assets be no less in the future than they are now, where asset stocks include the everyday concept of capital (machines, roads, and so on) as manmade capital, the stock of skills and knowledge (human capital), and the stock of environmental assets (land, trees, resources, and so on) (Pearce 1993; Solow 1986, 1993). By extension, then, the intragenerational requirement has as its condition that the asset base of the poor should not decline as a result of development. The basic logic of the constant and increasing capital base argument is that capital provides the capability to develop.

Thus the Bank's policy emphasis on restoring the economic base of the resettled (OD 4.30, paragraph 4) is wholly consistent with the idea of ensuring that the same, or an expanded, capital base is conferred on the disadvantaged. That is, treating resettlement as a development opportunity is an example of what is meant in practice by sustainable development.

Full and Proper Compensation

The economic costs of resettlement comprise three elements: (a) compensation to those displaced and associated rehabilitation investment costs, (b) compensation to the host community, and (c) administrative costs. We will focus on the first two elements.

Several potentially large sources of undercompensation exist even if governments and Bank staff pursue the existing guidelines. These are:

- Undercompensation because of the time lag between determining compensation and the time of resettlement
- Failure to account for nonmarket income and costs, which in turn comprise nonpriced environmental services, cultural assets, the psychological costs of dislocation, the value of community social cohesion, and the value of market access
- Lost consumer surplus from existing assets.

Project designers can overcome at least some of these sources of undercompensation by using valuation techniques borrowed from environmental economics.

UNDERCOMPENSATION DUE TO DELAYS. OD 4.30 and the existing economic guidelines (Cernea 1988, annex 2) approach the scale of desirable compensation for resettled people as follows: cost of replacement for losses plus costs of translocation plus transitional costs plus development or rehabilitation costs.

There are three sources of bias when delays are significant. The first arises if the living standards of the displaced community were rising at the time compensation was determined. Delays will therefore mean that the community would have been even better off at the time of the actual relocation. The second bias arises if, as is often the case, the project itself raises land values and the displaced population has to buy into the new neighboring land rather than being allocated land directly. The third arises from a failure to account for inflation.

THE COUNTERFACTUAL PROBLEM. Figure 2.1 illustrates the cost concepts involved in resettlement. The horizontal axis shows time and the vertical axis shows monetary units (which is not to imply that cash is always the appropriate means of compensation). The curve NR (for no resettlement) shows the path of asset accumulation without the project. This development curve, assumed for the moment to be rising, is interrupted by the project that will result in displacement. People's assets fall immediately because of the displacement and remain at a new low level for a further period as economic activity is built up at the new site (the transition period). If the resettlement package works, then a new development path is established as curve R. To meet the no-worse-off criterion, development path R has to involve faster development for a period than would otherwise have been the case to catch up with where those resettled would have been at time $t+x$.

It is the full replacement of capital assets that ensures the takeoff on path R, and it is the rehabilitation component of the package that

Figure 2.1.

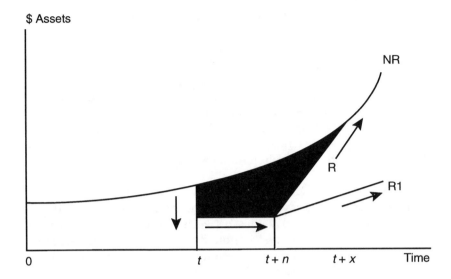

ensures that path R is steeper than path NR. Essentially, if the community was experiencing rising living standards before the project because of asset accumulation, replacing existing assets is not enough: the catching-up process will involve some additional asset creation. If path R continues to be steeper than NR after $t+x$, then the relocated community is better off as a result of the resettlement project, which is consistent with the Bank's aims.

By contrast, consider what would happen if the project made provision only for replacing assets. After the transition period (t to $t+n$), development would recommence along path R', but the resettled community would be worse off than it otherwise would have been, even though it is developing at the same rate as if the project had never occurred.

Strictly speaking, compensation for income loss caused by dislocation is the shaded area of figure 2.1; that is, the compensation arising from the fact that dislocation interrupted the community's development. This income loss compensation needs to be distinguished from asset loss compensation, which involves replacing capital assets as they existed at time t or setting up new and different assets in the host community. As several sources note (for example, World Bank 1993b), compensation for asset loss must be at replacement cost, not the worth of the asset. It is asset compensation that enables the achievement of path R.

Asset replacement is an adequate criterion for compensation only if project designers can assume that the displaced community was not experiencing growth and was not likely to experience growth, as shown in figure 2.2. Here assets are constant at time t and are expected to be constant in the future. Hence replacing assets will ensure a continued constant flow of income. The other situation in which replacement of assets is sufficient is if the adjustment period is extremely brief; that is, if the gap between t and $t+n$ is short. However, delays are often substantial.

Income compensation must be managed carefully, because the problem of dependency has been widely noted in communities that come to rely on the cash and food handouts in the new area (Butcher 1990; Cernea 1988). One way to avoid this problem is to place the obligation for reestablishing a new income-earning capacity primarily on the developer through the rehabilitation part of the resettlement scheme.

CHANGING LAND VALUES. The second source of bias arises because compensation at market values may be inadequate, because the development itself raises land values between the time compensation is agreed on and the time of dislocation (Butcher 1990). If compensation is in cash and is based on the situation before the price rise, then the dislocated population bears a direct cost. This must be accounted for and compensation must be adjusted, perhaps through contingency funds.

If compensation for property loss includes a direct allocation of the new land, either the developer or the government bears the cost. If

Figure 2.2.

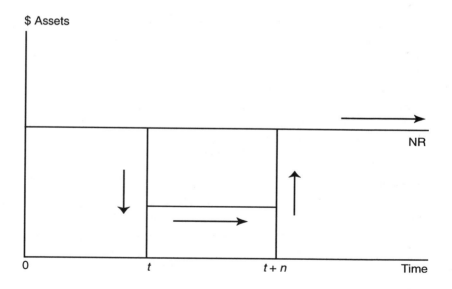

the developer seeks to reduce the commitment to provide new land of the same quality as those resettled had before the project, then some of the cost burden is transferred onto the resettlers. This can be avoided by carefully specifying both the quantity and quality of new land to be allocated to resettlers. Where this is done, the price rise should not affect resettlers. In some contexts they may actually gain, because the land price increases may reflect real land productivity gains from the project, for example from irrigation.

INFLATION. While the need to calculate all resettlement costs in real terms should be self-evident, in some situations no attempt has been made to estimate inflation rates. In China, for example, past projects have not taken inflation into account, with the result that delays in making payments reduced their real value to displaced populations (World Bank 1993a).

The theoretical ideal for payments has two main problems. The first problem is that the socioeconomic baseline survey at time t would need to assess not only assets and income at that point, but would have to secure some idea of how those assets and incomes would be likely to change over time. Historical evidence will almost certainly be absent unless the community happens to have been the subject of a previous survey, so there will be little evidence on which to base projections. A follow-up survey of four Bank projects by the Bank's Operations Evaluation Department demonstrated the importance of changes in asset formation (World Bank 1993b). In the Ghana Kpong hydroelectric scheme needs had clearly been underestimated because of changes in assets and population between the time of the survey and the time of the resettlement.

The second problem is that it is not easy to judge what the entire adjustment period is likely to be, so the size of the income compensation will also be unknown. No systematic evidence on adjustment periods is available. It is therefore unwise to assume that adjustment will be rapid. At best we can say that if there is any reason to assume that people's living standards were improving prior to the project and if the adjustment period is lengthy, then compensation at replacement cost for asset loss is a minimum requirement.

UNDERCOMPENSATION BECAUSE OF LIMITED CONCEPTS OF INCOME AND ASSETS. A proper theoretical classification of payments associated with displaced people would be as follows:

- Asset replacement costs
- Income compensation for the entire adjustment period

- Additional investment costs, over and above asset replacement, designed to secure an accelerated development path to compensate for the forgone growth of past income
- Any costs involved in actually moving the affected population, including administrative and transaction costs.

A comparison of the asset and income list above with the pro forma cost tables in Cernea (1988, annex 2) reveals that the latter omit the income compensation element except in a reference to "subsistence packages" (Cernea 1988, table 2). The additional asset formation or rehabilitation/development component is not clear in the pro forma tables either. The advantage of making it clear would be to draw attention to the need to ensure the inclusion of the extra rehabilitation financing. The importance of this component is that it appears to be significant for the success of resettlement schemes; that is, schemes where people's living standards are better after the project than before. Schemes that employed only asset compensation have been markedly less successful (World Bank 1993a, 1994, 1998). Revised pro forma tables are suggested later.

The terms income and assets need to be interpreted more broadly than has been the case to date. Income, for example, may be in cash or in kind, and it may be psychological in nature, for example, cultural and religious benefits. Similarly, assets may take the form of physical assets such as plows, tools, and buildings; livestock; access to the market place; and even nonphysical social goods, such as a community's social networks for mutual help (Cernea 1990).

Note that assets and incomes are closely related. For the farmer, land values will tend to be the capitalized value of the income to be earned from that land, assuming that any economic distortions (e.g., subsidies) have been netted out. The farmer's income will exceed the annuitized value of the land by amounts determined by off-farm incomes and nonmarket income from fuelwood, plants, wildmeat, and so on. The landless will not have land assets, but what they lose is access to employment, and hence income. Their incomes are the annual value of themselves as a human capital asset. Once this is recognized, it is possible to extend the compensation concept to both the landless and small businesses displaced by projects. For small businesses, assets will consist of nontransferable assets, usually the buildings, and transferable assets, such as tools and market access.

In practice, then, it is important to determine the nature of all the assets and income sources forgone because of dislocation. An example of nonmonetary income is the range of forest products that people relocated from tropical forest areas are likely to lose. A survey of the communities affected by the Pelagus/Bakun hydroelectric projects in Sarawak showed that important sources of nonmarket income were hunting and fishing, on which some groups depended substantially for food, and which would be lost on relocation (German Agency for Technical Cooperation and SAMA Consortium 1982). On actual relocation in Sarawak, those relocated also cited the loss of nonmarket benefits as a main source of "regret" (Furtado and associates 1991). They collected other forest products, such as rattan, dammar, garu, and jelutong, for cash sales, which would tend to be captured in any competent socioeconomic survey. The concepts of assets and income need to be kept broad to embrace nonmarket activities, the benefits of which may be lost on relocation.

Communities may also lose the pattern of social organization that prevailed before the project. Resettlement projects often treat the displaced community not as a social unit, but as an aggregation of individuals and families, paying little attention to the social structure of the community. On relocation, traditional communal rules and regulations may break down as traditional leaders lose their power over the allocation of rights to hunt and fish, to land, and so on—rights that effectively become the province of the government agency handling the resettlement. This is a social cost of resettlement for which compensation is extremely difficult. Careful project design and, where possible, integration of particular ethnic and social groups with similar host groups can minimize the problem.

UNDERCOMPENSATION BECAUSE OF NEGLECT OF THE CONSUMER SURPLUS. Welfare economics has shown that market prices do not capture the full economic benefits of a good or asset to the consumer or owner. The difference between the "willingness to pay" for the benefit in question and the market price is known as the consumer surplus. Figure 2.3 illustrates this concept. When the market price is Pm, the individual's willingness to pay is shown by the demand curve. The shaded area is the consumer surplus. If an asset is lost, proper compensation must be based not on the market price, but on the market price plus the consumer surplus. If the asset is replaced, the loss is the consumer surplus. Finally, if the asset has no market value because it is not traded (as with cultural or religious assets, for example), the surplus is again the relevant measure (the price is zero, but the surplus is positive).

The size of this surplus in the resettlement context is unknown because we have no real studies in developing countries on which to base an estimate. Some capital investments involving dislocation have been the subject of willingness to accept compensation (WTAC) surveys in

Figure 2.3

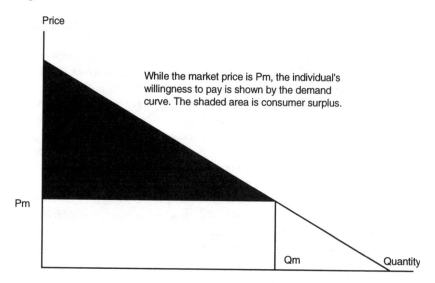

While the market price is Pm, the individual's willingness to pay is shown by the demand curve. The shaded area is consumer surplus.

the industrial world. Thus, London's Third Airport study of 1969–71 asked householders potentially affected by the development for their WTAC to be moved (Dasgupta and Pearce 1972, Schofield 1987). Unfortunately, the questionnaire used was flawed in that it did not indicate how far affected households would have to move. Moreover, it was an early example of the use of contingent valuation. Questionnaires have become far more sophisticated since that time.

OVERCOMING THE BIAS TO UNDERCOMPENSATION. It is evident that asset compensation could well involve undercompensation. The same may be true of the income approach. The issue is whether there are any ways to overcome this uncertainty about what the full and proper level of compensation should be. One approach is to supplement any asset or income inventory with a survey of willingness to pay (WTP) and WTAC.

WTP and WTAC surveys are common in environmental economics, where economists use them primarily to elicit economic valuations of nonmarketed environmental services, for example, the benefits of pollution reduction. They are just as important for marketed services or quasi-marketed services, for example, water supply. This applicability of WTA and WTAC surveys, or contingent valuation, to the spectrum of marketed and nonmarketed benefits (and costs) is important in the resettlement context.[6] Another failing of many socioeconomic baseline surveys, as already noted, is the omission of nonmarket sources of income, including cultural values and social cohesion. These are as much assets as anything else, and need to be accounted for. In the same way, there are psychological costs with dislocation.

Once these broader concepts of income and assets are recognized, it will be evident that compensation based on some official assessment of employment and property will understate the true value of the assets in the preproject situation. If contingent valuation can be made reliable, it has the virtue that it captures the dislocated population's own valuation of its assets and income construed in the broad manner described earlier. That is, it can capture the nonmonetary concepts of income and assets, including psychological costs, environmental services, market access, and cultural property.

Contingent valuation works by asking respondents to state their WTP to secure a given benefit and WTAC for giving up some benefit, usually (and preferably) in face-to-face interviews. A number of potential sources of bias exist, including hypothetical bias if the respondent is not facing the actual choice in question. However, modern questionnaire design has overcome many of the biases; investigators can test for the biases that remain to see if under- or overestimates are likely to arise. The hypothetical bias is likely to be minimal in the resettlement content because the threat of dislocation is a real one. (Hypothetical bias is not wholly absent, as several surveys have shown that people do not believe the event will happen until the day for relocation actually arrives [World Bank 1993b]).

As resettlement involves a loss, the relevant measure is the WTAC. In virtually all contingent valuation studies the means of compensation is money. That is not always appropriate for the main losses—land and housing—in the resettlement context, for reasons Cernea (1988) and others have pointed out. However, nothing in the contingent valuation approach says that money has to be the means of compensation. Nevertheless, cash compensation is appropriate for some losses that cannot be recreated instantly, for example, trees, and may work well for communities above the poverty line and where institutions are available for investing the money in new homes and so on (World Bank 1993b).

One possibility would be to survey communities about services that might be offered under a rehabilitation package and see what level of these might compensate for forgone preproject services. Such a questionnaire approach could be confined to nonmarket assets and services, or it could be extended to cover all assets. One obvious problem with WTAC questions is the potential for people to give inflated responses in the expectation that the responses will influence the actual level of compensation. Therefore, some thought needs to be given to mechanisms that will minimize such biases.

The contingent valuation literature has another important feature. In studies in industrial countries a fair degree of evidence indicates that WTAC measures exceed WTP measures, often significantly (Gregory 1986, also box 2.1). While the reasons for this disparity are disputed

---

Box 2.1. Contingent Valuation and Loss Aversion

Contingent valuation involves carefully structured questionnaires that ask respondents to indicate their WTP for a benefit or WTAC for a cost. Contingent valuation has been used extensively in environmental contexts, and applications have increased significantly in developing countries, mainly, but not exclusively, in connection with water supply and sanitation investments. WTP questions are more usual, but where anticipated losses are involved, WTAC questions are more appropriate. Economic theory suggests that WTP and WTAC should not differ much (they are the compensating variation and equivalent variation of welfare economics), but contingent valuation studies reveal a significant difference between them in practice, a result that may be caused by loss aversion. Some results from case studies in industrial economies are shown below for hypothetical contexts, that is, "what if" contexts where the answers do not involve any real transaction, and for real exchange contexts, where the survey uses actual money or goods.

Author	Context	WTAC/WTP ratio
Hypothetical surveys		
Hammack and Brown 1974	Marshes	4.2
Sinclair 1978	Fishing	2.9
Banford and others 1979	Fishing pier, postal service	2.7 to 2.8
Bishop and Heberlein 1970	Hunting	4.8
Rowe 1980	Visibility	2.6
Brookshire 1980	Hunting	2.6
Heberlein and Bishop 1985	Hunting	16.5
Real exchanges		
Knetsch and Sinden 1985	Lottery	4.0
Heberlein and Bishop 1985	Hunting	6.9
Coursey 1987	Tasting	1.4 to 2.6
Brookshire and Coursey 1987	Trees	2.1 to 5.6

Source: Kahneman, Knetsch, and Thaler 1990.

(Kahneman, Knetsch, and Thaler 1990), many believe that it reflects a general phenomenon of loss aversion, whereby individuals attach greater value to losses than to equivalent gains.[7] How far this asymmetry of valuation applies in the developing world is difficult to gauge, because no studies appear to have obtained WTP and WTAC measures. However, if it does apply, then compensation measures may well be understated by reference to the market prices of assets.

The WTAC approach might also assist with the problem of valuing public assets. Clearly, relocation involves the loss of access to and shares in communal assets. The Bank's approach is to replace those assets in the host community, replicating (and improving) the asset structure in the preproject situation as far as possible. This is a sound approach, but it could be supplemented by contingent valuation assessments to provide some idea of the valuations of those assets by individuals.[8] A further approach to valuing public asset losses is suggested later through the use of rules of thumb for compensating the host community.

The WTAC approach may prove unworkable in some contexts. In the resettlement case respondents are effectively asked to state the value of their assets, income, and other sources of well-being in the context of a development that they may well not understand or may not believe will actually take place. As Butcher (in Furtado and associates 1991) notes:

> The tendency to disbelieve anything will happen, together with their inability to conceive of the man-made lake, creates a very difficult situation in which affected people have to make rational choices on what to do. For many, their world is limited to their village and the land and forest around it; and anything beyond this has no significance for them other than its strangeness.

However, the observed ability of such groups to organize themselves when the threat of development is realized suggests that they may well be able to respond rationally to interviews involving WTAC questions. Moreover, the contingent valuation approach has an additional virtue: its compatibility with participation exercises. Because WTAC questions require that respondents understand the exact scenario for relocation, contingent valuation can be added to baseline social surveys fairly easily. At the same time, the questionnaires can encourage a sense of involvement in the project on the part of the affected population (box 2.2).

While there is little experience with WTAC/WTP valuations in developing countries, the evidence that is available suggests that such valuations can work and that they produce sensible results (box 2.3).

Box 2.2. Negotiating Compensation in China

Resettlement procedures in China have some of the characteristics of the kind of bargaining context to be found in contingent valuation procedures, even though contingent valuation is not used. Initial announcements about projects are followed by careful information campaigns targeting the specific populations. Counties negotiate with towns, villages, and households about compensation. Compensation offers are often refused, and negotiations subsequently focus on securing acceptance of the offer made or on modifying the offer. The extent of public discussion may vary from one project to another and the mechanisms of such negotiation differ from rural to urban resettlement programs.

Source: World Bank 1993a.

While the suggested approach obviously has its problems, contingent valuation surveys could be experimented with to see how answers match up with the replacement costs of assets. Theoretically, we would expect the WTAC to be greater than the value of replaced assets, reflecting the nonmarket element and the respondents' expectations about the change in the quantity (or value) of assets over time.

Box 2.3. Contingent Valuation in Madagascar

One of the few examples of the use of WTAC approaches in developing countries concerns the potential loss of access to a forest area of Madagascar because of a planned national park. The establishment of the park involves reduced access for nearby villagers, who rely on the forest for various environmental services. The project planners assessed their losses in two ways: by estimating the market value of the services lost (the opportunity cost approach) and by asking villagers for their WTAC to forgo the uses of the forest (contingent valuation). The contingent valuation should capture the nonmarket benefits of the forest.

The results are set out below. Although shown in dollars, the compensation was measured in terms of rice.

Market value of forest products *(US$ per household)*	*WTAC*
$91	$108

While the results are similar, it is significant that the contingent valuation measure is nearly 20 percent higher than the market price indicator.

Source: Kramer and others 1993.

PAYMENTS TO THE HOST COMMUNITY. As Cernea (1988) notes, the host community also bears costs in assimilating the displaced community: "empty green field" relocation sites are rare. However, the 1988 pro forma for economic and financial costing of resettlement projects does not overtly recognize the concept of compensating the host community (Cernea 1988, annex 2).

While assessing the losses of the relocated group is difficult, it is easier than assessing appropriate compensation for the host community. This is because the relocated group has identifiable losses, whereas while the host community has some known costs, it also faces anticipated but uncertain costs. These will be especially difficult to assess if the host community has little experience of assimilating settlers. The World Bank's Operations Evaluation Department's review of four projects (World Bank 1993b) also shows that failure to compensate hosts adequately (or at all), as in the Kpong hydroelectric project, can quickly render resettlement unsustainable. Experience with the construction of the Narayanpur dam in India also suggests that failure to anticipate environmental demands on the host area can cause significant social conflicts between host populations and resettlers (World Bank 1989).

The most difficult cost to estimate in this context is the effect of the expanded population on the host community's natural resources and environmental services. However, some fairly elementary rules of impact assessment can be applied. If fuelwood is an issue, estimating the extra demand should be possible by looking at demand in the host and in the dislocated community. Ideally, a resource inventory of the host area would indicate the potential for meeting the expanded demand. Otherwise, explicit provision will have to be made to establish woodlots for the specific purpose of providing additional supplies. Much the same holds true for water. Compensation might consist of funds for additional boreholes or even for communal taps. By far the most difficult problem will be estimating the effect of an expanded population on the receiving capacities for human and other waste.

Financing Resettlement

Resettlement packages need to be financed, and the costs of resettlement must be debited to the cost of the particular development project. Where the project yields benefits, for example, in the form of electricity or irrigation, beneficiaries should pay for the resettlement costs through a charge on the output, for instance, through higher electricity prices or irrigation charges. Because the resettlement costs occur early in the project cycle and the benefits come later, charges will yield revenues that can be used to pay back loans made specifically for the resettlement component of a project.

The Policy Context

Resettlement occurs mainly in the context of dams for irrigation, hydropower, and potable water. These investments are justified in terms of the net benefits they generate for society at large. Conventional measures of those net benefits are the economic rate of return and the net present value. These measures of social profitability are determined, in turn, by the quantities and prices of the project's outputs and inputs. As far as the Bank is concerned, shadow pricing of the costs and benefits of, say, a hydropower dam should ensure that the project is correctly evaluated. In terms of markets' actual workings, developing countries subsidize energy, including electricity, fairly systematically (Kosmo 1987, 1989). Electricity prices are, on average, about 30 percent of the costs of supply. If consumers paid the long-run marginal cost of supply, they would consume around 20 percent less electricity (World Bank 1992). Thus, if marginal cost pricing were employed, people would demand less electricity and fewer communities would be dislocated.

The problem of resettlement is, therefore, partly a problem of distorted energy and water pricing policies in the developing world. Those who are threatened with social dislocation should not pay for these economic distortions by being forced to bear the burden of economic inefficiency. Project interventions cannot solve these problems. Only macroeconomic and sectoral policy reform can correct the distortions.

Provided that those projects involving the Bank are properly evaluated, that is, shadow priced, one could argue that the Bank is not contributing to this element of unnecessary displacement. However, the shadow pricing requirement is somewhat stricter than marginal cost pricing. Marginal social costs should form the basis of the correct pricing rule (Goodland, Juras, and Pachauri 1991). This, in turn, means that electricity and water prices should reflect the environmental and social costs of production and distribution, as well as the private costs. This full costing of the outputs of projects is still not practiced on a sufficiently rigorous basis (Dixon, Talbot, and Le Moigne 1989). In addition to proper pricing, a careful consideration of the alternatives always needs to be made. As far as multipurpose dams are concerned, defining the alternatives is not easy because few alternatives are usually available to dams for irrigation or flood control. However, alternative sources of electricity are available, and planners should investigate these thoroughly (World Bank 1992).

From this discussion, it follows that at least some amount of displacement is due to economic distortions in the markets for the outputs from the projects in question, mainly water and electricity. The Bank can minimize its involvement in this unnecessary displacement by careful application of shadow pricing rules, but these must embrace projects' environmental and social consequences.

Resettlement and Project Rates of Return

One issue that frequently arises is whether resettlement costs make projects uneconomic. Gutman (1993) shows that if resettlement costs amounted to more than 10 percent of total project costs, 50 percent overruns in resettlement costs could have jeopardized up to 30 percent of a sample of projects reviewed. Where resettlement costs are less than 10 percent of project costs, overruns are not likely to result in unacceptable rates of return. The possibility that high resettlement costs could cause unacceptable rates of return appears to be a cause of some concern. (Similar concerns have been expressed about environmental costs.) However, if the resettlement costs are correctly calculated using the "no worse off" criterion, then projects with unacceptable rates of return should not go ahead anyway. Invoking a rate-of-return criterion for accepting and rejecting projects, and then denying its relevance when a proper accounting of costs produces a reject decision, would be contradictory.

Circumstances that give rise to such concerns are probably those in which the project is thought to be a national priority, perhaps because no alternative is available to meet projected energy or water demand. Apart from the fact that one alternative is always available, which is not to proceed with any development, the option of raising the price of the project's output is also available. While this may seem like a departure from correct shadow pricing, what such a procedure is actually doing is acknowledging the national need for the project and placing a premium on prices to reflect that need.

What is critically important is that arguments about national need and unacceptable rates of return should never be used to play down the importance of properly costing the resettlement component, or for that matter, any other component.

Guidelines for Gathering and Analyzing Economic Information for Resettlement

This section converts the conclusions of the previous sections into a set of principles and guidelines for carrying out the economic analysis of resettlement components in projects and for generating the economic information needed for such analysis. The guidelines also take into account the current Bank guidelines, as well as the arguments developed in two other studies in this volume (Cernea and Eriksen) and the findings of the Bank-wide resettlement review (World Bank 1994). Box 2.4 lists the cost components of resettlement according to their attributions into a pro forma that may facilitate and standardize the project economist's work.

The suggested principles and guidelines are as follows:

Box 2.4. A Revised Pro Forma for Assessing Resettlement Costs

The costs listed below are those that should be debited to any project that entails population displacement. All cost items should be allocated to the year in which they are likely to occur to permit standardized discounted cash flow analysis.

For financial appraisal, costs are estimated inclusive of taxes, subsidies, and so on. For economic appraisal, shadow pricing of significant items will be required using available conversion factors.

Cost categories vary according to the nature of project and the affected party.

Cost category	Comment
Administrative and transaction costs	
Baseline surveys of affected populations and host communities, census, land registration, participation exercises, staffing, offices, technical assistance.	Ensure that costs are estimated in both affected and host areas, and for the full projected resettlement period.
Compensation and resettlement costs: marketable assets	
Lost land: new land where possible.	Allow for productivity differences of new land, if any. Allow for potential higher price of new land—see guidelines.
Lost housing: replacement housing.	
Crops: new land compensates but not for the adjustment period when food and cash will be required.	Obligation on the developer to ensure that the transition and adjustment period is minimized.
Lost employment: new employment.	

FULL COST ANALYSIS. All projects that result in displacement of people require full cost analysis, where full cost means resource costs plus environmental costs plus social costs. The failure to engage in full cost analysis will result in unwarranted displacement effects.

COST MINIMIZATION. For any given level of project benefit (such as electricity or irrigation water), resettlement costs should be minimized. This can be done through careful analysis of alternative designs and optimal location of the project.

Cost category	Comment
Small business: new building.	See also "market access" below.
Public assets	
Infrastructure: expanded assets in the community.	Includes any provision of host community assets to induce acceptance of immigrants.
Environmental services	
Grazing lands, common resource rights: expanded assets in host community.	Depends on capacity in host community.
Water: cost of new boreholes. Cash payments appropriate if water has to be purchased.	Depends on capacity in host community.
Fuelwood, fodder, poles; cost of tree-planting schemes in host community. Cash payments appropriate if wood and fodder have to be bought, such as in transition period.	Depends on capacity in host community.
Compensation and resettlement costs: nonmarket assets	
Cultural assets. Costs of recreation.	Contingent valuation if recreation of assets difficult.
Social cohesion Psychological stability Environmental services	Use contingent valuation to determine values for cash or in-kind compensation (for example, wild meat).
Rehabilitation costs	
Investment costs of rehabilitation projects. Costs of extension, new works, retraining, credit, marketing.	

TRADEOFFS. Where a tradeoff between the amount or severity of displacement and the net benefits of the project can be identified, that tradeoff should be evaluated. A simple indicator might be computed, such as the number of families displaced per $1,000 of annual net benefits, so as to show the displacement cost in terms of the overall project benefits achieved.

WEIGHTING THE COSTS. Giving a higher weight to the cost of displacement, that is, in excess of the monetary value of assets and income lost, is warranted on two grounds: (a) equity, if the displaced population has less income or wealth than the likely beneficiaries, and (b) the probability that loss aversion exists, whereby people place a higher value on a $1 loss than on a $1 gain.

ATTENTION TO HOST COMMUNITIES. The concern that resettlers are no worse off after the project than before needs to be extended more explicitly to host communities where relevant. In determining whether resettlers and host communities are no worse off, attention must be paid to what would have happened in the absence of the project. Current guidelines assume a comparison between levels of well-being before and after the project. However, the relevant comparison is between the level of well-being that would have occurred without the project (allowing for the growth of incomes and assets) and the standard of living with the project.

Additionally, account must be taken of the feedback effect of the development on land values: in other words, compensation agreed on before the development is likely to be inadequate if land values rise by the time of the development. Land-for-land compensation avoids resettlers paying the costs of these price increases, provided the quantity and quality of the land they will receive is carefully specified.

EXTENT OF INVESTMENT. Some relatively simple rules of thumb might be used to compute the relevant level of compensation for the loss of public assets where a host community is involved. As a general rule, investment in expanded and new assets should take place up to the point where assets per capita or per family are the same or better than in the best off of the two communities. Where resettlement involves a green field site (newly developed land), assets per capita should be no less than they would have been in the displaced community in the absence of the project.

NO WORSE OFF. The "at least no worse off" criterion has strong justification in the philosophy of sustainable development, which requires that special attention be paid to the most disadvantaged members of a society and that development packages be implemented to ensure that displaced communities are no worse off in the future. The most important features of a rehabilitation package for sustainable development are likely to be secure land tenure and defined resource rights, extension, start-up funds and access to affordable credit.

NONMARKET SOURCES OF INCOME. The concept of income used when assessing incomes lost because of relocation must be extended to include nonmarket sources of income. Market values ignore nonmarket and intangible assets. Even when the emphasis is on replacement costs and not just on the market value of lost assets, the risk of understating true losses of well-being remains.

VALUATION BY RESETTLERS. An attempt should be made to assess the resettlers' willingness to accept compensation for the move by identifying *their* valuations of, at least, cultural assets and nonmarket benefits. Willingness to accept studies are also relevant to market assets because of the likely presence of consumer surplus, that is, valuations of assets over and above the market price of those assets.

CASH COMPENSATION. The form of compensation is likely to vary from context to context. In general, however, cash compensation should be confined to those assets that cannot be easily replicated in the resettlement area, for example, trees; where resettlers have the experience to invest money in new assets and have access to reasonably functioning markets; or where employment opportunities are available. Such contexts are more likely to arise in the higher-income countries.

ATTENTION TO NATURAL RESOURCES. Efforts must be made to assess the additional demands that resettlers will make on natural resources in the resettled area, especially fuelwood, water, and grazing lands. If the host community has spare natural resource capacity, the resettled area may be able to accommodate new demands, but planners must ensure that they assess the regenerative capacity of resources, such as forests and groundwater.

THE POLICY CONTEXT. Renewed attention needs to be paid to the policy context of projects entailing resettlement. Avoidance of resettlement can be maximized by ensuring that projects are subject to full social, environmental, and economic analysis; that they avoid externalization; and that they incorporate valuations of all impacts as far as possible.

WHO PAYS FOR RESETTLEMENT. Financing for resettlement should be regarded as part of the capital cost of a development project, with special attention paid to inflation and the means of financing resettlement. Because of inflation, compensation may be inadequate if it is not measured in real terms.

A second consideration is how resettlement is to be financed. The "beneficiary pays" principle suggests that the beneficiaries of the development project should pay the full costs of resettlement, not the people upon which displacement is imposed. This will happen automatically if the developer bears the full costs of resettlement rather than the government, because the costs are then internalized into the private costs of the development. Where the developer does not bear the full costs, the developing entity can be made to do so through a "development charge," which is a charge levied on the developer to repay a loan granted by the government.

Notes

1. Note that those who bear the costs of projects, the "developers," are already more than compensated by the expected flow of benefits from the project. Hence the issue is one of asking about compensation for externalities, costs that are not normally internalized.

2. The benefits and costs are all in terms of discounted values, which means adopting a discount rate.

3. A more technical point is that minimizing the sum of social, economic, and environmental costs does not necessarily mean that each component cost is minimized. Minimizing one component cost may raise costs in another component, for example, but we ignore this complication here.

4. This is not necessarily a recommendation for the social weighting of gains and losses, although the Bank did experiment with such weights in project appraisal for some time (see Squire and van der Tak 1975).

5. Traditionally, development practitioners thought that communal ownership resulted in the "tragedy of the commons" (Hardin 1968), but in reality, it is open access, defined as no ownership at all, that gives rise to excessive resource degradation. Communal management is often an excellent protector of resources because the community as a whole is perceived to bear the cost of degradation, not the individual alone (Baumol and Oates 1988; Bromley and Cernea 1989; Pearce and Turner 1990).

6. The literature on contingent valuation is huge. A definitive bibliography compiled by Carson and associates (1995) has some 2,100 entries. The main theoretical texts are Cummings, Brookshire, and Schulze (1986) and Mitchell and Carson (1989). Applications of contingent valuation in the developing world have primarily been in the context of water supply and sanitation (see, for example,

Altaf and others 1992; Boadu 1992; Briscoe and others 1990; North and Griffin 1993; Singh and others 1993; Whittington and others 1987, 1990; Whittington, 1992). For surveys of contingent valuation in developing countries see Pearce and Whittington (1994) and for a technical manual see Pearce, Whittington, and Georgiou (1993).

7. That is, the valuation function is kinked at the point that reflects the individual's existing situation (the reference point) rather than smoothly curved, as is assumed in neoclassical microeconomics. Loss aversion extends beyond environmental and dislocation effects and may even explain some stock exchange behavior. The reason that loss aversion is contrary to standard economic theory is that the theory of consumer behavior suggests that the compensating variation measure of consumer surplus (essentially WTP) should be approximately equal to the equivalent variation measure of consumer surplus (WTAC) (see Willig 1976).

8. Moreover, replacing assets may contain a further element of bias in that the surplus value attached to the asset in the preproject context may not be the same as in the relocation area: it could be higher or lower. Contingent valuation would secure some measure of this surplus.

References

The word "processed" describes informally reproduced works that may not be commonly available through libraries.

Altaf, M., H. Jamal, and D. Whittington. 1992. "Willingness to Pay for Water in Rural Punjab." Pakistan UNDP–World Bank Water and Sanitation Program Series No. 4. World Bank, Washington, D.C. Processed.

Baumol, W., and W. Oates. 1988. *The Theory of Environmental Policy*. 2nd edition. London and New York: Cambridge University Press.

Boadu, F. 1992. "Contingent Valuation for Household Water in Rural Ghana." *Journal of Agricultural Economics* 43 (3): 458–65.

Briscoe, J., P. F. de Castro, C. Griffin, J. North, and O. Olsen. 1990. "Towards Equitable and Sustainable Rural Water Supplies: A Contingent Valuation Study in Brazil." *The World Bank Economic Review* 4 (2): 115-34.

Bromley, D. W. 1991. *Environment and Economy: Property Rights and Public Policy*. Oxford, U.K.: Blackwell.

Bromley, D. W., and M. M. Cernea. 1989. *The Management of Common Property Natural Resources: Some Conceptual and Operational Fallacies*. Discussion Paper 57. Washington, D.C.: World Bank.

Butcher, D. 1987. "Report on Status of Resettlement in Bank Financed Projects and Corrective Actions Taken." World Bank, Washington, D.C. Processed.

_____. 1990. "Review of the Treatment of Environmental Aspects of Bank Energy Projects." PRE Working Paper, World Bank, Industry and Energy Department, Washington, D.C. Processed.

Carson, R., J. Wright, N. Carson, A. Alberini, N. Flores. 1995. *Bibliography of Contingent Valuation Studies and Papers*. La Jolla, CA: Natural Resource Damage Assessment, Inc.

Cernea, Michael M. 1986. "Involuntary Resettlement in Bank-Assisted Projects: A Review of the Application of Bank Policies and Procedures in FY79–85 Projects." World Bank, Agriculture and Rural Development Department, Washington, D.C. Processed.

_____. 1988. *Involuntary Resettlement in Development Projects: Policy Guidelines in World Bank–Financed Projects*. Technical Paper 80. Washington, D.C.: World Bank.

_____. 1990. *Poverty Risks from Population Displacement in Water Resources Development*. Development Discussion Paper 355. Cambridge, Massachusetts: Harvard Institute for International Development.

Cummings, R., D. Brookshire, and W. Schulze. 1986. *Valuing Environmental Goods: An Assessment of the Contingent Valuation Method*. Totowa, New Jersey: Rowman and Allanheld.

Curry, S., and J. Weiss. 1993. *Project Analysis in Developing Countries*. Basingstoke, U.K.: Macmillan.

Dasgupta, A. K., and D. W. Pearce. 1972. *Cost-Benefit Analysis: Theory and Practice*. Basingstoke, U.K.: Macmillan.

Dixon, John A., L. Talbot, and G. Le Moigne. 1989. *Dams and the Environment: Considerations in World Bank Projects*. Washington, D.C.: World Bank.

Furtado, J. dos R., A. Markandya, J. Mitchell, and D. W. Pearce. 1991. *Large Hydropower Dams in the Tropics: Development Assistance and Integrated Management*. London: Centre for Integrated Management for Overseas Development Administration.

German Agency for Technical Cooperation and SAMA Consortium. 1982. *Pelagus/Bakun Hydro-Electric Projects: Socio-Economic Aspects and Resettlement*. Kuching, Malaysia: Sarawak Electricity Supply Corporation.

Gittinger, J. P. 1982. *Economic Analysis of Agricultural Projects*. Baltimore, Maryland: The Johns Hopkins University Press.

Goodland, Robert, A. Juras, and R. Pachauri. 1991. "Can Hydro-Reservoirs in Tropical Moist Forest Be Made Environmentally Acceptable?" Policy and Research Division Working Paper 1991–23, World Bank, Washington, D.C. Processed.

Gregory, R. 1986. "Interpreting Measures of Economic Loss: Evidence from Contingent Valuation and Experimental Studies." *Journal of Environmental Economics and Management* 13: 325–37.

Gutman, P. 1993. "Involuntary Resettlement in the Hydro-Power Projects: A Review of Bank Performance during 1978–1992." World Bank, Industry and Energy Department, Washington, D.C. Processed.

Hardin, G. 1968. "The Tragedy of the Commons." *Science* 162: 1243–48.

Kahneman, D., J. Knetsch, and R. Thaler. 1990. "Experimental Tests of the Endowment Effect and the Coase Theorem." *Journal of Political Economy* 98 (6): 1325–47.

Kosmo, M. 1987. *Money to Burn? The High Cost of Energy Subsidies.* Washington, D.C.: World Resources Institute.

_____. 1989. "Commercial Energy Subsidies in Developing Countries." *Energy Policy* 17 (June): 244–53.

Kramer, R., M. Munasinghe, N. Sharma, E. Mercer, and P. Shyamsundar. 1993. *Valuing a Protected Tropical Forest: A Case Study in Madagascar.* Durham, North Carolina: Duke University, Center for Resource and Environmental Policy.

Mitchell, R. C., and R. T. Carson. 1989. *Using Surveys to Value Public Goods: The Contingent Valuation Method.* Washington, D.C.: Resources for the Future.

North, J. M., and C. C. Griffin. 1993. "Water Source as a Housing Characteristic: Hedonic Property Valuation and Willingness to Pay for Water." *Water Resources Research* 29 (7): 1923–30.

Pearce, D. W. 1999. "Sustainable Development." In D. W. Pearce, ed. *Ecological Economics: Essays on the Theory and Practice of Environmental Economics.* London: Edward Elgar.

Pearce, D. W., and R. K. Turner. 1990. *Economics of Natural Resources and the Environment.* Hemel Hempstead, U.K.: Harvester Wheatsheaf; Baltimore, Maryland: The Johns Hopkins University Press.

Pearce, D. W., and D. Whittington. 1994. *Economic Valuation of Environmental Costs and Benefits in Developing Countries: A Compendium.* Nairobi, Kenya: United Nations Environment Programme.

Pearce, D. W., E. Barbier, and A. Markandya. 1990. *Sustainable Development: Economics and Environment in the Third World.* London: Earthscan.

Pearce, D. W., A. Markandya, and E. Barbier. 1990. "Environmental Sustainability and Cost Benefit Analysis." *Environment and Planning* 22: 1259–66.

Pearce, D. W., D. Whittington, and S. Georgiou. 1993. *A Technical Manual for the Environmental Appraisal of Projects and Policies.* Paris: Organisation for Economic Co-operation and Development.

Schofield, N. 1987. *Cost-Benefit Analysis in Urban and Regional Planning.* London: Unwin Hyam.

Singh, B., R. Ramasubban, R. Bhatia, J. Briscoe, C. Griffin, and C. Kim. 1993. "Rural Water Supply in Kerala, India." *Water Resources Research* 29 (7): 1931–42.

Solow, R. 1986. "On the Intergenerational Allocation of Natural Resources." *Scandinavian Journal of Economics* 88 (1): 141–49.

_____. 1993. "An Almost Practical Step toward Sustainability." Lecture given to Resources for the Future, Washington, D.C. Processed.

Squire, Lyn, and H. van der Tak. 1975. *Economic Analysis of Projects.* Baltimore, Maryland: The Johns Hopkins University Press.

Stevenson, G. 1991. *Common Property Economics: A General Theory and Land Use Applications.* Cambridge, U.K.: Cambridge University Press.

UNIDO (United Nations Industrial Organisation). 1972. *Guidelines for Project Evaluation.* Vienna.

von Amsberg, J. 1993. "Project Evaluation and the Depletion of Natural Capital: An Application of the Sustainability Principle." Environment Department Working Paper 56. World Bank, Washington, D.C. Processed.

Ward, William A. and Barry J. Deren, with Emmanuel H. D'Silva. 1991. *The Economics of Project Analysis: A Practitioner's Guide*. Washington, D.C.: World Bank.

Whittington, D. 1991. "Willingness to Pay for Improved Sanitation in Kumasi, Ghana." World Bank, Infrastructure and Urban Development Department, Washington, D.C. Processed.

_____. 1992. *Willingness to Pay for Water in Rural Punjab, Pakistan*, UNDP–World Bank Water and Sanitation Program, Report 4. New York: UNDP.

Whittington, D., M. Mujwahuzi, G. McMahon, and K. Choe. 1989. *Willingness to Pay for Water in Newala District, Tanzania: Strategies for Cost Recovery*. Water and Sanitation for Health Project, Field Report 246. Washington, D.C.: U.S. Agency for International Development.

Whittington, D., J. Briscoe, X. Mu, and W. Barron. 1990. "Estimating the Willingness to Pay for Water Services in Developing Countries: A Case Study of the Use of Contingent Valuation Survey in Southern Haiti." *Economic Development and Cultural Change* 38 (2): 293–311.

Willig, R. 1976. "Consumers' Surplus without Apology." *American Economic Review* 66 (4): 589–97.

World Bank. 1989. "Staff Appraisal Report: India–Upper Krishna (Phase II) Irrigation Project." Report No. 7406-IN. Washington, D.C. Processed.

_____. 1990. Operational Directive 4.30: "Involuntary Resettlement." Washington, D.C. Processed.

_____. 1991. Operational Directive 4.20: "Indigenous People." Washington, D.C. Processed.

_____. 1992. *World Development Report 1992: Development and the Environment*. New York: Oxford University Press.

_____. 1993a. "China: Involuntary Resettlement." Report 11641-CHA. China and Mongolia Department. Washington, D.C. Processed.

_____. 1993b. "Early Experience with Involuntary Settlement: Overview." Operations Evaluation Department. Washington, D.C. Processed.

_____. 1994. "Resettlement and Development: The Bankwide Review of Projects Involving Involuntary Resettlement 1986–1993." Washington, D.C. Processed.

_____. 1998. "Recent Experience with Involuntary Resettlement: OED Overview." Washington, D.C. Processed.

World Commission on Environment and Development. 1987. *Our Common Future*. Oxford, U.K.: Oxford University Press.

3

Comparing the Economic Planning for Voluntary and Involuntary Resettlement

John H. Eriksen

Editor's Note   This chapter provides the most detailed comparative study of *voluntary* population settlement programs and *involuntary* resettlement programs undertaken in the literature. Using a careful secondary analysis of data, the author reveals wide disparities in the ways in which several governments have treated the two types of resettlement over essentially the same time period. In almost all cases, these differences have been to the detriment of those forcibly displaced. Country economic planners appear to systematically undertreat involuntary relocation. The few positive exceptions signaled by the author not only reinforce the findings, but also convincingly demonstrate that involuntary resettlement does not necessarily have to become a development setback. These exceptions prove that the process can protect, even benefit, those relocated.

The study uses a simple yet ingenious methodology. Five sets of development projects were identified in five countries according to criteria that make comparisons among the projects legitimate. Each pair consists of a project supporting voluntary resettlement and a project in the same country containing an involuntary resettlement component. For some countries, more than a pair of projects could be identified, so a total of 18 projects were studied. Appraisal reports and completion reports provided both *ex ante* and *ex post*. All of the projects were cofinanced by the World Bank and offer some of the largest sets of data available for development projects—much more than the data typically available for projects financed from domestic sources alone. Several variables—from type of resettlement to household income, from type of farm model envisaged to type of risk assessment—are examined, as are some of the assertions expressed in the literature about differences between voluntary and involuntary resettlement projects in design, strategy, economic analysis, and financial allocations.

The findings of this comparative analysis persuasively demonstrate that, independent of the complexity of forced displacement, failures originate partly from subjective errors of strategy and from inadequate or absent economic and financial analysis of resettlement components at project appraisal stage. The study argues that changes of paradigm and method are imperative, because marginal fixes will not improve the outcomes of involuntary resettlements. The facts highlighted in this chapter and its recommendations invite the full attention of everyone involved in planning resettlements, from decisionmakers to practicing planners, economists and social researchers.

This chapter compares projects supporting *voluntary* resettlement with those supporting *involuntary resettlement*. The purpose of this comparative analysis is to identify the differences or similarities between voluntary and involuntary resettlement operations. This analysis uses five sets (or pairs) of projects in five countries, with each set containing both types of projects (thus each set contains two or more projects). Several criteria were used to select appropriate project pairs for comparison: both projects had to take place in the same country, during approximately the same period. And both had to have resettlement components that focused on restoring families' incomes by installing identical or very similar sets of agricultural enterprises. Project pairs also were selected to reflect a broad geographical spectrum, with cases drawn from Asia, Africa, and Latin America.

The first section compares the planning approach and characteristics of resettlement activities in Brazil, China, India, Indonesia, and Ghana. The second section further analyzes the different farm "models" used in planning project resettlement operations. The analysis of the individual projects also reviews the economic assumptions made about the baseline income of resettlers and planners' expectations as to their future after resettlement, including farm production, off-farm income, and so on. The final section lists recommendations for improving the design and implementation of resettlement operations.

The specific resettlement activities compared in this study were components of the following World Bank projects:

- In Brazil, the Sobradinho involuntary resettlement under the Paulo Afonso IV Hydroelectric Project and the voluntary resettlement projects under the Northwest Regional Development (Polonoreste) Program, which includes the Agricultural Development and Environmental Protection Project, the Mato Grosso Rural Development Project, and the New Settlements Project
- In China, the involuntary resettlement under the First and Second Shuikou hydroelectric projects and the voluntary resettlement under the Red Soils Area Development Project
- In India, the involuntary resettlement under the Gujarat Irrigation projects I and II and the voluntary resettlement under the Rajasthan Canal Command Area Development and the Rajasthan Command Area and Settlement projects
- In Indonesia, the involuntary resettlement under the Thirteenth Power (Cirata Dam) Project and the voluntary resettlement under the Transmigration I, II, III, and IV projects
- In Ghana, the involuntary resettlement under the Kpong Hydroelectric Project and the agricultural development under the Volta Region Agricultural Development Project.

A number of issues arose in connection with the analysis. First, data and time constraints imposed some limitations on this comparative analysis, the comprehensiveness of the available data sets, and the availability of comparable pairs of projects. The selection criteria—country, time period, and sector focus—limited the number of involuntary/voluntary resettlement pairings appropriate for comparative analysis. Second, because the study required complete and detailed data sets on project planning and implementation processes over time, four of the five resettlement pairings selected involved projects initiated in the 1970s or early 1980s. Thus the sample did not capture recent improvements in the way the Bank handles involuntary resettlement projects. Third, the involuntary resettlements were all components of major infrastructure development projects, dams, irrigation, or both. These projects, with their large-scale construction activities, demanded massive displacements. As such, they represent only one type of involuntary resettlement. The study utilized World Bank staff appraisal reports (SARs), project completion reports (PCRs), and project performance audit reports (PARs), and in some cases, additional documents from project files.

Programmatic Characteristics of the Projects

The pairs of projects reviewed presented striking contrasts in their approaches to resettlement. In four pairs—those in Brazil, India, Indonesia, and Ghana—project designers and implementers clearly treated the involuntary resettlement component as subordinate to construction processes and schedules (for a discussion of this "engineering bias" in connection with reservoir planning see Cernea 1991) and as an economic externality (see the study by Cernea in this volume)—with poorly identified costs and no defined "benefits." Planning objectives appear to have been to internalize as few of the costs of resettlement as possible and to ignore the real costs or possible benefits of the resettlement component in internal rate-of-return calculations. SARs and PCRs often discussed involuntary resettlement activities in the same section as the analysis of the project's environmental impact. This way, the mitigation of resettlement problems had to be put in place during the life of the project, not ahead of time, and would not impinge upon or disrupt the central process of infrastructure development.

By contrast, in the case of *voluntary* resettlement, project designers and implementers treated such activities, whether spontaneous or government-assisted, as either the central focus of their activities or as an integral part of a long-term, regional process to develop agriculture. In both Brazil and Indonesia, for example, planners and the settlers themselves saw the transmigration of a large number of families from densely settled to "frontier" areas as vital steps in both regional development and nation building. In India, the settlement of landless families on newly developed irrigation schemes in desert areas of Rajasthan had a high priority in terms of both regional economic development and settlement of border areas. In Ghana, while there was no resettlement per se, area development for smallholder farmers had a high priority within the government.

In voluntary resettlement projects, the costs of providing potable water supplies, social infrastructure, agricultural extension services, and road construction between farms and markets were internalized as line items within project budgets. Thus these activities were designed and implemented as building blocks of a larger process of social and economic development.

The First and Second Shuikou projects and the Red Soils Project in China present a different approach to planning and implementing involuntary and voluntary resettlement activities in that resettlement activities were handled as central to the project and as an opportunity for long-term agricultural development in a frontier area.

A review of the paired projects revealed that, in each, the primary determinants of the approach to resettlement were the government's policies and attitudes and the composition of the teams charged with project design and implementation. Evidence suggests that interventions by Bank staff during supervisory missions may have mitigated some of the worst impacts of poor resettlement planning after its effects became evident: for example, in the Sobradinho component of the Paulo Afonso Project in Brazil. However, prior to the World Bank's adoption of its resettlement policy, Bank input into project design seems not to have influenced borrowers' handling of resettlement issues.

More significant is that several individual voluntary resettlement projects were implemented sequentially under the Northwest Regional Development (Polonoreste) Program in Brazil and the transmigration programs in Indonesia. Thus the greater success of the voluntary resettlement programs could be a result of the cumulative effects of the experience gained during individual projects.

Bank Financial Participation in Resettlement

Table 3.1 shows that the degree of financial participation by the Bank in the projects under review varied considerably; however, a pattern is evident. Bank participation as a percentage of total project costs *was generally lower in the involuntary resettlement projects than in the voluntary schemes.* And whereas the Bank's financial participation percentagewise tended to increase (sometimes significantly) between appraisal and loan closure relative to total project costs in voluntary resettlement (often because the total investment in the project ended up less than anticipated), in involuntary resettlement costs the Bank's participation remained at the same level, or even declined, over the life of the project.

An interesting observation is that where Bank financial participation was lowest as a percentage of total project costs, project performance with respect to involuntary resettlement was judged to be the poorest. For instance, in the Paulo Afonso IV Project, where Bank participation was only 5.7 percent, performance was so poor and the impacts so negative that the lessons derived provided a major argument for instituting the first Bank policy on social issues in involuntary resettlement operations (Cernea 1993).

Relationship between Scale and Success

The number of people resettled varied considerably from country to country and among the paired projects within each country (see table 3.2). The largest numbers of participants were resettled voluntarily

Table 3.1.   World Bank Financial Participation in Involuntary and Voluntary Resettlement

Country/project	Total project funding (millions of US$)	World Bank funding (millions of US$)	Percentage of Bank participation
Brazil			
Paulo Afonso IV	692.6[a]	81.0	11.7
Hydroelectric	1,413.9[b]	81.0	5.7
Agricultural Development and Environmental Protection	199.3[a]	67.0	33.6
	132.2[b]	71.5	54.1
Mato Grosso Rural	76.8[a]	26.4	34.6
Development	43.8[b]	22.7	51.8
New Settlements	182.0[a]	65.2	35.8
Indonesia			
Thirteenth Power	625.7[a]	278.3	44.5
	609.2[b]	269.6	44.3
Transmigration I	56.8[a]	30.0	52.8
Transmigration II	242.0[a]	144.1	59.6
Transmigration III	185.8[a]	101.0	54.4
Transmigration IV	121.0[a]	63.5	52.5
	63.9[b]	38.6	60.4
India			
Gujarat Irrigation	170.5[a]	85.0	49.9
	353.8[b]	85.0	24.0
Gujarat Irrigation II	350.0[a]	175.0	50.0
	248.7[b]		
Rajasthan Canal	174.0[a]	83.0	47.7
Command Area	183.6[b]	83.0	45.2
Development			
Rajasthan Command Area and Settlement	110.6[a]	55.0	49.7
	n.a.	n.a.	n.a.
China			
Shuikou	1,087.8[a]	140.0	12.9
Hydroelectric	n.a.	n.a.	n.a.
Second Shuikou	321.0[a]	100.0	31.2
Hydroelectric	n.a.	n.a.	n.a.

Table 3.1. *(continued)*

Country/project	Total project funding (millions of US$)	World Bank funding (millions of US$)	Percentage of Bank participation
China (continued)			
Red Soils Area	122.2[a]	40.0	32.7
Development	110.3[b]	44.7	40.5
Ghana			
Kpong Hydro-	236.5[a]	39.0	16.5
electric	250.6[b]	39.0	15.6
Volta Region	48.7[a]	29.5	60.6
Agricultural	43.8[b]	28.8	65.8
Development			

n.a. Not applicable.

Notes: Involuntary resettlement projects in the table are as follows: in Brazil, the Paulo Afonso IV Hydroelectric Project; in Indonesia, the Thirteenth Power Project; in India, the two Gujarat Irrigation Projects; in China, the two Shuikou Hydroelectric Projects; and in Ghana, the Kpong Hydroelectric Project.

a. Projected figures from staff appraisal reports.

b. Actual figures from project completion reports.

in India and Indonesia: some 432,000 people in the two Rajasthan irrigation projects in India and 133,850 people under the four transmigration projects in Indonesia.

Voluntary resettlement in agricultural development projects in Brazil, India, Indonesia, and Ghana were more successful than the involuntary resettlements, according to Bank evaluations, suggesting that the large scale of the resettlement activity does not significantly contribute to failure of the component.

Average Cost of Resettlement per Participant

Table 3.2 presents a breakdown of the costs of resettlement activities by project, family, and individual. The data vary considerably in terms of quality and comprehensiveness, a fact that creates a number of problems when attempting to analyze the costs of resettlement. The first problem is that in many projects, particularly those in the mid-1970s and early 1980s, the procedures for the financial analysis of projects with resettlement components did not follow a standard format for enumerating resettlement costs. The involuntary resettlement projects in Brazil, India, and Indonesia initially reported only the costs of land acquisition

Table 3.2. Characteristics of the Paired Involuntary and Voluntary Resettlement Projects

Country/project	Number of families resettled	Number of persons resettled	Total resettlement costs ($ million)	Resettlement costs per family ($)	Resettlement costs per capita ($)	Ratio of resettlement costs to GDP
Brazil						
Paulo Afonso IV Hydroelectric	9,700[a]	70,000	120.2	12,392	1,717	1.95
	7,200[b]	51,969	236.2	32,806	4,545	5.17
Agricultural Development and Environmental Protection	18,200[a]	87,000	199.3	10,951	2,291	1.23
	11,330[b]	70,000	132.2	11,668	1,889	10.93
Mato Grosso Rural Development	10,000[a]	47,800	76.4	7,640	1,598	0.78
	6,497[b]	39,632	43.8	6,742	1,105	0.54
New Settlements	15,000[a]	72,000	182.0	12,133	2,528	1.23
Indonesia						
Thirteenth Power	10,121[a]	40,000	92.8	9,167	2,319	3.80
	11,052[b]	43,655	92.8	8,395	2,125	3.48
Transmigration I	8,369[a]	33,476	52.8	6,787	1,697	6.29
	7,232[b]	28,928	57.3	7,923	1,981	7.34
Transmigration II	30,000[a]	120,000	242.0	8,067	2,017	5.04
	19,622[b]	78,488	140.1	7,140	1,785	4.46
Transmigration III	2,000[a]	8,000	185.8	92,900[c]	23,225[c]	38.07
	2,000[b]	8,000	131.0	65,500[c]	16,375[c]	26.84
Transmigration IV	5,400[a]	27,000	121.0	22,407	4,482	7.35
	4,466[b]	18,434	63.9	14,317	3,469	5.68

India					
Gujarat Irrigation and	18,630[a]	111,780	1.8	95[d]	16[d]	—
Gujarat Irrigation II	15,700[b]	94,200	344.1	21,917[e]	3,653[e]	19.23
	20,050[a]	120,300	248.7	12,404[f]	2,067[f]	10.88
Rajasthan Canal Command Area Development	33,000[a]	198,000	174.0	5,273	879	6.28
Rajasthan Command Area and Settlement	39,000[a]	234,000	110.6	2,836	473	2.49
China					
Shuikou and Second Shuikou Hydroelectric	14,522[a]	67,239	207.0	14,254	3,079	10.26
Red Soils Area Development	19,000[a]	61,000	122.0	6,421	2,000	6.67
	13,619[b]	33,646	110.3	8,099	3,278	10.93
Ghana					
Kpong Hydroelectric	1,140[a]	5,700	11.5	10,439	2,018	n.a.
	1,089[b]	7,000	5.4	4,957	771	n.a.
Volta Region Agricultural Development	60,000[a,g]	336,000	48.7	812[h]	145[h]	n.a.
	90,000[b]	504,000	43.8	487[h]	87[h]	n.a.

n.a. Not applicable.

a. Figures from SAR.

b. Figures from PCR.

c. Figure includes site selection and other planning costs for an additional 200,000 families—only 2,000 families actually resettled under the project.

d. Land acquisition costs only.

e. Total cost per beneficiary family and per capita calculated for Gujarat Irrigation Project.

f. Total cost per beneficiary family and per capita calculated for Gujarat Irrigation II Project.

g. Total beneficiary families, no resettlement in this project.

h. Total cost per family and per capita.

and direct compensation. For the Kpong Hydroelectric Project in Ghana, and particularly for the Shuikou I and II projects in China, the financial analyses for involuntary resettlement were much more meticulous at appraisal and appear to have enumerated virtually all the costs of reestablishing the income levels of the displaced populations.[1] This may explain why the per capita resettlement costs are so similar for the China projects, but so divergent for the paired projects in the other countries.

A second difficulty was the large differences between the anticipated and actual cost figures reported for resettlement activities in all the countries. For example, the appraisal report for the Paulo Afonso IV Project in Brazil projected costs of US$12,392 per family and US$1,717 per capita, whereas the PCR indicated that actual costs had amounted to US$32,806 per family and US$4,545 per capita.[2] In most of the other projects, the actual costs of resettlement were lower than the initial estimates. Moreover, one sees PCRs simultaneously reporting that (a) on the one hand, the Bank's evaluators correctly concluded that project planners significantly underestimated the actual size of the populations to be displaced, and (b) on the other hand, because of defective project performance in implementing involuntary resettlement, several projects actually provided compensation and services to significantly fewer displaced people than estimated. The PCRs generally attributed this to poor project implementation, revisions in project objectives during implementation, and exchange rate fluctuations.

A third difficulty was that the number of people included in a particular project tended to change significantly during implementation. In the case of the Northwest Regional Development (Polonoreste) Program in Brazil, where flows of spontaneous migrants were high, one can understand why it was difficult to obtain an accurate estimate of the size and composition of voluntary resettlement populations *ex ante*. In the involuntary resettlement projects, however, where the affected areas were defined in advance, the poor specification of both the size and composition of the groups to be displaced appears to have been primarily a function of inadequate initial field surveys by project planners (World Bank 1994; 1996, p. 131).

Therefore an analysis of the economics of resettlement was difficult, given the constant shifts in funding levels and the number of people to be resettled throughout the implementation of most of the projects surveyed. We can conclude (a) that the available statistical data, given the unrefined methods used in financial planning, do not permit us to demonstrate a relationship between the amount of money spent on resettlement per family or per capita and the project's success at restoring resettlers' incomes, even though individual observations and reports suggest such a relationship; and (b) that when a development strategy common to both involuntary and voluntary resettlement activities is applied systematically from the outset, as in China, it is likely to lead to similar per capita costs for projects (excluding the costs of compensating resettlers for their land).

Duration of Resettlement Operations

Table 3.3 shows the length of Bank involvement in the surveyed resettlement projects. Currently, a full comparison of the pairs of projects is possible only for Brazil, Indonesia, and Ghana. In Brazil and Indonesia, no appreciable differences in the duration of implementation are apparent between involuntary and voluntary resettlement activities, except that the voluntary resettlement projects had slightly shorter implementation periods than the infrastructural projects entailing involuntary resettlement within the same country. In Ghana, by contrast, the Kpong Hydroelectric Project lasted 69 months, whereas the Volta Region Agricultural Development Project took 111 months. What is probably more signifi-

Table 3.3.   Comparison of Effective Length of Projects with Resettlement Operations

Project	Loan dates (Board approval to loan closing)	Effective length of Bank involvement in project (months)
Involuntary resettlement		
Paulo Afonso IV Hydroelectric	06/04/1974 to 06/30/1983	97
Thirteenth Power	06/02/1983 to 05/08/1991	95
Gujarat Irrigation	05/25/1978 to 06/30/1984	73
Gujarat Irrigation II	04/29/1980 to 04/30/1989	96
Kpong Hydroelectric	03/01/1977 to 12/31/1982	69
Voluntary resettlement		
Agricultural Development and Environmental Protection	12/01/1981 to 09/06/1990	93
Mato Gross Rural Development	03/25/1982 to 12/31/1988	80
Transmigration I	07/21/1976 to 04/13/1983	81
Transmigration II	05/29/1979 to 12/31/1986	91
Transmigration III	03/22/1983 to 01/10/1989	69
Transmigration IV	05/24/1983 to 08/08/1991	98
Rajasthan Canal Command Area Development	07/16/1974 to 06/30/1983	107
Red Soils Area Development	09/09/1986 to 06/30/1992	70
Volta Region Agricultural Development	03/20/1980 to 06/30/1989	111

Note: Project dates taken from project completion reports.

cant is that several individual voluntary resettlement projects were implemented sequentially under the Brazilian Northwest Regional Development and the Indonesian Transmigration Programs. Therefore, it is possible that the greater success of the voluntary resettlement programs is a function of the cumulative effects of several individual projects, which learned lessons from prior phases.

Use of Bank Resources for Resettlement

Table 3.4 presents an estimate of staff weeks and professional skills devoted to most of the projects reviewed. The levels of Bank staff and con-

Table 3.4. World Bank Staff Inputs in Involuntary and Voluntary Resettlement Projects in Staff Weeks and by Skill Mix

	Inputs into		
Country/project	*Preappraisal/ appraisal*	*Negotiations*	*Supervision*
Brazil			
Paulo Afonso IV	73.3	7.4	102.3
Hydroelectric	E and Eng	n.a.	n.a.
Agricultural	128.8	8.0	153.8
Development and	E, A, M, F, Ls,	A, E, F, and	E, En, An, Eng,
Environmental	Ed, S, Ts,	An	Ts, A, M, Dm,
Protection	Eng, and An		H and Ec
Mato Grosso Rural	97.4	6.9	139.3
Development	E, C, A, H, R, En,	n.a.	E, C, A, En, H, S,
	F and I		F, I, R, LO, Ls, Ts,
			An and Cs
Indonesia			
Thirteenth Power	55.9	13.7	104.5
	Eng and F	n/a	Eng, E, F and O
Transmigration I	n.a.	n.a.	43.4
	n.a.	n.a.	A, E, C, Ps, F
			and H
Transmigration II	n.a.	n.a.	n/a
	n.a.	n.a.	A, E, An, Ls, Ae
			and Eng
Transmigration III	110.9	16.0	109.5
	n.a.	n.a.	A, C, Ms, Ls, E,
			Ae and Rs
Transmigration IV			
	49.8	6.7	88.0
	E, Eng, A, Ts	An, A, E, and	E, Eng, A, Ts,
	and An	Rp	S and M

sultants allocated to involuntary and voluntary resettlement projects had to be estimated because there is no uniform system for reporting those levels. The available data indicate, however, that the voluntary resettlement and agricultural development projects generally benefited from a much broader mix of specialist skills during both preparation and appraisal activities than did the projects involving involuntary resettlement.

Agricultural and livestock specialists, agronomists, soil scientists, foresters, and commodity processing experts appear to have devoted a substantial amount of time to the design and implementation of most voluntary resettlement projects. This is perhaps because the projects were conceived as agricultural or integrated rural development

Table 3.4. *(continued)*

	Inputs into		
Country/project	*Preappraisal/ appraisal*	*Negotiations*	*Supervision*
India Gujarat Irrigation	172.9 n.a.	2.1 n.a.	205.9 E, Eng, F and Wm
Rajasthan Canal Command Area Development	97.7 A, E, Eng, R and Fr	7.0 n.a.	133.6 A, E, Eng and R
China Red Soils Area Development	112.6 E, A, Rc, Ls, Fs, Ap, M and S	3.7 n.a.	60.3 E, A, Rc, Ls, Fs and Ap
Ghana Kpong Hydroelectric	n.a. n.a.	n.a. n.a.	16.5 C, F and An
Volta Region Agricultural Development	74.0 A, E, Ls, Ex, C and F	8.0 n.a.	99.5 A, E, Ex, M, C and Fss

n.a. Not applicable.

Notes: Skill codes are: A = agronomist/agriculturalist; Ae = agricultural economist; An = anthropologist; Ap = agroprocessing specialist C = civil engineer; Cs = community development specialist; Dm = demographer; E = economist; Ec = ecologist; Ed = education specialist; En = environmentalist; Eng = engineer; Ex = agricultural extension specialist; F = financial analyst; Fr = forestry specialist; Fs = fruit crop specialist; Fss = fisheries specialist; H = rural health specialist; I = institutional specialist; Lo = legal specialist; Ls = livestock specialist; M = management specialist; Ms = cartographer/mapping specialist; O = unspecified other skill specialist; Ps = procurement specialist; R = road engineer; Rc = rural credit specialist; Rp = rubber processing specialist; Rs = remote sensing specialist; S = soils specialist; Ts = tree crop specialist; and Wm = water management specialist.

activities. In addition, these projects made greater use of rural development specialists and social scientists in project preparation and supervision.

By contrast, few involuntary resettlement projects had broad participation by Bank staff beyond those needed for the basic analysis required to plan and supervise the projects' physical infrastructure components. Because the Bank did not use social specialists (sociologists and anthropologists) before 1980, when its own resettlement policy was first adopted, the overall average for the projects included in this study is low. Whereas the engineering and construction aspects of the infrastructural projects entailing involuntary resettlement benefited from the participation of Bank staff and consultants throughout the project cycle, their resettlement components appear to have been designed primarily by recipient country staff, with little Bank oversight. Information on the mix of local preparation staff is not available, but social specialists were rarely part of local teams.

Nature and Quality of Baseline Surveys

Baseline surveys for involuntary resettlement projects should accomplish at least three basic objectives:

- They should specify the size and composition of the populations to be displaced.
- They should provide a quantitative analysis of existing levels and sources of household income to aid in formulating precise income restoration targets.
- They should provide detailed assessments of the income restoration potential of the resources, land, irrigation water, occupational training, cash payments, and so on to be made available to the displaced households under each resettlement option proposed.

Although data collection efforts improved modestly in the 1980s, the involuntary resettlement projects surveyed generally did a less than satisfactory job of assembling an accurate database on the populations to be displaced. The almost casual attitude of project planners toward displacees becomes clear when one compares the level of data provided in most appraisal documents for physical structures with the cursory, data-free discussion of the resettlement "program."

In most cases, the planners of involuntary resettlement activities attempted to specify the size and composition of populations to be displaced by extrapolating from existing census data or other local records and making projections of population growth through the period of infrastructure construction. However, the documents for the Thirteenth Power Project in Indonesia (appraised after the adoption of the Bank's resettlement policy, see table 3.3) refer to a two-year anthropological, socioeconomic, and ecological baseline study conducted by a local university before actual resettlement activities began.

The Paulo Afonso IV Project in Brazil, specifically the resettlement program linked to the creation of the Sobradinho reservoir, exemplifies the poor initial specification of the size and composition of the populations to be resettled. Such superficial survey work directly led to not only a serious underestimation of how many people would be affected by the reservoir's construction but to a complete misunderstanding of how those people would respond to the proposed resettlement options.

Baseline surveys for the involuntary resettlement projects surveyed were particularly deficient in providing accurate information about the levels and sources of household income in the populations to be displaced and in valuing fixed assets that would be lost. The persistence of this deficiency in project planning and appraisal is particularly serious given the Bank's current attempts to build into involuntary resettlement projects a structured process of income restoration (see Cernea 1988). If one cannot specify in precise terms the nature and sources of baseline income flows and asset holdings within households to be displaced, one has a very limited basis, if any, upon which to formulate a resettlement options package. One also has no baseline from which to set goals, measure "income restoration," and monitor progress.

Finally, with the exception of the Shuikou I and II projects in China, the resource packages provided to households do not appear to have undergone serious multidisciplinary analyses to ensure their potential to restore income levels. Nor have the capacities of different types of households to respond to these packages been assessed.

Quality of Resettlement Plans

The documents on planning for involuntary resettlement demonstrated four different approaches to the problems caused by infrastructure development, as follows:

- In the Paulo Afonso IV Project in Brazil, the resettlement plan had miscellaneous descriptive information (for example, generalized descriptions of the geology, soils, and vegetative cover in the

Sobradinho reservoir area and qualitative and summary descriptions of the farming systems in place), along with a general statement of the objectives of the resettlement program. The Bank rejected this document.

- In the Gujarat irrigation projects, resettlement planning appears to have been limited to a restatement of the government of India's policy on compensation for displaced people and the operational procedures for obtaining such compensation in the case of involuntary resettlement.

- In the Thirteenth Power project in Indonesia, the resettlement plan offered four options for displaced people: resettlement from Java to outlying areas of Sumatra and other islands, participation in the development of aquaculture in the new reservoir, occupational training, and simple cash compensation. The outcomes: the displacement and resettlement activity was handled under the Transmigration Program already in place, the results of the aquaculture program were satisfactory, the proposed occupational training program was subsequently canceled, and the cash compensation program proceeded without major difficulties.

- In Ghana, a team from the Faculty of Architecture of Kumasi University of Science and Technology prepared "conceptual designs of the resettlement villages and construction of the township" (appraisal report). A team from the University of Lagon was contracted to "prepare the agricultural resettlement program" (appraisal report for the Kpong Hydroelectric Project). However, as the actual resettlement plan for this project was not found for this review, the influence of these university teams on the quality of the planning is unknown.

None of these four so-called resettlement plans proposed a well-articulated and appropriately phased program, nor did they contribute to a structured process for restoring the incomes after displacement.

The case of the Shuikou I and II projects in China presents an interesting contrast to the prior approaches. The local planners and the Bank (which sent its senior sociologist on the appraisal mission) treated the resettlement component of the projects as a genuine development opportunity—not as an uncomfortable and undesirable project component. They created an upland agricultural development project and treated project planning and implementation similar to that of the Red Soils Area Development voluntary resettlement activity. The plan aimed to reclaim uncultivated land on steep hillsides by using bench terracing for cultivating tree crops and for creating new village sites, without encroaching further on already cultivated lands. The Fujian Provincial Resettlement Office and local agricultural development agencies were assigned responsibility for executing the plan in recognition that the engineering agency in charge of the actual dam construction "lacked the authority or the capabilities needed for managing the resettlement work." Resettlement planning brought together a broad array of local specialists to work with groups of displaced families with the specific objective of arranging resettlement "so that physical and human resources can continue to be at least as productive and living conditions at least as convenient as they were before."

Differences among Implementing Agencies

PAULO AFONSO IV HYDROELECTRIC POWER PROJECT. In the case of the Paulo Afonso IV Hydroelectric Power Project in Brazil, the Companhia Hidro Eletrica do Sao Francisco (CHESF) was responsible for the project's design and implementation, including that of the resettlement component. At appraisal Bank staff projected that CHESF would be able to "contract out" the responsibility for resettling about half the families to be displaced by the dam construction to the Instituto Nacional de Colonizacae e Reforma Agraria (INCRA). Under this plan, INCRA was to be responsible for resettling the rural population affected by reservoir construction and CHESF was to be responsible for resettling the urban population affected. However, after discovering that not all the displacees met INCRA's eligibility requirements for the resettlement program and that many eligible individuals did not want to migrate to INCRA's distant agricultural resettlement sites, CHESF was forced to assume major responsibilities for resettling both rural and urban populations in the immediate area of the Sobradinho reservoir. This was a complex sociocultural and technical task for which CHESF, as a power agency, was not staffed or otherwise prepared to undertake.

The PCR for this project concludes that CHESF and the government of Brazil had complied with the strict conditions of the resettlement covenant, but with "migration results far different from what had been expected." Moreover, the evaluators stated that:

A major lesson of this project related to the importance of the resettlement component is that planning for resettlement was as important as planning for the hydroelectric project; and that the

inclusion of covenants providing for resettlement did not ensure the effective preparation and implementation of such
plans. A companion lesson is that, for resettlement efforts on the
scale of that experienced at Sobradinho, explicit consideration
should be given to establishing a separate project. The status of a
separate project would help to assure appropriate levels of government funding and interest.

GUJARAT IRRIGATION I AND II. For India's Gujarat irrigation projects, which together included financing for about 15 dams, three agencies were responsible: the national Ministry of Water Resources, the
Central Water Commission, and the State Irrigation Department. The
government of Gujarat was responsible for resettling about 5,700 families (some 30,000 to 35,000 people) from villages that would be submerged by the reservoirs. To facilitate the socioeconomic
reestablishment of the displaced families, the government was to ap-
point a rehabilitation committee for each dam and irrigation scheme
that would comprise representatives of the resettled families, government officials, and voluntary agencies active in the areas. A director of
rehabilitation from the State Irrigation Department was to supervise
and coordinate the resettlement.

However, matters did not turn out as envisaged, and the analysis carried out at project completion pointed to organizational, institutional,
and financial causes. Once again, local preproject planning had been
deeply flawed, in fact utterly incomplete, with regard to resettlement and
rehabilitation. During implementation, political commitment to full reestablishment was inadequate. Inside the Bank, these projects had also been
largely processed before the new policy (1980) took hold. According to
the PCR for the Gujarat Medium Irrigation Project (Phase I):

> Resettlement planning was not considered an integral part of
> the overall preparation of subprojects under Phase I. Although
> the legal framework and administrative arrangements existed,
> resettlement actions tended to be implemented in an ad hoc
> manner and were not consistently included in the implementa-
> tion schedules for project construction works. Moreover, since
> the government lacked effective institutionalized monitoring
> procedures, it was unable to determine to what extent the com-
> pensation packages it offered displaced persons enabled them
> to set up sustainable income-generating arrangements. In rec-
> ognizing these deficiencies, the government agreed to prepare
> and implement detailed resettlement plans for nine subprojects
> under Phase II of the project. The progress of resettlement activi-

ties is now monitored regularly . . . Furthermore, special evaluation studies are being undertaken to analyze the standard of living of displaced persons in five subprojects and to provide the government with feedback on its compensation package.

Despite the optimistic expectations for improved government work in the Phase II Project, formulated in the Phase I PCR, the subsequent Phase II PCR had to paint a somewhat discouraging picture:

> The project fell well short of achieving the project's established goals and objectives in both quantitative and qualitative terms despite two extensions, totaling three years . . . Project implementation continued to experience delays, both avoidable and unavoidable, leading to significant performance deficiencies right from the early stages of the Credit. . . . Furthermore, it would not be reasonable to blame "start up" delays since several major components were on-going at appraisal. Except for some specific works and components which moved ahead reasonably well, the overall implementation of the project was less than satisfactory. . . . Numerous revised implementation schedules were loosely formulated by the government at regular intervals during each semi-annual review; still, the subprojects persistently lagged behind the targets which had been revised only a few months before.

THIRTEENTH POWER PROJECT. Overall implementation of the Thirteenth Power project in Indonesia was the responsibility of the National Electricity Authority (PLN), a public corporation charged with the generation, transmission, and distribution of electricity and with the planning, construction, and operation of electricity supply facilities. On-site project implementation was the responsibility of a project manager responsible to PLN headquarters staff in Jakarta. NEWJEC of Japan was the consulting engineer and was responsible for the design and construction supervision on the project. Finally, a special board of consultants (BOC) was appointed to review the investigations and design for the project.

A resettlement coordinating board (RCB) coordinated compensation and resettlement for people with homes and other major interests in the reservoir areas. The implementation of resettlement by the National Electricity Board was to (a) execute an environmental and resettlement plan of action satisfactory to the Bank, (b) monitor resettlement and environmental activities closely, and (c) furnish the Bank with quarterly reports on the progress of environmental and resettlement activities. The PCR reported that:

The resettlement component was based on the experience with the Saguling hydroelectric project . . . and was carefully planned. It was implemented on schedule and in accordance with a plan agreed between the Government of Indonesia and the Bank at the time of project appraisal. All families who lost land or property were given fair compensation in cash, based on procedures agreed with the Bank. The owners of private land were compensated based on the market value of the land, and the users of state forest lands were compensated through purchase and transfer of equivalent acreage of forest land in other locations.

In addition to compensation for the loss of land and other property, the Cirata project also necessitated the resettlement, as of August 31, 1989, of 8,469 families from the reservoir area and 2,593 families from above the reservoir area. . . . About 34 percent of the affected families were resettled through the Transmigration and Nucleus Estate and Smallholder (NES) programs. Those who elected to remain in the area were assisted through training in aquaculture and industrial skills. Both of these training programs were reserved for members of households who had not received any other form of compensation. The aquaculture program, which was modeled on a similar program developed for the Saguling Hydroelectric Project, was particularly successful.

The project included follow-up surveys that were carried out at one-year intervals for three years (the last one in 1990), following the impoundment of the reservoir. Among the positive impacts of the project, the surveys identified electrification and improved roads. Among the negative impacts, the surveys noted the increased population density in the host villages, leading to reductions in average size of landholding, working hours per person, income, and nutrition levels. The authors of the surveys concluded that these impacts should be regarded as transitional, given the timing of the surveys shortly after the resettlement.

KPONG HYDROELECTRIC PROJECT. In Ghana, the Volta River Authority was responsible for planning and implementing the resettlement program. This authority had one prior experience with resettlement when the Akosombo Dam was built and nearly 80,000 people had to be moved. In this case, serious problems arose with the agricultural program and the housing and water supply activities, partly because of poor planning by the authority, and partly because of its reliance on other government agencies for inputs that were not always forthcoming. The net result was that some of the resettlement towns created were deserted or they gradually deteriorated (for an in-depth socioanthropological description and analysis of this resettlement operation, see Chambers 1970). Thus the preparation of the Kpong Project provided a rare opportunity for a power authority to learn from the planning failures of a recent, larger project on the same river and to avoid repeating the same resettlement failures. (For a discussion of the extent to which the Kpong project learned from the resettlement experience gained in Akosombo, see Adu-Aryee 1993).

A recent Bank report (World Bank 1993b) states that despite improved planning in the preparation and appraisal phases, "Kpong's resettlement process was deficient in some elements of execution. . . . One weakness in plan preparation, however, caused settlers dissatisfaction at Kpong—underassessment of needs." The evaluation team concluded that while surveys of populations to be resettled must be done well ahead of the actual resettlement, constant focused monitoring is needed during implementation so that the resettlement process can be adjusted to respond to changing circumstances.

The Kpong resettlement team faced nearly all the same problems as at Akosombo, despite specific attempts to address them. These problems included working under time pressure, satisfying land needs, avoiding conflicts, receiving inadequate support from qualified agricultural staff, and encountering failures in the handing over of responsibilities from the Volta River Authority to assigned local support agencies. The evaluation team concluded that the problems might have been corrected without delay under more stable macroeconomic conditions. But even though Bank supervisory missions identified resettlement problems and proposed solutions at the time, the country authorities responsible for actual implementation did nothing. In addition:

> Financial management of resettlement caused avoidable problems and conflicts despite established policies and guidelines. Overall resettlement cost accounting was poor. Valuations and land compensation payments were treated as matters to be dealt with after resettlement. And valuations for compensation were not done, which meant that compensation for land taken for resettlement was not paid, causing opposition to resettlement. According to the evaluators: The overriding lesson from Kpong's resettlement program is that more attention must be paid to plan implementation. There were generally sound policies, acceptable plans, a suitable organization, and a seasoned staff

with very relevant resettlement experience. Yet the program faced avoidable [economic and financial] problems which were not adequately solved.

SHUIKOU HYDROELECTRIC I AND II. In the Shuikou Project in China (phases I and II), several agencies shared responsibilities for engineering and construction design, implementation, and supervision. The Fujian Provincial Electric Power Bureau was to be the project's owner, in accordance with its program of economic reforms and to ensure that large hydroelectric projects like Shuikou are constructed as efficiently as possible. The Ministry of Water Resources and Electric Power set up a special organization, the Shuikou Hydroelectric Project Construction Corporation, to organize project construction and manage the main civil works contract. And the East China Hydroelectric Power Investigation and Design Institute was responsible for project design.

Implementation of the resettlement plan was the responsibility of the government of the province of Fujian, which in April 1986 set up the Resettlement Office for the Shuikou Project, with separate divisions for handling the resettlement of state-owned enterprises and the resettlement of agricultural households. The Resettlement Office was independent of the Shuikou Hydroelectric Project Construction Corporation but coordinated its activities with it. It was to have one consolidated budget covering the entire costs of resettlement and was to be assisted by the line bureaus of the provincial and county governments. Resettlement suboffices were also established under each county government within the province. The Resettlement Office was responsible for regular monitoring and reporting on resettlement progress and on progress made toward restoring the productive base and welfare of the dislocated population, and for the midterm review of resettlement impacts and other studies.

The implementing agencies for the Shuikou resettlement were operating in a policy framework that guided resettlement planning and implementation. This policy framework was formulated in 1982 as the State Council's *Statute for Land Requisition for Construction Use by the State*. The basic principles of this country policy are so clearly stated and so relevant to all the other involuntary resettlement projects surveyed that they are repeated here in full:

> The basic principles of this policy aim at enabling the affected population to become economically and socially re-established on a sound productive basis, to restore their communities, to attain at least the same standard of living as prior to relocation, and to fully reconstruct and develop the affected means of pro-

duction. The inhabitants of an inundated village are to be resettled in the same county, and within the same township, if
possible, on higher ground at the nearest adjacent location. Relocation at new sites will aim at preserving the integrity of the
original social units, village communities, neighborhood
groups, and extended families. Resettled persons will be assisted to resume, wherever possible, their original occupations,
or to get training for off-farm employment in new locations.
Compensation will be paid for lost assets and dwellings at realistic levels (recently increased by governmental decision) and
public facilities will be reconstructed.

These explicit policy principles guided a systematic planning effort
for the resettlement carried out by an interdepartmental task force of the
government of the province of Fujian as part of project preparation. This
resulted in a full-fledged resettlement and reconstruction plan, based
primarily on agricultural development and on local industries, that was
included as a component of the project.

After having substantially helped design the resettlement strategy
at appraisal, Bank social specialists carried out full reviews of the
Shuikou resettlement process in April and July 1991. In both cases, the
assessment of resettlement was positive, but both missions expressed
concern about the approach to monitoring and reporting physical progress and about the possibility of individual hardship because of the time
lag between reservoir impoundment and new systems (such as fruit
trees and fishing) reaching full production. By 1992, however, these concerns had been either addressed or overtaken by events, and physical resettlement activities were completed on schedule. The authorities also
took two additional steps to strengthen the resettlement program:
(a) they launched an independent evaluation of the resettlement on a
sample of 15 to 20 percent of those resettled to provide timely warning of
problems in reestablishing incomes and general welfare; and (b) they
provided substantial additional financing by establishing two funds
to ensure that the local government could continue to help resettlers
fully reestablish their standard of living after external project support
ended.

CONCLUSIONS. The review of these individual project experiences
led to the following conclusions:

- The primary implementing agencies for all the involuntary resettlement projects surveyed had mandates oriented almost exclusively toward installing major infrastructure for power generation

or irrigation. This lack of focus on resettlement in the context of development projects is not unusual (see Pearce in this volume).

- The implementing agencies initially had little internal staff capacity for, or institutional interest in, handling the resettlement problems caused by their construction activities. This problem was aggravated by the lack of a well-articulated national policy on involuntary resettlement (Brazil), by a failure to implement the general policies that had been developed (India); or by the absence of the macroeconomic and administrative environments within which successful resettlement could be carried out, despite a good initial planning effort (Ghana).

- Some of the implementing agencies demonstrated willingness to learn from their previously unsatisfactory experiences with resettlement to improve their performance in subsequent projects. For instance, in Ghana, the Volta River Authority drew upon its experiences with the Akosombo project to improve preparation of the Kpong project; the National Electricity Authority in Indonesia improved its performance in Cirata by drawing on prior experiences with the Saguling project; and even the Companhia Hidro Eletrica do Sao Francisco in Brazil, after a disastrous performance with resettlement in Sobradinho, improved its handling of resettlement activities significantly in later projects (World Bank 1993a, pp. 15–16).

- The Chinese experience at Shuikou was the only involuntary resettlement surveyed that succeeded in putting together a complete and effective implementation program for displaced families. This program was executed through local agencies and based on a well-articulated national policy for involuntary resettlement.

Resettlers' Participation in Decisionmaking

The surveyed documentation provides little evidence that the involuntary resettlement projects in Brazil, India, and Indonesia made significant efforts to engage those scheduled for resettlement in the decisionmaking that shaped the their options or modified procedures. In retrospect, project planners' erroneous judgments about how families destined for resettlement would react to the options presented to them demonstrate a pattern of poor communication between planners and resettlers and of planners' underestimation of the importance of participatory approaches.

The involvement of representatives of populations to be displaced in the Shuikou projects in China appears to be, in our study, the only fully successful attempt by a government to set up a genuinely interactive process between project management and those affected by displacement. The key to this success appears to be that management of the resettlement component was independent of the infrastructure development process and decentralized down to the county level, where local government officials had better knowledge of and were more sympathetic towards the people being displaced than officials at higher levels of government.

Accuracy of Cost Projections

Given the lack of a uniform Bank format for enumerating the projected costs of resettlement at appraisal, it was impossible to compare actual resettlement costs as reported in PCRs with the costs projected at appraisal on a line item basis. Nevertheless, the limited *ex ante* and *ex post* cost information available for the projects surveyed indicates that cost projections were not particularly accurate.

As table 3.2 shows, in the Paulo Afonso IV Hydroelectric Project in Brazil, planners underestimated resettlement costs by about $20,000 per family, an error of 165 percent. Flawed planning for involuntary relocation, combined with poor estimates of inflationary trends, completely invalidated the initial cost projections, whereas cost projections for the voluntary resettlement projects in Brazil, which were implemented at roughly the same time, diverged much less from actual costs. In fact, it is most likely erroneous to assume that the two types of resettlement can be correctly planned with the same approach, as their very socioeconomic nature, requirements, and impacts are deeply different.

The principal reason for actual costs being less than the original cost estimates for the voluntary resettlement components of the Transmigration III and IV projects was the premature termination of the program. In the Transmigration I and II projects underestimates apparently occurred because these projects served fewer families than anticipated, but per capita costs were higher than estimated.

In Ghana, officials involved in the Kpong Hydroelectric Project initially estimated that US$10,439 per family would be needed to resettle 1,140 families, but they actually spent the equivalent of US$4,957 per family to resettle 1,089 families. In this instance, however, the largest part of the difference in costs was attributable to planners' inability to predict inflation and the effects of devaluation of the cedi in the context of a deteriorating macroeconomic situation.

In the Gujarat Irrigation Projects in India, cost projections turned out to be inaccurate for two reasons. First, they laid out only the land acquisition costs for the project's resettlement activity, without the additional support needed for the resettlers. And second, the Indian planners redesigned and enlarged the project almost immediately after the Bank appraisal had been completed and the initial credits negotiated.

In the case of the eight voluntary resettlement or agricultural development projects that could be evaluated, the percentage error in the cost projections ranged from an underestimate of some 17 percent to an overestimate of approximately 40 percent.

As table 3.2 shows, cost projections for the projects surveyed are approximately evenly split between those appraisals that underestimated costs and those that overestimated them. The reasons for inaccurate cost estimates varied from project to project, but one common reason was poor correspondence between the projected and actual number of people served by the projects' resettlement activities. In most cases, projects provided resettlement services to fewer displaced people than anticipated.

Inclusion of Transition Costs and Grants

The projects entailing involuntary resettlement surveyed in Brazil, India, and Indonesia were initiated in the 1970s and early 1980s. In all cases, cost estimates for resettlement were aggregated under one or two categories: land acquisition and preparation costs and the costs of resettlement. There were no line item breakdowns to indicate if any funds were allocated to support displaced persons in transition. In addition, the breakdown between loan and grant funding for resettlement activities was not clearly indicated.

In the Kpong Hydroelectric Project in Ghana, the appraisal report broke down resettlement costs into categories that included land purchase, land clearing, dike construction, housing, schools, water and sewerage, moving expenses, administrative expenses, and contingencies. Unfortunately, subsequent evaluation reports failed to enumerate actual resettlement costs using the same categories.

In contrast to the involuntary resettlement operations, several of the voluntary resettlements did enumerate grant funding to migrating families for temporary transition costs. The transition support was usually provided in kind as access to cereals and other foodstuffs when cropping systems were being established or as subsidies for special credit arrangements to establish crops or purchase equipment. In these instances, transition support was viewed as part of the income regeneration process.

Agricultural Characteristics of the Projects

The set of 12 tables (Tables 3A.1 to 3A.12) consolidated into Annex 1 of the present study compares the principal characteristics of the resettlement projects surveyed, variable by variable. For the most part, the specific characteristics reviewed were drawn from Kinsey and Binswanger (1993). The objective was to compare the structuring of involuntary and voluntary resettlement programs within each country and each project's structure against the variables or characteristics Kinsey and Binswanger identify as being important to the success of resettlement programs.

Analysis of the Resource Base

For projects involving agriculture, in-depth knowledge of the physical environment is essential for decisions on:

- The appropriate agricultural and livestock enterprises to be promoted
- The types and levels of agricultural inputs necessary to establish and sustain those enterprises over time
- The time necessary to establish those enterprises and bring them to a mature and stable state
- The levels of income generation possible from those enterprises and the risks involved.

Unlike urban resettlement efforts, resettlement aimed at restoring the incomes of farm families must deal with climatic and biological factors as an integral part of project design and implementation. This is particularly true when resettlement occurs in frontier areas on marginal soils, as was the case with most of the resettlement programs reviewed. In these situations, project planners must attempt to collect all relevant data on the resource base in the project area, assess the agronomic implications for crop and livestock enterprises, and, where major knowledge gaps exist, take the time and provide the resources needed to fill in the gaps.

None of the involuntary resettlement efforts reviewed benefited from comprehensive analyses of the resources available to displaced families for agricultural enterprises. In Brazil and Indonesia, the two power authorities essentially avoided responsibility for any resource analysis related to agriculture by contracting out the agricultural resettlement components of the projects to other agencies. Consequently, examination of the natural resource bases in the resettlement areas and the implications for agricultural enterprises did not take place.

In the Indian and Chinese involuntary resettlement projects, the resource analyses were fairly general and not site-specific, but at least some attempt was made to link the proposed farming systems to the resource bases underlying them. In both cases, it was significant that the area development activities were carried over two project phases, extending the total period available to install the resettled populations.

In Ghana, planners designed the siting of new resettlement villages around four basic objectives: (a) to retain villagers' rural, riverine life style, while providing the means for self-development; (b) to supply sufficiently good farmland and water in proximity to the resettlement areas; (c) to maintain health, especially with respect to bilharzia; and (d) to respect land tenure rights and traditional, tribal, and clan groupings. No attempt was made to change the existing traditional farming systems as part of the resettlement program. Consequently, resource conditions were not analyzed in relation to any specific income restoration objective. A Bank consultant visited Ghana to discuss public health aspects related to construction of the Kpong head pond, but no agricultural consultants were supplied to help assess the agricultural conditions facing settlers displaced by the construction.

In contrast to the involuntary resettlement activities, all the voluntary resettlement projects were planned with a central focus on agriculture and rural development. The appraisal reports for these projects contain much more detailed and location-specific discussions of resource conditions and relate them directly to the agricultural enterprises to be promoted and their income-generating potential. In many cases, the *ex ante* projections of incomes to be generated from crop and livestock enterprises proved to be optimistic, but the initial efforts by project planners at least provided points of departure for monitoring and analyzing actual income generation during project implementation.

Appraising Sources of Household Income

For all the projects reviewed, preproject analyses of the income sources and flows of the families to be resettled, to the extent they existed at all, were poorly done and were rarely based on current field survey data. For the involuntary resettlement programs, displaced families were often classified as rural or urban, as if these labels constituted mutually exclusive categories. Such imprecise labeling led to assumptions in planning that all members of rural families were available full-time for work in agricultural enterprises and that the incomes of rural families were derived entirely from agriculture.

Experience gained from agricultural projects around the world casts doubt on such facile planning assumptions. A better approach for planners would have been to assume that most so-called farm families in developing countries follow a diversified income strategy aimed at ensuring family survival. To define realistic strategies for income regeneration, planners must develop much more refined profiles of the different subgroups within any population to be relocated, so that they can better tailor the resettlement options to the affected individuals. This requires that resources be made available for high-quality field survey work to set baseline parameters for planning diversified income regeneration strategies as an integral part of any resettlement effort.

Simultaneously with establishing baseline parameters, any income regeneration strategy requires that serious efforts be made to analyze and project family income flows from all employment sources available in the designated resettlement area, and not just from the agricultural enterprises being promoted. While the voluntary resettlement projects generally did a better job of projecting potential income flows from agricultural enterprises, the voluntary resettlement projects in China and Indonesia were the only ones to deal, in even general terms, with nonagricultural and off-farm activities.

Participant Selection Criteria

Although information on participant selection criteria for the voluntary resettlement projects is scant, project documents indicate that most of these projects did have the latitude to select applicants for the available resettlement openings. While the Transmigration Program in Indonesia and the Rajasthan irrigation schemes in India used the most selection criteria, essentially all the voluntary resettlement programs exerted some control in shaping the composition of the groups relocated. While the relevance of some of the selection criteria used as indicators of family success in establishing viable agricultural operations is questionable, the criteria used in the voluntary resettlement programs were generally more detailed than those used in the involuntary resettlements, providing a better basis for eliminating unsuitable candidates.

In the involuntary resettlement operations, some of those with legitimate loss claims were unsuitable by background, skill level, or disposition for resettlement options based on agricultural activities. The problems were compounded because the projects presented the displaced families with a narrow range of nonagricultural resettlement options, and thereby reduced the potential for channeling candidates less suitable for agricultural enterprises into other types of employment. This indicates that planners of involuntary resettlement operations should pay more attention to the range of resettlement options presented to displaced families, the array and intensity of support services provided to nascent agricultural enterprises, and the time requirements for reestablishing family incomes following displacement.

Range of Income-Generating Options

For participants in the voluntary resettlement programs, the process of evaluating family employment options essentially took place outside the context of the particular resettlement project. Candidates submitted themselves to a project's selection process and thereby demonstrated a positive commitment to the proffered agricultural opportunities. In other words, they self-selected themselves for the opportunities offered, having weighed them against available alternatives.

The involuntarily displaced families had no choice. They were destined to suffer losses and had to devise alternative economic survival strategies based in most instances on a narrow range of options, usually cash compensation and outmigration; entry into an agricultural resettlement scheme; or, occasionally, participation in training programs for nonagricultural employment. Only in the Shuikou projects in China did project planners attempt to tailor the assistance provided to reestablishing families in the full range of income-generating activities they had employed before displacement. In all the other involuntary resettlement projects, those displaced were asked to fit in with the narrow range of options provided through the project. While this approach may have been the most convenient one for project planners, it was not necessarily the most appropriate way to restore family income flows expeditiously.

Farm Models Envisaged

For all projects where at least one farm model was defined, planning favored the development of smallholder farm operations based primarily on family labor. In the Red Soils Area Development Project in China, collective farming was offered as an alternative in one county, but the PCR subsequently reported that it had been unsuccessful. In the Transmigration Program in Indonesia, some of those resettled as smallholder farmers participated in contract farming agreements for rubber production.

In the involuntary resettlement project components, with the exception of the Kpong Hydroelectric Project in Ghana, the farm models implemented involved major changes from the farming systems previously practiced by those displaced—from lowland and riverbank farming to hillside systems in Brazil and China, from dryland to irrigated crop production in India, and from highly intensive crop production on Java to less intensive crop production on other Indonesian islands.

At appraisal, planners of the involuntary resettlement projects in Brazil and Indonesia did not present any specific farm models as the bases for resettlement planning, and in China and India they stipulated single generalized farm models. In Ghana, however, planners did not attempt to change the preexisting traditional farming system when moving displaced populations to new resettlement villages.

By contrast, with the exception of the Rajasthan irrigation scheme in India, the voluntary resettlement projects all evaluated two or more different farm models. In Brazil, for example, two of the voluntary resettlement projects promoted five and seven farm models, respectively, compared to none for the involuntary resettlement at Sobradinho. In addition, the farm models promoted were not only far more detailed at appraisal, they were also more intensively monitored during implementation, and in some cases were modified in the follow-on projects. This was particularly evident in the Transmigration Program in Indonesia and the Northwest Regional Development Program in Brazil.

Allocation of Land Holdings: Size, Criteria, and Land Tenure

In Brazil, Ghana, and India, planners for neither the involuntary nor the voluntary resettlements attempted to tailor the size of landholdings allocated to the labor or capital endowments of recipient families. The selection criteria used for the New Settlements Project in Brazil did, however, favor the recruitment of "large, physically able" families for the 25- to 40-hectare farms allocated.

In the Transmigration Program in Indonesia, farm sizes were fixed at 3.5 or 5.0 hectares depending on plot location and the farm model being promoted, and selection criteria were designed to recruit nuclear families with no more than five members and with no members older than 60.

Only the projects in China embodied a deliberate policy to allocate land commensurate with capacities—and in the Shuikou projects, the previous occupations—of the families being recruited or displaced. The projects also restricted the size of land allotments so as to foster intensive input use and crop production. The objective of this latter policy was to facilitate farm families' ability to incorporate crop residues and organic fertilizers into the soil of their small plots and thereby build up the land's productive capacity more rapidly.

Measures that guarantee long-term access to land through owner-ship or lease rights introduce a major element of stability into develop-ing agricultural systems. In the projects reviewed, documents for the involuntary resettlement projects did not provide clear statements of what land tenure systems were to be put in place, whereas the appraisal reports for the voluntary resettlement projects often contained detailed plans for cadastral surveys and land titling processes. Unfortunately, most of the projects suffered from slow land titling processes, often issu-ing land titles to only a small percentage of new settlers during the life of the project. Where the lack of an effective land titling process directly af-fected farmers' access to agricultural credit services as, for example, in Brazil, this deficiency had doubly stressful consequences for families in the midst of a difficult transition process.

Types of Infrastructure Provided

The level of infrastructure provided varied significantly both among the involuntary resettlement programs and between the voluntary and in-voluntary resettlements. In Brazil under the Paulo Afonso IV Hydro-electric Project, INCRA was to provide basic infrastructure for displaced families at its distant resettlement scheme, but poor knowledge of the families' intentions led to expenditures on houses and other infrastruc-ture that were never used because families refused to move to the scheme. Faced with unanticipated numbers of families remaining in the vicinity of the reservoir, the World Bank eventually persuaded the Bra-zilian power authority to provide a range of facilities—houses, schools, health facilities, and roads—for displaced families at the reservoir.

In Indonesia, some of the families subjected to involuntary resettle-ment were absorbed into the Transmigration Program and had access to the wide range of facilities provided under that program. These in-cluded housing, all-weather roads, wells, village health centers, and community centers. However, when displaced families in Indonesia had the option to take the transmigration route for their resettlement, only a fraction agreed to do so, while many preferred to not move far from their area of origin.

No infrastructure appears to have been constructed specifically for the families displaced by the installation of irrigation systems in the Gujarat projects in India. By contrast, the Rajasthan voluntary resettle-ment projects provided for a wide range of infrastructure to be installed in direct support of the agricultural development process. This is, once again, a clear instance of inadequate and unjustified differences in plan-ning approaches and resource allocation. In Ghana, the development of new villages for those displaced by the Kpong Hydroelectric Project centered mainly on social infrastructure, housing, schools, and water and sewerage systems, and construction of dikes for irrigation and fishing. Infrastructure developed under the Volta Region Agricultural Development Project concentrated on providing area centers to supply agricultural inputs, power and water supply systems, agricultural research and extension facilities, and health and education facilities.

Finally, planning for the Shuikou Hydroelectric and Red Soils Area Development in China was equally comprehensive with respect to basic facilities provided: roads, water supply systems, and market centers. The Red Soils Project, however, provided a considerably broader array of infrastructure in support of agricultural activities, including warehouses, sprinkler irrigation systems, and agricultural research and extension facilities.

Overall, planners of the voluntary resettlement projects did a better job of detailing and constructing infrastructure that was directly relevant to the agricultural development processes envisaged, whereas planners of the involuntary resettlement projects tended to emphasize the replacement of social infrastructure (schools, health facilities, community centers) that families and villages lost as a result of displacement.

Sources of Resettlement Services

The documents for the voluntary resettlement programs provide more details about the importance of these services to the success of the overall agricultural development process. However, for most of the projects reviewed, the real problem with services for settler families was not with their specification during project preparation and at appraisal, but with their actual delivery during project implementation. The PCRs for many of these projects reiterate the same basic deficiencies in project implementation: inadequate support for agricultural research to develop appropriate technology packages for the technical problems of frontier areas, inadequate extension coverage, problems with the supply of agricultural inputs, and poor access to agricultural credit for farmers.

Degree of Risk Assessment

Discussions of risk in the appraisal reports for the involuntary resettlement projects were in every case wholly devoted to the investment risks to the Bank and other donors. Despite the literature on the risks and failures of involuntary resettlement, there was no indication that project planners had analyzed the comparative risks to the displaced families or that they had tailored any elements of the resettlement plans to mitigate against a perceived risk to the displaced families in the income restoration process. At the time when the projects under review were appraised, the Bank had not yet developed the impoverishment risks framework which explains how forced displacement can inflict, rather than reduce, poverty (Cernea 1990, World Bank 1994).

Plans also failed to recognize the risk to resettled families from insufficient time allotted to their recovery of livelihood. The period of assistance was limited to the time span necessary to complete the project's civil works components, with no account taken of the time needed to establish agricultural enterprises and stabilize the income restoration process. In most of the involuntary resettlement components, even the advanced farm families were still establishing their new agricultural operations when project support officially ended. Many of those further behind simply gave up on the process. In hindsight, given that the projects were directed at establishing displaced families in frontier areas with marginal soils, the income restoration processes should have been planned in two phases: a system establishment phase of at least four to six years and a system stabilization phase of another five years.

Planners of the voluntary resettlement projects produced preparation and appraisal reports that discussed the risks to farmers of initiating agricultural enterprises on soils of uncertain productive capacity and the risks to the attainment of project objectives from inadequate provision of key support services for those farmers. The project planners also attempted to counteract specific risks through deliberately tailored components of the agricultural package. Such counter-risk measures included supporting agricultural research to produce technological innovations adapted to the on-farm environment, undertaking processing and marketing studies to identify appropriate crops, constructing roads to facilitate input supply and crop marketing, and so on.

Conclusions and Recommendations

This comparison of pairs of voluntary and involuntary projects showed that even though involuntary resettlement is a more difficult undertaking than voluntary resettlement, it consistently received less attention from project planners during conventional planning. The exceptions were only the China projects. Not only were voluntary resettlements more carefully prepared, but more financial and physical resources were devoted to their implementation, whereas given the nature of involuntary resettlement the reverse should be the case. More financial support is needed in involuntary resettlement because in such situations all families must leave, including those less equipped for the risks and hardships of relocation; no selection to recruit those families most likely to succeed in the new environment is possible; forcibly removed families lose their former assets, while voluntary resettlers can maintain them, leave them to kin, or sell them into strong markets; and return migration is not an option for involuntary displacees if the resettlement does not work. Thus, involuntary resettlement should receive more attention to ensure adequate planning.

The planning of the voluntary resettlements incorporated input from a range of experts, including experts on rural development and agriculturists; prepared detailed programs to help farmers adapt to new physical and socioeconomic environments; and internalized resettlement costs within project budgets. Planners of involuntary resettlement components of projects treated them as an unfortunate side effect of the main (usually infrastructure) project, with poorly defined costs and no defined benefits. Table 3.5 summarizes several traditional differences in the planning and appraisal of the voluntary and involuntary resettlement operations analyzed in this study.

The success of involuntary resettlement in terms of restoring settlers' incomes seems to largely depend on planning and implementation. In the early projects we analyzed, the implementing agencies lacked the mandate, resources, commitment, and capacity for an undertaking of this nature, and those to be resettled did not participate in making the decisions that would affect their lives—perhaps their very survival.

China appears to have been an exception. Project planners gave equal attention and priority to voluntary and involuntary resettlement, handling involuntary resettlement as a genuine opportunity for development rather than as an additional burden caused by the project activity triggering resettlement.

In light of the preceding analysis, several recommendations are presented here, divided between those directed at the programmatic aspects of resettlement and those directed at the agricultural aspects.

With respect to the programmatic aspects of resettlement project, we believe that project planners should:

- Provide the resources and take the time during project preparation to define in detail the populations likely to be displaced by infrastructure construction. Base the definition of these populations on data collected from on-site surveys, not on secondary, indirect, or obsolete information.
- Define an income restoration objective for each displaced population in precise terms and then design specific project components to accomplish that objective.
- Ensure that any project with a land-based resettlement component be designed, negotiated, and supervised by a multidiscip-

Table 3.5.   A Comparison of the Design and Management of Involuntary and Voluntary Resettlement

Aspect of project	Involuntary resettlement	Voluntary resettlement
World Bank staff input	Concentration on civil works for main project component and none of Bank's rural development expertise brought to bear.	Diverse mix of specialists used to review technical, social, and economic soundness of proposed farm models.
Managerial focus	On the infrastructure building component of the project.	On resettlement as the core of an agricultural development project in which the new farm's viability was critical to the project's overall success.
Assessment of income generating potential of new sites	No detailed, systematic analysis of resources available to displaced families.	Resource conditions faced by farmers related to realistic appraisals of income generating potential of enterprises being promoted.
Farm models	Either single, generalized farm model offered or no model.	Several farm models presented; help given to settlers to develop off-farm sources of income.
Risk	Risk assessment restricted to investment risk faced by donors; risks to displaced and relocated farmers not analyzed.	Risks to farmers initiating agricultural enterprises in new, unfamiliar areas are assessed along with risks from uncertain delivery of support, and backup plans prepared.
Duration	Provisions limited to time needed to complete main physical infrastructure, with insufficient assistance provided to ensure stabilization of new farm enterprises.	Provisions made to support settlers until full farm development.

linary team, including competent agricultural and social science specialists.

• Treat involuntary resettlement activities as important independent and parallel components of infrastructure projects, not as inconvenient and subordinate appendages to them.

• Adopt realistic time horizons to accomplish the defined income restoration objectives. Break down the resettlement period into a system establishment phase of about four to six years and a system stabilization phase estimated to be at least five years.

- Offer the widest possible range of compensation and resettlement options keyed to the specific needs of the displaced populations and always include some cash payment as part of the option package.

- Encourage decentralized management of resettlement activities through established local institutions, including nongovernmental agencies and local citizens' advocacy groups, backed by established government institutions and resources. Avoid using centralized bureaucracies, such as power authorities, irrigation departments, or ministries of agriculture, as the implementing agency for resettlement activities, as they are ill-equipped to deal with those tasks. Also avoid ad hoc institutional structures set up to deal with only the short-term exigencies of relocation and not with the longer-term issues of rehabilitation.

- Introduce a standard format for enumerating the full costs and potential benefits of any involuntary resettlement activity and insist that these costs and benefits be internalized in all *ex ante* and *ex post* financial and economic analyses.

- Introduce a standard format for enumerating both donor and recipient country staff and consultant inputs used in project preparation, appraisal, negotiations, and supervision by staff months and skills represented, so that staff input can be analyzed and compared.

With respect to the agricultural aspects of resettlement, our study suggests that project planners should:

- Strengthen site-specific analysis of the resources available to resettled families and use appropriate agricultural skill specialists in project planning and implementation so that the resource analysis can be directly linked to defined agricultural development processes. This would provide a realistic basis for designing project elements that directly address the resource constraints facing settler families and provide a more focused agenda for project monitoring.

- Fund detailed analysis of the preproject income flows and sources of farm families to be displaced to provide better baseline definitions of the resettlement populations and to set realistic points of departure for planning and monitoring the income restoration processes.

- Set participant selection criteria for the agricultural options provided so as to encourage outmigration from agriculture for families with low prospects of succeeding in the income restoration process.

- Broaden the range of resettlement options offered to encourage employment in agricultural support enterprises, such as crop processing and marketing, transportation, and input supply.
- Encourage experimentation with a range of farm models to better accommodate the varying capacities and capital endowments of families to be resettled and the different natural resource situations.
- Tailor land allocations for displaced families to both the physical characteristics of the available resource base and the endowments of individual families, namely, the size of the family's labor force for agricultural work, capacity to invest, and so on.
- Ensure greater stability in the income restoration process by providing the legal arrangements needed for rapid land titling or other guarantees of long-term land tenure for displaced families.
- Concentrate project resources on providing infrastructure directly related to fostering and sustaining the agricultural income restoration process. Developing roads from farms to market centers, rural water supplies, crop processing and marketing facilities, and local agricultural research and extension stations are likely to have a greater impact on livelihood restoration when linked with installing a broad array of social services.
- Encourage better analysis of and funding for agricultural support services directly relevant to the income restoration process.
- Resist attempts to restrict displaced families' use of on-farm resources.
- Introduce a requirement that project preparation and appraisal documents include comprehensive economic and agricultural risk and constraint analyses, considered from the pragmatic perspective of the resettled farming population.

Appendix
Characteristics of the Agriculturally Based
Resettlement Projects Surveyed

The set of tables that follow provides researchers, practitioners and other interested readers with additional information collected during this comparative research. The characteristics described in these tables for the pairs of compared projects refer to:

Table 3A.1. Resource Base
Table 3A.2. Household Income
Table 3A.3. Type of Resettlement Undertaken
Table 3A.4. Range of Resettlement Options
Table 3A.5. Type of Farm Model Envisaged
Table 3A.6. Size of Land Holding Allocated
Table 3A.7. Criteria for Land Allocation
Table 3A.8. Conditions of Land Tenure
Table 3A.9. Type of Infrastructure Provided
Table 3A.10. Source of Resettlement Services
Table 3A.11. Type of Risk Assessment
Table 3A.12. Restriction Placed on Settlers

Table 3A.1.   Resource Base

Country/project	Analysis of the resource base
Brazil	
Paulo Afonso IV	Perfunctory analysis of the geologic, climatic, vegetative, and soil conditions in the vicinity of the reservoir. Information not correlated with productive capacity for income regeneration.
Agricultural Development and Environmental Protection	Good analyses of land capability and present use, land tenure conditions, social infrastructure, baseline ecological conditions; research conducted on specific crops and their potential. Good data and discussion on socio-economic conditions faced by settlers and the constraints on various farming systems.
Mato Grosso Rural Development	Good set of resource base analyses very similar to those in the Agricultural Development and Environmental Protection Project.
New Settlements	The project is the Phase III follow-on activity to the Agricultural Development and Environmental Protection Project and depends to a large extent on information and data gathered under the Northwest Regional Development Program.
Indonesia	
Thirteenth Power	Agricultural resettlement was managed by the national Transmigration Program at sites on islands other than Java. No analysis of resource base and its relationship to income regeneration.
Transmigration I Transmigration II Transmigration III Transmigration IV	The four Transmigration Projects were phased over time but carried out essentially the same activities. Good general descriptions of each resettlement area. Agricultural research conducted crop trials at various project sites to determine appropriate farming techniques and income potential.
India	
Gujarat Irrigation	Most information on the resource base is general description at the state, not project, level. No specific discussion of resources nor of an income regeneration process for displaced persons.
Gujarat Irrigation II	Resource analysis similar to Gujarat Irrigation. Most resource information related to construction aspects of project, not to agriculture or income regeneration for displaced families.

Table 3A.1. *(continued)*

Country/project	Analysis of the resource base
India (continued) Rajasthan Canal Command Area Development	Good analysis of soil and water resources in the project area. Analysis directly relates resources to agricultural potential. Research results and long-term crop production figures used to assess income generation potential.
Rajasthan Command Area and Settlement	This project is a follow-on of the Rajasthan Canal Command Area Development Project. Resource analyses were extended to new areas to be developed.
China Shuikou Hydro-electric	Limited discussions of area resources related primarily to construction activities, not the resettlement program. Some discussion of capabilities of hillside lands for crop production, fruit tree production, establishment of economic trees, and permanent forests.
Second Shuikou Hydroelectric	The Second Shuikou Project is a follow-on effort. The appraisal document does not provide any significant additional information on the resource base for resettlement. It does report that the resettlement program was proceeding very satisfactorily.
Red Soils Area Development	Good comprehensive analysis of the key resource conditions in the project area—climate, topography, soils and land use—and the techniques needed to bring the area into viable agricultural production.
Ghana Kpong Hydro-electric	Essentially no analysis of the resource base as it related to crop, livestock, or fishery enterprises.
Volta Region Agricultural Development	Good analyses of ecology and climate, soils, infrastructure and social services, socio-economic situation, land use, farm structure, and crop production.

Table 3A.2.   Household Income

Country/project	Appraisal of household income
Brazil	
Paulo Afonso IV	Very general analysis of income groups in poorly defined rural population. General description of existing production systems.
Agricultural Development and Environmental Protection	Limited discussion of preproject household incomes; good analysis of income generation potentials of farming models being proposed.
Mato Grosso Rural Development	Limited discussion of preproject household incomes; good analysis of income generation potentials of farming models being proposed.
New Settlements	No real discussion of preproject settler income sources and flows; calculations of indicative farm family income from agricultural enterprises based on generated farm budgets.
Indonesia	
Thirteenth Power	Project financed a two-year anthropological, socioeconomic, and ecological baseline and impact study (including censuses and property inventories). No evidence that information from this study was used in the appraisal report.
Transmigration I Transmigration II Transmigration III Transmigration IV	No evidence that settlers income status and/or sources were investigated in detail, except as an element in the candidate selection process. Considerable work was devoted to determining the viability of the various farm models used and their income generation potentials over time.
India	
Gujarat Irrigation	General information from state records on general population characteristics. Some discussion of per capita income levels with and without the project, but the information appears to come from secondary sources.
Gujarat Irrigation II	General information from state records on general population characteristics. Some discussion of per capita income levels with and without the project.

Table 3A.2. *(continued)*

Country/project	Appraisal of household income
India *(continued)*	
Rajasthan Canal Command Area Development	Little discussion of preproject income status of settlers, but very good discussions of financial requirements of anticipated cropping and their relationship to credit needs and farmers' ability to pay water charges.
Rajasthan Command Area and Settlement	Income analysis discusses two groups of settlers under two different farm models. It is of similar quality to the Phase I project.
China	
Shuikou Hydroelectric	Little discussion of the income status of families being displaced other than for purposes of detailing compensation. No specific calculations are offered on the projected income regeneration process for displaced persons, although there is a detailed budget for total resettlement costs and one calculation of expected costs and revenues for resettlement in one county.
Second Shuikou Hydroelectric	No additional information is provided.
Red Soils Area Development	Little discussion of preproject incomes and sources among settlers. Good preliminary analysis of the income generation potentials for eight different farm models. Analyses of market demand for certain crops—mandarin oranges and ramie—may have been suspect.
Ghana	
Kpong Hydroelectric	Essentially no analysis of farm family incomes before or after resettlement.
Volta Region Agricultural Development	Analysis of pre and post project farm budgets. Limited discussion of family incomes focused entirely on agricultural enterprises.

Table 3A.3.   Type of Resettlement Undertaken

Country/project	Type of resettlement
Brazil	
Paulo Afonso IV	Involuntary resettlement with groups classified as urban or rural.
Agricultural Development and Environmental Protection	Government-assisted voluntary resettlement, some assistance to families who had migrated spontaneously.
Mato Grosso Rural Development	Government-assisted voluntary resettlement, some assistance to families who had migrated spontaneously.
New Settlements	Government-assisted voluntary resettlement for qualified new settlers.
Indonesia	
Thirteenth Power	Involuntary resettlement. Agricultural component of resettlement involved out-migration from Java to other islands under the Transmigration Program.
Transmigration I Transmigration II Transmigration III Transmigration IV	Three types of voluntary resettlement. Officially sponsored migrants had their travel paid and were settled on settlement schemes. Spontaneous migrants paid their own fares, but were settled on a settlement scheme and received some assistance (food, building materials, and so on). Free migrants who paid their own fares and settled wherever they found available land, other than the settlement schemes.
India	
Gujarat Medium Irrigation	Resettlement involved involuntary displacement of families from dam construction and reservoir areas.
Gujarat Medium Irrigation II	Resettlement involved involuntary displacement of families from dam construction and reservoir areas.
Rajasthan Canal Command Area Development	Project involved voluntary settlement of landless rural populations, subject to eligibility conditions.
Rajasthan Command Area and Settlement	Project involved voluntary settlement of landless rural populations, subject to eligibility conditions. Farm families from other sites within the existing perimeters were also voluntarily resettled in newly developed areas.

Table 3A.3. *(continued)*

Country/project	Type of resettlement
China Shuikou Hydro-electric	Project entailed involuntary resettlement of both urban and rural families. Rural families were resettled from lowland sites to hillside farms.
Second Shuikou Hydroelectric	Project entailed involuntary resettlement of both urban and rural families. Rural families were resettled from lowland sites to hillside farms.
Red Soils Area Development	Voluntary resettlement in the Red Soils area based upon a set of eligibility criteria.
Ghana Kpong Hydro-electric	Project entailed involuntary resettlement of rural farm families.
Volta Region Agricultural Development	No resettlement. Project focused on agricultural development of pre-existing smallholder farming systems.

Table 3A.4.   Range of Resettlement Options

Country/project	Resettlement options
Brazil	
Paulo Afonso IV	To move to distant INCRA resettlement scheme; receive cash settlement and move; remain in the vicinity of the reservoir for temporary employment, farming on the uplands, or work in a fisheries scheme.
Agricultural Development and Environmental Protection	Four farming models offered to qualified settlers based on coffee, cocoa, livestock, and rubber production. Fruit tree model was added later.
Mato Grosso Rural Development	Seven farm family income models are analyzed based on production of bananas, rubber, coffee, livestock production, and farm sizes (from less than 20 to more than 100 hectares).
New Settlements	Generalized farm model for farms of less than 50 hectares producing a combination of perennial and annual crops, including coffee, rubber, and tropical fruit trees.
Indonesia	
Thirteenth Power	No farm models were discussed in the available documents. Presumably, displaced families were eligible to participate in the same farm models that were used in the Transmigration Program.
Transmigration I Transmigration II Transmigration III Transmigration IV	A wide variety of farm models were designed, implemented, and evaluated over the total implementation period. Initial model was based on food and perennial tree crop production on 5-hectare farms. Other models involved development of low-lying swamp areas, upland, and forest areas for annual and perennial crops and livestock. Models were adjusted over time based on survey data collected on income generation and technical parameters.
India	
Gujarat Irrigation	Two generalized farm models outlined in the appraisal report. Both anticipate smallholder family farms growing a variety of crops under irrigation during the *kharif* and *rabi* seasons. Farm size varies from 2 hectares in mainland Gujarat to 5 hectares on Saurashtra.
Gujarat Irrigation II	Displaced families were to receive cash compensation for lost assets and replacement land. Land purchase costs to be paid only after farmer negotiated purchase and presented evidence to government agents.

Table 3A.4. *(continued)*

Country/project	Resettlement options
India (continued)	
Rajasthan Canal Command Area Development	Smallholder farms of 6.32 hectares allocated to qualified landless families. Farm model is a two-season irrigated system, with production of a range of crops.
Rajasthan Command Area and Settlement	Smallholder farms of 6.32 hectares allocated to qualified landless families. Farm model is a two-season irrigated system, with production of a range of crops.
China	
Shuikou Hydroelectric	Specific agricultural model was not presented. Displaced families were compensated for lost assets and resettled on hillside farms. According to land capability, farm production was to be a combination of annual crops, fruit trees, and forestry products.
Second Shuikou Hydroelectric	Specific agricultural model was not presented. Displaced families were compensated for lost assets and resettled on hillside farms. According to land capability, farm production was to be a combination of annual crops, fruit trees, and forestry products.
Red Soils Area Development	Smallholder individual farms and cooperative farming system. Eight farm models were evaluated, with cultivated areas ranging from 0.6 to 2.1 hectares of cultivable land, plus woodlots. Crops included irrigated rice, tea, oranges, and forest products.
Ghana	
Kpong Hydroelectric	Resettlement options were limited to cash reimbursement or moving to new resettlement villages.
Volta Region Agricultural Development	No resettlement activity in this project.

Table 3A.5.   Type of Farm Model Envisaged

Country/project	Type(s) of farm model envisaged
Brazil	
Paulo Afonso IV	No detailed farm model was presented in appraisal documents or resettlement plan.
Agricultural Development and Environmental Protection	Five smallholder farm models were offered to qualified settlers based on coffee, cocoa, livestock, and rubber production.
Mato Grosso Rural Development	Seven smallholder farm models were analyzed based on production of bananas, rubber, coffee, and livestock production.
New Settlements	One generalized smallholder farm model was discussed in the appraisal report, but three farm models were evaluated in the financial analysis. Two models based on production of annual crops and coffee and one based on annual crops and fruit trees.
Indonesia	
Thirteenth Power	No specific farm model was offered in the appraisal document. Since the displaced families entered the Transmigration Program, the farm models described below pertained to this project.
Transmigration I Transmigration II Transmigration III Transmigration IV	A wide variety of farm models were designed, implemented, and evaluated.
India	
Gujarat Irrigation Gujarat Irrigation II	Farm model under the Gujarat schemes is one for smallholder family holdings of irrigated cropland. Model is for diversified crop production over the *kharif* and *rabi* seasons.
Rajasthan Command Area Development Rajasthan Command Area and Settlement	Farm model under the Rajasthan schemes was smallholder farms of 6.32 hectares of irrigated land. Diversified crop rotations during the *kharif* and *rabi* seasons.

Table 3A.5. *(continued)*

Country/project	Type(s) of farm model envisaged
China Shuikou Hydro-electric Second Shuikou Hydroelectric	Shuikou resettlement provided for smallholder hillside farms producing, according to land capability, a combination of annual crops, fruit trees, and forestry products.
Red Soils Area Development	Two farm models were used in the Red Soils area. One was based on individual smallholder farms and the other on cooperative farming with individual house plots. Eight different cropping models. Crops included irrigated rice, tea, oranges, and forest products.
Ghana Kpong Hydro-electric	No new farm model was envisaged. Project planners sought to maintain pre-existing "traditional" smallholder farming systems at new village sites.
Volta Region Agricultural Development	There was no resettlement in this project. Interventions sought to strengthen existing smallholder farming systems on a commodity-by-commodity basis.

Table 3A.6.   Size of Land Holding Allocated

Country/project	Size of land holding allocated
Brazil	
Paulo Afonso IV	No detailed information is available on the size of land holdings allocated.
Agricultural Development and Environmental Protection	Information on the size of land holdings granted is very confusing. Apparently original model was for standardized 100-hectare farms, but new settlements had no standard sizes. Instead, size was determined on the basis of soil fertility, topography, and availability of farm labor.
Mato Grosso Rural Development	Land holdings for farms varied from less than 20 to more than 100 hectares.
New Settlements	Farm sizes variously reported as less than 50 hectares and between 25 and 40 hectares.
Indonesia	
Thirteenth Power	If Transmigration farm models applied, land holdings allocated should have been between 3.5 and 5 hectares per family.
Transmigration I Transmigration II Transmigration III Transmigration IV	Depending on the phase of the Transmigration Program, land holdings allocated per family varied between 3.5 and 5 hectares.
India	
Gujarat Irrigation Gujarat Irrigation II	Land holdings allocated ranged from 2 to 5 hectares per family, depending on location.
Rajasthan Command Area Development	Farm size invariable at 6.32 hectares of irrigated land.
Rajasthan Command Area and Settlement	

Table 3A.6. *(continued)*

Country/project	Size of land holding allocated
China	
Shuikou Hydro-electric Second Shuikou Hydroelectric	Size of holdings allocated varied according to family size, size of previous holdings, and occupation prior to displacement. Holdings in all cases were equal to or greater than those lost through displacement.
Red Soils Area Development	Size of holdings included cultivated areas ranging from 0.6 to 2.1 hectares, plus woodlots.
Ghana	
Kpong Hydro-electric	No information on the size of plots allocated to resettled families. Under the "traditional" system, plots apparently averaged about 2 hectares.
Volta Region Agricultural Development	No land was allocated under this project.

Table 3A.7.   Criteria for Land Allocation

Country/project	Criteria for land allocation
Brazil	
Paulo Afonso IV	Displaced families classified as "rural" and subject to loss of assets in the reservoir area.
Agricultural Development and Environmental Protection	Settler eligibility criteria were: area of origin, educational level, and years of previous agricultural experience. Later experience showed that success was determined more by whether settlers had been farm owners or managers and whether they had had a stable residence in the past.
Mato Grosso Rural Development	No comprehensive set of criteria is listed. Emphasis was apparently on "smallholder" farm families, defined as families having access to less than 200 hectares of land.
New Settlements	Settler eligibility criteria were stated as: physically able candidates with large families who have experience in agriculture but are not landowners, and who have not participated in any previous INCRA settlement project.
Indonesia	
Thirteenth Power	Eligible for resettlement if the displaced family lost property or use rights in the reservoir area and meets eligibility requirements.
Transmigration I Transmigration II Transmigration III Transmigration IV	Eligibility criteria for the Transmigration Program: Indonesian citizenship; married; aged 20 to 45, with no family member older than 60 years; agricultural experience and skill; maximum family size of five; nonpregnant wife; good political record; good police record; agreement to follow transmigration regulations; and has never transmigrated before.
India	
Gujarat Irrigation Gujarat Irrigation II	Displaced families are entitled to land allocations at least equal to their former holdings. If their holdings were less than 2 hectares, they were to be allocated at least 2 hectares.

Table 3A.7. *(continued)*

Country/project	Criteria for land allocation
India (continued) Rajasthan Command Area Development Rajasthan Command Area and Settlement	Priorities for land allocation: pre-1955 landless farmers (temporary cultivators); post-1955 farmers (temporary cultivators); landless farmers belonging to the village in which land is distributed; landless farmers belonging to the Tehsils in which the land is distributed; landless farmers of other Tehsils in the district; and other landless farmers belonging to other districts of Rajasthan.
China Shuikou Hydroelectric Second Shuikou Hydroelectric	Families displaced by Shuikou construction and/or reservoir filling and with rural occupations were eligible to participate in the resettlement and receive new terraced hillside land.
Red Soils Area Development	Farmers were selected by county governments and state farms from among applicants who possess requisite experience and managerial skills, long-term farm residence, and resources to contribute about 30 percent of the on-farm development costs (including land development, buildings, crop establishment, livestock, and farm machinery and equipment) in the form of cash or labor.
Ghana Kpong Hydroelectric	No criteria discussed other than family lost land and/or use rights due to project construction activities.
Volta Region Agricultural Development	No land was allocated under this project.

Table 3A.8.   Conditions of Land Tenure

Country/project	Conditions of land tenure
Brazil	
Paulo Afonso IV	Most displaced families apparently never received clear titles to the land allocated.
Agricultural Development and Environmental Protection	INCRA's performance on land titling was slow. A total of 14,393 titles were actually issued—about 60 percent of the total projected.
Mato Grosso Rural Development	Area was divided into two tenure regularization projects in which legitimacy of land claims was investigated by INCRA. Squatters found to have legitimate claims were to receive a "license to occupy" their farms. This was an adequate guarantee to obtain long-term credit and was eventually to lead to granting of an outright land title.
New Settlements	INCRA had acquired all property rights to the areas considered for settlement and corresponding reserve areas. Project funding is provided for mapping, surveying, demarcation, and land titling, but no specific titling process is indicated.
Indonesia	
Thirteenth Power	Presumably land tenure arrangements were as per the Transmigration Program.
Transmigration I Transmigration II Transmigration III Transmigration IV	Under the Transmigration Act, settlers are entitled to obtain land rights in accordance with prevailing laws. Settlers receive land in a two step process. First, they are granted land right of use [Hak Pakai], and, after proving their land has been developed and improved, they can be granted full ownership [Hak Milik].
India	
Gujarat Medium Irrigation Gujarat Irrigation II	No clear indication of farmer status of land rights. Apparently they have land use rights and access to a fixed water rotational schedule.

Table 3A.8. *(continued)*

Country/project	Conditions of land tenure
India (continued) Rajasthan Command Area Development Rajasthan Command Area and Settlement	Exact status of land tenure rights is unclear. Apparently most farmers receive their holdings as the result of a lottery among qualified farmers. Payments are made against long-term tenure guarantees. Over the life of the two projects, payments varied from Rs. 16,777 to Rs. 29,000 payable over 15 years without interest. Full title is given at this time.
China Shuikou Hydroelectric Second Shuikou Hydroelectric	No specific indication of the status of land tenure. Appraisal report discusses allocation of house plots but not individual ownership of land.
Red Soils Area Development	Use rights for the land were to be granted by the county governments or the state farms on a renewable, long-term basis.
Ghana Kpong Hydroelectric	roject did not alter traditional land use rights, which vary by ethnic group.
Volta Region Agricultural Development	Project did not alter existing land use patterns, which vary by ethnic group and location within the project area.

Table 3A.9.   Type of Infrastructure Provided

Country/project	Type of infrastructure provided
Brazil	
Paulo Afonso IV	Infrastructure provided by INCRA at the distant resettlement site is not detailed, except for the report that INCRA built 3,500 houses for anticipated resettlement population, of which 2,000 remain vacant at the end of the project. Specific infrastructure in the vicinity of the reservoir known to include: settler houses, schools, health facilities, and roads.
Agricultural Development and Environmental Protection	CODARON was to provide access and farm-to-market roads, rural service centers, schools, health posts, and warehouse/drying sheds. Social infrastructure included schools, rural water supply, health and sanitation facilities.
Mato Grosso Rural Development	Infrastructure very similar to that provided by the previous project.
New Settlements	Infrastructure provided is very similar to the previous project.
Indonesia	
Thirteenth Power	No specific infrastructure development for resettled families is discussed in the appraisal report.
Transmigration I Transmigration II Transmigration III Transmigration IV	Fully financed settlers received a house; all-weather main and village roads were built; one hand-dug well was provided for each of five families; and village health posts and village centers were constructed.
India	
Gujarat Medium Irrigation Gujarat Irrigation II	There is no reference in the appraisal documents for either of the Gujarat projects of any infra-structure built specifically for the families displaced by dam construction and irrigation tanks. The major infrastructure created is the irrigation network itself.

Table 3A.9. *(continued)*

Country/project	Type of infrastructure provided
India (continued) Rajasthan Command Area Development	Other than the irrigation systems, infrastructure included: village water supplies and major and minor roads. Afforestation, water channel lining, and land shaping operations were also included in the projects.
Rajasthan Command Area and Settlement	
China Shuikou Hydroelectric	Infrastructure included: roads, water supplies, market centers, and replacement of public buildings lost in the reservoir area. Building materials were provided to displaced families to reconstruct houses.
Second Shuikou Hydroelectric	
Red Soils Area Development	Infrastructure included: enlargement of small reservoirs, canal construction, installation of pumping stations and sprinkler irrigation systems, rural electrification, road and bridge construction, housing, schools and clinics, administrative buildings, warehouses, laboratories and extension stations, and livestock sheds.
Ghana Kpong Hydroelectric	Infrastructure included: settler housing, schools, water supply and sewerage systems, irrigation, and fishing dikes.
Volta Region Agricultural Development	Infrastructure included: village input supply centers, research/extension facilities, roads, water supply, power distribution networks, schools, and health facilities.

Table 3A.10.   Source of Resettlement Services

Country/project	Source of resettlement services
Brazil	
Paulo Afonso IV	INCRA was to provide support services in the distant resettlement site. Services in the vicinity were assumed from state agricultural extension and health services. Access to these services was apparently spotty or nonexistent for most displaced persons.
Agricultural Development and Environmental Protection	Full range of services, including agricultural research, extension, credit, supply of improved seeds, input supply services, crop processing and marketing, and soil survey and mapping were planned
Mato Grosso Rural Development	Services provided are very similar to those under the previous project.
New Settlements	Services provided are very similar to those under the previous project.
Indonesia	
Thirteenth Power	No discussion of agricultural or social services to be made available to displaced farm families.
Transmigration I Transmigration II Transmigration III Transmigration IV	A broad range of agricultural and social services were to be provided to settlers, including agricultural research, extension, input supply, assistance in cooperative organization, and credit. The projects also had complementary health and education services for the settler communities.
India	
Gujarat Irrigation Gujarat Irrigation II	Resettled families would presumably have the same access to the agricultural input supply, research, extension, and credit services as the other farm families in the Gujarat schemes.

Table 3A.10. *(continued)*

Country/project	Source of resettlement services
India (continued)	
Rajasthan Command Area Development	Settler families would have access to agricultural input supply, research, extension, and credit services in the Rajasthan schemes.
Rajasthan Command Area and Settlement	
China	
Shuikou Hydroelectric	Farmers had access to agricultural research and extension, credit, tillage, transport, crop processing, and marketing services.
Second Shuikou Hydroelectric	
Red Soils Area Development	Farmers had access to agricultural research and extension, credit, tillage, transport, crop processing and marketing services.
Ghana	
Kpong Hydroelectric	Project documents do not report introduction of any new services for the resettled populations.
Volta Region Agricultural Development	Project strengthened existing agricultural research and extension services and created village input supply centers, nutrition extension, credit, and irrigation development services.

Table 3A.11.   Type of Risk Assessment

Country/project	Type of risk assessment
Brazil	
Paulo Afonso IV	Essentially no *ex ante* risk analysis for the plight of the displaced persons. Any statements of risk are related to the donor's risk in the project.
Agricultural Development and Environmental Protection	Brief but intelligent qualitative discussion of crop production risks related to soils and crop diseases. Also discusses weaknesses in the extension service and consequences for settlers.
Mato Grosso Rural Development	Principal production risk discussed is the unknown nature of the resources in the frontier areas— soils and climate—and the need for effective agricultural research to develop effective cultivation and soil conservation techniques.
New Settlements	Risk statements are similar to the previous projects. Some comments on need to have better selection procedures for settlers.
Indonesia	
Thirteenth Power	All risk statements are directed at the risk to the donor from hydroelectric projects. No statements on risks to displaced persons.
Transmigration I Transmigration II Transmigration III Transmigration IV	Risk statements over the course of the projects build on implementation experiences and discuss mainly the risks associated with poor institutional performance of some agencies. Discussion of the relative deficiencies of some of the farm models tried in terms of income generation potential.
India	
Gujarat Irrigation Gujarat Irrigation II	There is some discussion of investment risks implicit in irrigation projects in India, but there is no discussion of risks to displaced families or farmers.
Rajasthan Command Area Development Rajasthan Command Area and Settlement	Risk statements discuss relative absence of risks in the project. Conclusion is that there are no greater risks in Rajasthan than in other irrigation projects in India. No real discussion of risk at the farm level.

Table 3A.11. *(continued)*

Country/project	Type of risk assessment
China	
Shuikou Hydro-electric	No specific risk statements dealing with farm operations.
Second Shuikou Hydroelectric	
Red Soils Area Development	No specific risk statements dealing with farm operations.
Ghana	
Kpong Hydro-electric	Planners attempted to reduce risks of a poor resettlement process by studying the mistakes made in the Akosombo project upstream.
Volta Region Agricultural Development	Risk statements primarily related to need to provide agricultural support services to farm families.

Table 3A.12.   Restriction Placed on Settlers

Country/project	Restriction placed on settlers
Brazil	
Paulo Afonso IV	Not defined.
Agricultural Development and Environmental Protection	Farmers can cultivate up to a maximum of 10 hectares of their land, of which not more than half can be in perennial crops.
Mato Grosso Rural Development	Not defined.
New Settlements	Not defined.
Indonesia	
Thirteenth Power	Not defined.
Transmigration I Transmigration II Transmigration III Transmigration IV	Settlers had to follow instructions on the allocation of land within their farming systems. Of the 5-hectare allocations, one hectare had to be planted to rubber; 0.2 hectare was to be used for home gardens. Before issuance of full ownership title, settler performance was subject to review by government officials.
India	
Gujarat Irrigation Gujarat Irrigation II	No information on any restrictions placed upon resettled families.
Rajasthan Command Area Development	No information on any restrictions placed upon settler families.
Rajasthan Command Area and Settlement	
China	
Shuikou Hydroelectric	No restrictions indicated.
Second Shuikou Hydroelectric	
Red Soils Area Development	No restrictions indicated.
Ghana	
Kpong Hydroelectric	Not defined.
Volta Region Agricultural Development	None. This was not a resettlement project.

Notes

1. The appraisal of the Shuikou project took place in 1986 immediately after the completion of the Bank's first internal review of resettlement operations and benefited much from the conclusions and effects of that review on the Bank's in-house work (see Cernea 1995).

2. This absolute numbers appear relatively large because of an artifact in compilation: the total costs of resettlement includes also compensation for infrastructure (for example, roads, bridges, and other items) that does not accrue to the families themselves, but they are part of the total costs computed for the overall component.

References

The word "processed" describes informally reproduced works that may not be commonly available through libraries.

Adu-Aryee, V. Q. 1993. "Resettlement from Akosombo to Kpong." In M. M. Cernea and S. E. Guggenheim, eds., *Anthropological Approaches to Resettlement: Policy, Practice, and Theory.* Boulder, Colo.: Westview Press.

Cernea, M. M. 1988. *Involuntary Resettlement in Development Projects: Policy Guidelines in World Bank-Financed Projects.* Washington, D.C.: World Bank.

_____. 1990. *Poverty Risks from Population Displacement in Water Resources Development: Policy and Operational Issues.* DDP 335. Cambridge, Mass.: Harvard University, HIID.

_____. 1991. "Socio-Economic and Cultural Approaches to Involuntary Population Resettlement." *Guidelines on Lake Management* 2:177–88.

_____. 1993. "Anthropological and Sociological Research for Policy Development on Population Resettlement," in M. M. Cernea and Scott Guggenheim, eds., *Anthropological Approaches to Resettlement: Policy, Practice, and Theory.* Boulder, Colo.: Westview.

_____. 1995. "Social Integration and Population Displacement: The Contribution of Social Science." *Economic and Political Weekly* (India) 31 (June 15): 1515–23.

Chambers, Robert, ed. 1970. *Volta Resettlement.* London: Pall Mall Press.

CHESF (Companhia Hidro Eletrica do Sao Francisco). 1975. *Projeto Sobradinho: Resettlement Plan for the Population Reached by Sobradinho's Reservoir.* São Paulo, Brazil.

FAO (Food and Agriculture Organization of the United Nations)/World Bank. 1975. "Report of the Brazil Mato Grosso Land Settlement Project: Preparation Report." Report No. 44/75 BRA:17. FAO/World Bank Cooperative Programme. Rome. Processed.

_____. 1980. "Report of the Brazil Rondonia Rural Development Project Preparation Mission," vols. I and II. Report No. 52/80 BRA:21. FAO/World Bank Cooperative Programme. Rome. Processed.

Gulyani, S. 1992. "Rethinking Resettlement: Employment, Negotiation, and Land in Singrauli, India." Master's thesis, Department of Urban Studies and Planning, Massachusetts Institute of Technology, Cambridge, Mass. Processed.

Gutman, P. 1993. "Involuntary Resettlement in the Hydro Power Projects: A Review of the Bank Performance during 1978–1992." World Bank, Washington, D.C. Processed.

Indonesia, Government of the Republic of. 1982. "Physical Planning for Transmigration Terms of Reference, Phase II, Phase III A, Phase III B." Jakarta. Processed.

Kinsey, B. H., and H. P. Binswanger. 1993. "Characteristics and Performance of Resettlement Programs: A Review." World Bank, Washington, D.C. Processed.

Shuikou Reservoir Resettlement Office. 1991. "Shuikou Hydroelectric Project Part II: Supplementary Information on Resettlement." Fujian Provincial Government, Fouzhou, China. Processed.

World Bank. 1978. "The World Bank and the Settlement of Agricultural Lands: An Issues Paper." Washington, D.C. Processed.

_____. 1985. "The Experience of the World Bank with Government-Sponsored Land Settlement." Report No. 5625. Washington, D.C. Processed.

_____. 1987. "World Bank Experience with Rural Development 1965–1986." Report No. 6883. Washington, D.C. Processed.

_____. 1992. "World Bank Approaches to the Environment in Brazil: A Review of Selected Projects, vol. V, The (POLONORESTE) Program." Report No. 10039. Washington, D.C. Processed.

_____. 1993a. "Early Experience with Involuntary Resettlement: Overview." World Bank, Operations Evaluation Department, Washington, D.C. Processed.

_____. 1993b. "Early Experience with Involuntary Resettlement: Impact Evaluation on Ghana Kpong Hydroelectric Project (Loan 1380-GH)." World Bank, Operations Evaluation Department, Washington, D.C. Processed.

_____. 1994. "Resettlement and Development: The Bankwide Review of Projects Involving Involuntary Resettlement, 1986–1993." Environment Department, Washington, D.C. Processed.

_____. n.d. "Economic Alternatives for Displaced Populations: Resettlement and the Shuikou Hydroelectric Development Project in China." Washington, D.C. Processed.

The author also referred to numerous World Bank appraisal reports, project completion reports, and other internal documents relating to the projects reviewed.

4

Economic Dimensions of Urban Resettlement: Experiences from Latin America

María Clara Mejía

Editor's Note   The economic dimensions of urban involuntary resettlement have been studied even less than the economics of rural population displacement. To this vast "field-in-waiting," the study by María Clara Mejía makes a substantive contribution and recommends a rich agenda of topics for further inquiry.

After a general overview on urban resettlement in Latin American countries, the study focuses on key economic issues regarding house replacement for resettlers. It discusses affordability of new housing, subsidized rehousing solutions with full or partial payment by the project, and other financing alternatives that emerged in Brazil, Argentina, and Colombia. Because failure to understand the complexity of the resettlement process has caused chronic underestimation of its costs in urban project budgets, María Clara Mejía "deconstructs" the general concept of urban resettlement costs in some 15 specific cost categories germane to resettlement operations. Detailed tables provide information on average resettlement costs per family and as a percentage of total project costs.

The study also discusses the World Bank's participation in resettlement financing, which in some projects has been increased during implementation to levels higher than those defined at appraisal time. The analysis found that reliance on local financing alone for resettlement has increased the likelihood of delays and problems. The availability of external (nonlocal) financing is helpful because it can meet costs that otherwise tend to be left "unrecognized"; it also enhances the commitment by governments to deliver local financing and facilitates better implementation.

Reestablishing income-generating activities for resettlers in urban settings confronts a host of economic problems that are specific to large human agglomerations and different from rural resettlement. Among them are the costs of urban services, distance to jobs and cost of transportation, scarce demand for labor, and limited customer bases in newly constructed locations. The study explores possible responses and concludes with numerous practical recommendations for the preparation and implementation phases of future urban projects entailing resettlement.

<hr>

The involuntary displacement and consequent resettlement of populations has been a major concern of the World Bank and other international development agencies during the past two decades. During this period, investigators from a variety of scientific fields have conducted research on the impacts of official policies and procedures—or lack of policies—for resettled populations. Most such efforts have focused on "megaprojects" for hydroelectricity and irrigation in rural areas, while the experience with involuntary displacement of urban populations, especially in the slums and poverty belts of large cities, has been less systematically assessed. A disciplined effort to understand the specific features of urban resettlement would help in designing operational policies, strategies, and procedures that are compatible with the socioeconomic and political realities of the urban context.

Current knowledge of the economic dimensions of urban resettlement is rudimentary. This paper draws on recent experience in Latin America with planning, implementing, and evaluating urban resettlement operations, discussing the challenges of dealing with the economic costs, financial arrangements, and impacts of the relocation process on family income, employment, and economic activities generally. While the cases reviewed here illustrate many important lessons regarding the economic dimensions of involuntary resettlement, the point we would like to stress is that such economic dimensions require much more attention from professional economists in all resettlement operations. Several of the operations discussed in this study are still under implementation, and the analysis, though empirical, is necessarily preliminary.

The cases presented here are drawn from World Bank–assisted urban projects in Latin America and the Caribbean. In the 1970s and 1980s Bank-financed projects involving involuntary resettlement in the region were mostly located in rural locales, but by the middle of the current decade the majority of such resettlement-related projects in Latin America were in urban areas. This chapter seeks to improve understanding of the resettlement process in active projects and those under preparation during the past five to seven years.

We readily recognize that the Bank–assisted projects discussed here account for only a small fraction of the *total* urban involuntary resettlement occurring today in Latin America, since the largest part of forced relocation takes place outside Bank projects under domestically financed projects. But the economic and sociocultural issues are more or less the same, notwithstanding the source of financing. With 70 percent of the region's population residing in urban areas, and the pace of urbanization still accelerating, urban development projects and resulting involuntary displacement are increasing as well (Burki and Edwards 1995).

During the past decade, Latin American countries and implementing agencies have made considerable progress in the design of resettlement plans, adoption of participatory strategies for decisionmaking, and restoration and improvement of living standards for those displaced. Despite this progress, however, too frequently the scope and nature of involuntary displacement are not clearly identified during project preparation. There is little planning for resettlement, the economic reconstruction of the livelihoods of affected people is inadequately addressed, financing is insufficient, and unexpected results occur due to failures that could have been avoided or minimized through a comprehensive approach to the economic dimensions of resettlement.

Studying the economic characteristics of urban resettlement operations and analyzing operational problems will help to significantly increase benefits, reduce social costs, and enhance the feasibility of urban development projects in Latin America (Cernea 1992). Accordingly, this chapter will analyze some of these characteristics, describe current procedures in projects under implementation, show the main difficulties in the planning and execution of urban resettlement, and make operational recommendations for overcoming those difficulties.

Overview of Urban Displacement and Resettlement in Latin America

Magnitude of Urban Population Displacement

One of the most significant changes in development in the past 10 to 12 years has been the growing number of urban, transportation, and water supply investments. The Bankwide resettlement review found that in the Bank's overall project portfolio these sectors accounted for 22 percent of all projects, 53 percent of all projects involving resettlement, and 47 percent of people displaced (about 950,000 people) (World Bank 1996).

The Bank currently has more than 100 urban projects either under implementation or in preparation in Latin America and the Caribbean. Most are directed toward the construction and improvement of services, urban infrastructure, environmental sanitation, territorial zoning, and management of urban river basins in large and heavily populated cities. Due to the high population density of urban areas, many of these operations will inevitably involve involuntary displacement.

Table 4.1 shows urban projects in Latin America and the Caribbean as of September 1995 for which involuntary resettlement operations are under way and for which resettlement plans have been agreed upon by the Bank and the borrower governments. Preliminary estimates indicated that a total of over 30 projects that will entail involuntary resettlement of urban populations have been scheduled for approval between 1996 and 1999 (World Bank 1995a). Past experiences have shown that due to lack of detailed design, uncertainties in defining technical components, and a paucity of analysis of the economic dynamics in urban settlements, resettlement needs have been often established only during the advanced stages of preparation or even during implementation. But while the number of households affected is relatively easy to count, the impact of resettlement on the economic and social systems of the urban population is not readily apparent and requires careful examination during the planning phase.

The 10 projects in table 4.1 displace almost 100,000 people and serve as a context for our discussion.[1] These numbers, of course, are likely to change from year to year because of the growing weight of urban projects in the Bank's portfolio, and because there are anticipated projects for which resettlement needs are not yet fully determined.

Causes and Rationale for Involuntary Displacement in Urban Areas

Displacement of urban populations is generally the result of (a) disorderly growth and consequent reordering of urban living space, (b) improvement of highly deteriorated sanitation and environmental conditions, (c) improvement of other urban infrastructure facilities, (d) specific social or poverty alleviation policies, and (e) the effects of natural disasters. This last case typically involves moving at-risk populations to avoid future disasters. In this case, the resettlement is an objective in itself and may be highly beneficial to the displaced population, provided sound resettlement plans are implemented.

Table 4.1. Population Displacement in Selected Urban Development Projects

Country	Project	Displaced population[a]
Argentina/ Paraguay	Highway VIII	204[b]
Argentina/ Paraguay	Yacyretá Hydroelectric II	15,000
Brazil	Paraná Water Quality and Pollution Control	9,000
Brazil	Minas Gerais Water Quality and Pollution Control	12,522
Brazil	São Paulo Water Quality and Pollution Control	24,144
Brazil	Rio Flood Reconstruction and Prevention	22,200
Brazil	Ceará Urban Development and Water Resource Management	2,000[c]
Brazil	Belo Horizonte and Recife Metropolitan Transportation	4,368
Brazil	Minas Gerais Urban Development (Ipatinga)	4,500[d]
Colombia	Santa Fe 1 Water Supply and Sewerage Rehabilitation and Private Sector Development	390
Total		94,328

Note: Actual and anticipated displacement in projects under implementation or preparation as of September 1995; this table reflects the group of projects analyzed in this paper; the Bank's portfolio of urban projects with resettlement components in Latin America and the Caribbean includes several other recent projects in Colombia, Peru, Guatemala, Brazil, and Guyana.
    a. Some numbers were estimated using an average household size of six residents.
    b. Residents without legal title. No data are available on legal owners to be displaced by the project.
    c. The first four dams of this project will displace about 2,000 people in rural areas where water supply reservoirs are being built. The total population to be affected by the 39 dams is not yet determined, but an unknown number of urban families will be displaced.
    d. Population displaced in Ipatinga. The number to be displaced in other municipalities of Minas Gerais by the next phase is under assessment.

The importance of water and sanitation projects in response to soaring urban growth in Latin America is beyond question. Such projects improve the health and living conditions of hundreds of thousands of people in metropolitan areas. For example, in the project for Bacia de Guarapiranga in the São Paulo region, more than 72,000 families will benefit from rehabilitation of urban slums. The same project will also protect the water supply of more than 3 million families. But such projects often imply considerable social and economic costs as well. The reorganization and improvement of urban areas inevitably involves displacement of marginalized populations living on public or private lands, in slums, and in highly degraded areas.

But the relation between the objectives of urban development projects and involuntary displacement is not always justifiable. Some of the occurring displacements are unnecessary, and they are caused by poor project design, failure to optimize social costs and benefits, or exclusion of relevant actors from the decisionmaking process. For instance, in most of the projects discussed in this chapter, displacement has been reduced significantly by changing initially proposed project design by using more appropriate technology and broadening public consultation, without seriously affecting project costs or objectives (see table 4.7).

Specific Conditions in the Urban Context

Is urban displacement and resettlement different from that in rural areas? And if so, how?

Diverse and complex factors define the specific features of urban resettlement—the internal conditions of each country, the nature of some projects, the dynamics of urban growth and demographics, the urban land tenure problem, and the institutional arrangements for urban projects. Below are some of the characteristics specific to resettlement in the urban context.

• The pattern of settlement is relatively recent. On average, 65 percent of the urban population affected by Bank-assisted projects in Latin America and the Caribbean has lived in the affected area for five years or less, while only about 15 percent of families have lived in the area for more than 20 years.[2] That is to say, these populations have already relocated to their present location in the recent past, some as rural migrants, some from town and cities. This feature is in striking contrast to typically long-established rural settlements.
• Because of the scarcity and the high price of urban land, it is increasingly difficult to find affordable and suitable land for resettlement in urban areas, and real estate prices are subject to runaway speculation. This is a serious obstacle. Building upward rather than outward is increasingly seen as the most adequate resettlement alternative. The expenses for doing so may be justifiable when compared with the high sociocultural costs and the disruption of social and economic activities caused by resettlement to a more distant area.
• Urban communities display a high capacity for adaptation, self-management, and resettlement resulting from previous expe-

riences in relocating themselves (Peattie 1970). The ability of the urban poor to self-relocate and to manage compensation packages should be studied more deeply, but what is important is that their experience in this regard is much greater than that of rural populations. The Rio Flood Reconstruction Project is a good example. In the face of delays and bureaucratic inefficiencies, and fearful of squatters, 63 families that were going to be displaced occupied the allocated resettlement site on their own. The self-resettlement was orderly and calm, and it created favorable conditions for future negotiations between the communities and project management.

- The number of families in affected areas is always changing because of pressures on urban living space, inability of the government to prevent such movements, project delays, and so on. The constant threat of massive new influxes makes traditional field studies, planning processes, and lengthy negotiations difficult. This is especially problematic when projects are planned but then delayed for many years (such as the Yacyretá Hydroelectric Project and the Rio Flood Reconstruction Project), during which poor people move into the area hoping to receive a resettlement package.

- The reliance of slum dwellers on the so-called informal economy has not been sufficiently studied or taken into consideration in resettlement planning. While informal activities allow greater mobility, they also create dependence on the surrounding environment, which provides informal or temporary job opportunities in the commercial and industrial centers of cities. The unsanitary, dangerous, and impoverished living conditions of many slum dwellers should not obscure the fact that a vibrant and essential economic life drew them here in the first place (Lomnitz 1977, Peattie 1970, Perlman 1982). Efforts at "urban modernization" or rehabilitation of deteriorated downtown areas underestimate the centrality of this fact. This makes site selection critical to restoring employment, income, and social networks.

- The socioeconomic and political landscape of cities is constantly changing, affecting the various social actors (institutions, groups, and individuals) and requiring continual adjustments in the agreements established in development projects. Relocation of populations and housing solutions for low-income groups has undeniable political significance (Lomnitz 1977). It does not take extensive research to understand that, beyond the main objectives, these projects indirectly (a) legalize and regulate the occupation of urban lands, (b) allocate access to public services, (c) create new economic opportunities for commercial and industrial businesses, (d) increase land values and influence low-income housing, and (e) produce political capital for electoral purposes.

- Resettlement "naturally" tends to become intertwined with public housing programs and is therefore subject to official housing agencies' parameters on financing strategies and recovery of investments, real estate appraisal, housing standards, and expropriation procedures. This deflects attention from the heart of resettlement—reestablishing the economic basis for improved livelihoods.
- Institutional and administrative complexity. Urban projects usually include a number of components involving many sectors of the economy and a multitude of agencies and institutions. Land use regulation, building codes, environmental zoning, public services provision, and other issues related to resettlement often entail the participation of many agencies. This complicates decisionmaking, dissemination of information, and planning and implementation of resettlement programs.
- Slum dwellers are considered third-class citizens. Many public officials tend to view people living in slums as squatters, thieves, prostitutes, and drug dealers, who are therefore less worthy of meaningful consultation and participation strategies or well-designed resettlement plans. Yet slums are like parallel cities whose marginalization and lack of government assistance have fostered specific survival strategies. Relocating their inhabitants involuntarily disrupts an entire lifestyle and the social network established among neighbors (Perlman 1982).
- Perhaps one of the most outstanding characteristics of urban resettlement processes is the impact on poor families with no legal land titles, who frequently account for the vast majority of the affected population in highly degraded urban areas. Although this feature may also be found in rural resettlement, it is even more challenging in the urban context.

There are some special conditions in the case of slum improvement programs that hinder traditional planning processes and create new social and technical challenges:

- Resettlement needs can be determined precisely only when project design is ready for each slum, which in many cases practically merges planning and implementation into a single stage.
- Additional resettlement may be necessary during construction due to unforeseen property damage and other impacts caused by small

variations in the work plan and other strictly technical requirements.

- Displacement of some families is often necessary to provide
services and improve the standard of living of the rest of the community, which divides the population into affected and benefited groups.
- A parallel strategy is required to keep out new squatters during the
period from project design to registry and relocation of the existing
families. In the case of São Paulo, for instance, it is estimated that
this process usually takes six to 10 months.

Another special case is that of linear projects such as construction or
improvement of roads, laying out electrical grids, and installing pipes
for water and sewers that affect urban areas. On the one hand, these undertakings require isolated, noncontiguous relocations that must be
planned on a case by case basis. On the other hand, the impact on most
houses and property is only partial, and the families can usually stay in
the same location as long as their homes are rebuilt. This is quite different from cases in which the loss of property or housing is total and
where the project affects an entire community.

Displacement of populations in high-risk areas also has special
characteristics. Despite the social and economic costs, resettlement of
families frequently threatened by landslides, floods, or risky environmental conditions is highly desirable as long as housing provisions are
acceptable and the economic recovery program ensures the improvement of living conditions. It is a case that requires special procedures
and policy considerations.

Economic Issues in House Replacement Alternatives

During the past four years several countries in Latin America and the
Caribbean have designed and implemented a range of policies to address problems related to urban resettlement. These policies follow the
general lines of the World Bank's resettlement policy but also reflect the
specifics of each country and each project.[3] More important, they are the
result of social, economic, and political agreements among the agencies
and institutions participating in project implementation. Some of the sa-
lient issues addressed are described below.

Land Titles and Property Compensation

The Bank's policy is to provide compensation regardless of whether the
person has legal title. Some countries in Latin America still base resettle-

ment policy on whether the displaced people have legal title to land, while others base their policy on social vulnerability regardless of the legal status of the land on which those to be displaced reside.[4] Compensation for legal landowners is generally considered a buyer-seller transaction between the state and private individuals.

Houseowners without title, on the other hand, are considered squatters, or "illegal inhabitants," of public or private property who should bear more of the financial burden of resettlement through partial payment of housing solutions, legal prohibitions on property exchange, or lower-quality housing solutions. Commonly, they receive compensation only for personal property but not for the lot itself. However, it is recommended that borrowers recognize de facto property rights as part of the compensation package. Usually replacement of houses and land is the best strategy to ensure recovery of the previous standard of living.

Monetary Compensation

The Bank's view is that delivering only monetary compensation, while acceptable in select cases, often jeopardizes living standards, especially for low-income groups. Such compensation often ends up in the hands of moneylenders and intermediaries, or is spent on old debts, consumer goods, or other expenses that do not ensure the reestablishment of homes, communities, and social networks. There have been few *ex post* evaluations of groups that received cash compensation, so the true dimensions of this problem in Latin America and the Caribbean have not been measured, but current work in Argentina and Colombia is addressed precisely to this lacuna. For those without legal title, monetary compensation often does not allow for full replacement, since it does not include payment for land.

Socioeconomic Development

Since involuntary displacement can destroy previous means of livelihood, all resettlement operations must be development programs. There is need for alternative employment strategies for the displaced, including preferential hiring in the project itself and in the public sector when appropriate. However, most current urban resettlement programs are based only on housing replacement. Economic and social assistance programs are mentioned only tangentially, and financing, human resources, and participation of social development agencies are inadequate. Usually it is the social workers directly involved who promote the community and solicit support from state agencies.

By contrast, in the El Salvador Earthquake Reconstruction Project, the Italian government collaborated in a resettlement plan that included integrated programs of socioeconomic development. The programs were generated employment (construction at each phase provided employment for the families displaced in the previous phase), created a development agency to be managed by the relocated families, and generated family income through creation of microenterprises. The case of Yacyretá is another example, with routine socioeconomic assistance programs before, during, and after actual resettlement (Mejía 1996).

Subsidized Solutions versus Partial Payment

Policies also vary in the degree of subsidy or financing required of the families themselves. In some cases the entire cost of housing and resettlement is covered by the project (Minas Gerais, Santa Fe 1, Colombia Power Market, Yacyretá), while in others the displaced families must pay a share of the housing costs (São Paulo, Paraná, Rio de Janeiro). Without trying to settle the debate over whether to require those displaced to cover part of the resettlement cost, the following points should contribute to the discussion.

- The Bank's basic policy is that the risks of impoverishment involved in forced relocation must be avoided (Cernea 1997). Because the population is *forcibly* displaced, it should not have to bear *any* of the resettlement costs and also should have a variety of resettlement options. Additional financial burdens must not be placed on low-income families that are already at risk of impoverishment due not only to precarious income but also to labor instability. As an illustration, in projects examined here, between 15 and 25 percent of the families affected earn less than the minimum wage. Even those that appear capable of making modest payments might be at risk of losing their homes due to economic crises, inflation, and currency devaluations. Forced imposition of a debt when no other alternative is offered is not acceptable to the Bank.
- Faced with declining budgets, needs for investment recovery, and increasing land and construction prices, housing agencies tend to transfer, openly or surreptitiously, part of the resettlement costs to the displaced people. Agencies also fear that not requiring squatters to pay part of the resettlement cost will encourage new occupations of public land.
- Some civil servants in charge of resettlement think that having to pay part of the housing cost makes the resettled families feel more

rooted, increases their sense of ownership, and creates greater social discipline and capacity for self-management. In the projects under implementation in Latin America, housing subsidies to
families vary from 65 percent for families with income greater than
three times the minimum wage to 75 percent for families with up to
three times the minimum wage, and as much as 95 percent for families with less than a single minimum wage.

• The involuntarily displaced communities themselves have repeatedly rejected being forced to assume housing costs. In the "Sitio do
Livramento" in Rio de Janeiro, 95 percent of the families failed to
make their monthly payments due to unstable incomes and the financing terms imposed. A recent survey by a local housing agency
revealed that 70 percent of families that were resettled for more
than one year were not making their monthly payments. The
Yacyretá project also illustrates reluctance to pay even by families
considered well off.

Housing Replacement Alternatives

Table 4.2 shows the resettlement solutions offered to different groups
in urban projects in Latin America. It shows the variety of approaches

**Table 4.2. Compensation Alternatives Offered to the Displaced
Population**

Country/project	Displaced	Alternatives
Brazil– São Paulo Water Quality and Pollution Control	Legal owner	There are no legal owners of land to be dis-placed in the project.
	Landholder without legal title	1. Financed house provided by the housing development agency. Alternatives offered depend on family income, in accordance with normal agency regulations. Monthly payments vary from $11 to $226. Compensation for improvements is not paid because the new homes are already highly subsidized. A legal agreement (*Termo de Compromiso*) is signed upon moving into the house. 2. Letter of credit for up to $15,000. 3. For extremely poor families (less than one minimum wage) exchange for shack worth up to $1,700 in another slum, or construction of home in the same slum, without financing restriction.

77.2 (continued)

Country/project	Displaced	Alternatives
	Renter	Same alternative as for house owners without titles. No indemnification paid to original owners if the units have not been legalized.
Brazil–Minas Gerais Water Quality and Pollution Control	Legal owner	Monetary compensation at market replacement price.
	Landholder without legal title	1. Monetary compensation of at least $6,000 for houses and improvements. 2. House in state housing company development, with no financial obligation. Resident signs a legal agreement (*Posse Provisoria*) that prohibits the family from selling the house for ten years.
	Renter	One year rent payment at market prices. Property owners are given the same option as the house owners without title.
Brazil–Paraná Water Quality and Pollution Control	Legal owner	1. Monetary compensation at market replacement price. 2. Exchange for developed lot with no payment by property owner.
	Landholder without legal title	1. Developed lot financed under state housing company rules: 60 to 120 monthly payments up to 20 percent of minimum salary 2. Modular house financed in conjunction with the developed lot.
	Renter	Basic package of building materials to families recently displaced by floods (Trevisan area). The materials will be financed jointly with the urbanized lot.
Brazil-Rio Flood Reconstruction and Prevention	Legal owner[a]	1. Monetary compensation. 2. Home in state housing company housing development.
	Landholder without legal title	Unit in the state housing company development with monthly payments equivalent to 15 percent of the minimum wage, one-year grace period.
	Renter	1. Unit delivered by state housing company with monthly payments equivalent to 15 percent of the minimum wage, one-year grace period. 2. Monetary compensation for house and improvements. Property owner is not compensated if units are not legalized.

(Table continues on the following page.)

Table 4.2 *(continued)*

Country/project	Displaced	Alternatives
Brazil–Belo Horizonte and Recife Metropolitan Transportation	Legal owner	Monetary compensation at market value or a minimum payment sufficient to buy another property, whichever is higher. Assistance is provided in finding a replacement property.
	Landholder without legal title	1. Compensation at market values. 2. Housing in housing units for poorest families.
	Renter	1. Financial assistance provided to help rent another property. 2. Indemnification for commercial house.
Argentina/Paraguay–Yacyretá Hydroelectric II	Legal owner	1. Indemnification for lot, house, and improvements at market replacement price. 2. Full restitution of the lot, house, and material losses. Exchange of current house for unit built by the project in development with community services and infrastructure.
	Landholder without legal title	Monetary compensation for material losses.
	Renter	Monetary compensation for material losses.
Colombia–Santa Fe 1 Water Supply and Sewerage Rehabilitation and Private Sector Development	Legal owner	1. Monetary compensation for 120 percent of replacement value of house and lot. 2. Replacement of house at no cost to owner. 3. Monetary compensation for economic losses in domestic and commercial activities.
	Landholder without legal title	1. Indemnification for 100 percent of house and lot replacement value. 2. Replacement of the property at no cost to owner. 3. Monetary compensation for effects on economic activities.
	Renter	Financial assistance equivalent to six months' rent for tenants with less than two years' residence, and twelve months' rent for tenants with more than two years of residence.

a. When the parents' marital status is not legalized, the house is registered to the woman.

currently used, which depends on the internal policies and the institutional and legal frameworks within each country.

Table 4.3 presents in more detail the basic menu of strategies available for providing housing. The alternatives actually used depend on families' capacity for self-management of their resources as well as on local financial and market constraints and possibilities. Each strategy

Table 4.3. Housing Alternatives

Housing alternatives	Description
Chess game	For families with income below the minimum wage, the project buys a house in the same slum and gives it to the displaced family. The family that sold the house is moved into housing financed by the state housing company. In São Paulo, 14 families out of the 80 already resettled have chosen this option.
Exchange for partially subsidized housing in developments built by housing agencies or under contract by private firms	The family promises to make monthly payments in accordance with their income level (Rio de Janeiro, São Paulo).
Exchange for fully subsidized house in development built by the project	Those displaced receive a single-family home in a new housing development built by the project (Minas Gerais, Yacyretá, São Paulo).
Exchange for single-family housing with shared social area	In Rio de Janeiro, the family promises to make monthly payments based on its income level.
Apartment buildings	Delivery of a financed apartment (São Paulo, 80 families).
Letter of credit	The displaced family receives a document giving them credit to buy an existing house worth up to $15,000 (in São Paulo, this tool has yet to be used).
Renting with option to buy	The renting family moves to a unit that belongs to the local housing agency. The family continues to make monthly rent payments, but part of them goes toward an escrow account to allow for the possibility of purchase in about five years.
Financed lot with services	The renting family moves to a developed urban lot. The project provides technical assistance to dismantle, move, and rebuild the existing home.
Lot with services and basic building supplies	For families left homeless by flooding, financing is provided to enable the family to buy the building supplies and the lot (Paraná).

involves a different set of pros and cons, and deciding which approach to use is a complicated task that requires careful analysis of the conditions in each project and location, as well as consultation with the population being resettled.

Socioeconomic Profile of the Affected Population

Socioeconomic characteristics are an important consideration in determining appropriate urban resettlement strategies. The baseline information available for Latin America and the Caribbean urban resettlement projects is drawn from registries and censuses that provide an economic and demographic profile on which to base compensation and indemnification. The socioeconomic data presented assist in understanding the risks of impoverishment associated with resettlement, but they are by no means exhaustive.

With the aim of contributing to the discussion regarding the appropriateness or inappropriateness of the strategies and policies adopted in the resettlement process of urban population in Latin America and the Caribbean, socioeconomic characteristics of the displaced population are summarized here. Although each project has census and land registry data that at least include the communities to be displaced in the first phases, these data do not clearly delineate the sociocultural characteristics of the displaced population, nor are the socioeconomic data complete.

FAMILY INCOME. The Paraná Water Quality and Pollution Control Project stands out at the extreme low end of family income—37 percent of the families received less than a single minimum wage, compared with 5 percent in the Rio de Janeiro metropolitan area. In general the great majority of the families to be displaced received less than two times the minimum wage. While the proportion varies, the socioeconomic vulnerability of this extremely poor segment is indisputable. Special social assistance for relocation will be needed.

EMPLOYMENT. Average unemployment among the displaced population is about 15 percent, though in Rio de Janeiro it exceeds 40 percent. Furthermore, about 25 percent of the population on average is underemployed or relies solely on incidental work. With 40 percent either unemployed or underemployed, this population is highly vulnerable and requires special support during resettlement. It can also be expected that relocation of this group in a new settlement far from its current one will significantly affect job and income opportunity.

WOMEN IN URBAN RESETTLEMENT. The gender of heads of households is another important factor, with implications for program design such as financing and titling of real estate, accommodating special socioeconomic needs, and building community support infrastructure. Households headed by women who work outside the home have a greater need for kindergarten or day care facilities. For example, in the Rio Flood Reconstruction Project, about 66 percent of households are headed by women, whereas in Paraná (Curitiba) only 15 percent are headed by women. Unfortunately, in the other samples there is no breakdown of data by gender. Though gender influences participatory strategies and attainment of economic outcomes, it is insufficiently considered.

LENGTH OF RESIDENCE. A high percentage of families have lived in the neighborhoods for five years or less, while about 15 percent have resided there for more than 20 years. This influences both the heterogeneity of the neighborhood and the degree of participation in the community social network.

HETEROGENEITY OF THE POPULATION. The heterogeneity of populations in the so-called poverty belts has been clearly confirmed by the technicians responsible for conducting socioeconomic surveys and negotiations with the affected communities. Significant indicators of heterogeneity include:

- Income structure—ranges from less than one minimum wage to more than eight wages per household
- Quality and size of houses—from disposable materials to brick; from 18 square meters of floor space to 120 square meters and more; from one floor to as many as four floors
- Family size—from one person to more than nine
- Level of community organization—from rudimentary forms to officially recognized organizations with representation in policymaking bodies at local and state levels.

The previous data show the general, widely recognized socioeconomic characteristics of slum dwellers: the majority of the population is extremely poor, unemployment and underemployment are marked features, a significant number of households are headed by women, and there is great internal variation. The point here is that these features, while mentioned in surveys, are poorly reflected in resettlement policies and in resettlement plans.

Economic Reconstruction and Participation

Consultation and participation by the affected families is a critical step in designing socially, financially, and technically feasible resettlement programs to restore the economic productivity of resettlers. This is the only way to ensure a fit between proposed economic and social programs and the social and cultural realities in which people live. All the projects reviewed here include consultation with affected communities to guarantee the social feasibility of relocation and rehabilitation programs. The difficulties now are mainly operative: When to consult? Whom to consult? Which actors are most relevant? Through which mechanisms should we consult? Which type of decisions and actions should the communities participate in? How to prevent manipulation of the communities by outside parties? Some of these questions are elaborated on below.

Is it possible to begin consultation and participation at the earliest stages of the project? There is a myth that participation at the early stages will lead to cost overruns and unnecessary delays. It is also feared that sharing information and consulting with the affected population will create unrealistic expectations and attract new squatters to the project site. But the experience of current projects in Latin America and the Caribbean have demonstrated that this is not the case. Two exceptions should be mentioned: in the Yacyretá and the Rio Flood reconstruction projects, the massive invasions of people seeking housing were produced by several years of delays in project implementation—a major reason to avoid delay.

These and other experiences show that far from hindering the planning process, participation actually reduces tensions, conflicts, and negative social impacts; builds trust and collaboration; avoids delays due to lack of agreement at the community level; and improves the feasibility of the project. Participatory mechanisms such as holding a referendum on decisions made by community leaders also help prevent manipulation of the community by outside parties. There is no evidence that participatory processes cause delays and cost overruns. Such difficulties are more due to planning inadequacy, implementation weaknesses, or insufficient resources that actually hinder participation. In the Paraná Water Quality and Pollution Control Project, for example, project delays and changes paralyzed the work of a committee composed of a local planning agency and community associations, and heightened criticism and distrust of the project.

Consultation mechanisms and strategies vary, but follow the same general pattern:

- Preliminary meetings with neighborhood associations or organized interest groups to survey public opinion and gain preliminary consent for the resettlement plan
- Agreement on basic policy and plans, especially the resettlement
  site, housing design, compensation and indemnification, and replacement of community property
- Family-by-family negotiations once the cadastre and census are
  completed.

As the process advances, consultation evolves into more active
participation, not only in the decisionmaking process, but also in such
areas as construction of housing, house hunting (for self-resettlement),
and protection of unoccupied sites. In some cases, after settling into the
new site, the communities begin to manage services such as transportation, community centers, schools, hospitals, garbage collection, and
road maintenance.

In the late 1980s and early 1990s, consultation and participation generally were initiated only after the project had already been approved.
Communities were simply informed at the implementation stage that
they would be displaced, and under what conditions. Consultation was
limited to decisions related to the resettlement itself, and participation
was negligible, almost nonexistent. However, in projects approved more
recently—such as Colombia Santa Fe 1, Colombia Power Development,
and Belo Horizonte and Recife Metropolitan Transportation—and in
others under preparation, consultation began at the early stages of project
planning. The borrowers agreed to present the resettlement policy and
consult directly with the affected community about resettlement as a
condition for Bank approval. Likewise, before final approval of
Yacyretá II, the resettlement plan underwent an extensive process of
consultation, including discussions with community organizations,
affected groups, unions, nongovernmental organizations, universities,
and others.

The economic cost of neglecting consultation and participation
can be considerable. Delays in execution of contracts, resulting con-
tractor claims and commitment charges due to lack of agreement by
the affected population, and protracted negotiations to make unacceptable proposals acceptable can elevate project costs to unnecessary levels. On the other hand, the costs of the consultation process
are rarely internalized in the planning and implementation budgets
and timetables of the projects under consideration, so that funding
consultations with the affected population tend to be underestimated
and understaffed.

Participatory strategies still are aimed more at avoiding conflict than at including stakeholders and displaced communities in decisionmaking and in sharing responsibilities central to the project and to people's lives. Developing a strategy that decentralizes decision-making and finding new alternatives related to urban renewal, development, and sanitation continue to be important goals.

Principal Difficulties in Planning and Implementation

Planning

Beyond many variations in past resettlement planning, in most cases we can identify the same basic pattern:

- Projects are conceived by the development agency in charge of preparation and design.
- Resettlement policy is established by each agency based on local circumstances rather than on national social policy.
- Social and economic information on the affected population is unreliable, incomplete, and usually based on secondary sources.
- The resettlement site is selected based on the availability of public land rather than on what is desirable for the displaced population.
- Prevailing state or municipal housing policy is automatically adopted regardless of its adequacy for involuntary resettlement.
- Consultation with the affected population is rarely conducted prior to project approval and generally is limited to a small group of local authorities and state agencies.

The typical planning process for urban resettlement faces many difficulties. Three of the most important, explained more fully below, are lack of an official resettlement policy at the national or state level, inadequate definition of project subcomponents at the time of appraisal, and lack of social and economic analysis of adverse resettlement consequences within the project preparation process.

Lack of an official resettlement policy that defines institutional responsibilities, rights of those displaced, financing mechanisms, land acquisition, compensation, indemnification, and titling is one of the most common problems in resettlement planning. No Latin American or Caribbean country has a national policy for involuntary resettlement caused by development projects, nor are we aware of any comprehensive sectoral resettlement policy except for the one in the Colombian electricity sector.

Inadequate definition of subcomponents, especially those involving public works construction, hinders early identification of the scope and nature of involuntary displacement. Problems in resettlement programs are frequently a direct consequence of socially unfeasible designs in the preparation phase. Some subcomponents lack basic design elements, even at times failing to clearly identify the area affected. In the case of slum upgrading and rehabilitation projects, the need for displacement may not be known until the project nears completion. This complicates planning of specific elements, defining a feasible framework for relocation, and budgeting of human resources and funds.

Lack of social and economic analysis in the project planning process, and perpetuation of an engineering perspective—from which resettlement tends to be seen as an obstacle to the advancement of the public works projects, instead of an integral economic and social reconstruction program—is probably the biggest obstacle. Physical elements of resettlement, such as land and housing, generally are taken into account during project planning. But the subtle interdependency between the population and its economic environment, and an assessment of socioeconomic impacts before, during, and after the actual move, are usually missing, weakly addressed, or little more than a phrase in a document.

Implementation

Although each project runs into difficulties related to specific undertakings or local conditions, it is possible to identify common problems that are the rule rather than the exception. The most important of these are presented below (some will be discussed in more detail later).

- Constant change in project design has been one of the most important factors complicating resettlement planning in the projects studied here. In almost all of the projects the prevailing resettlement plan is different from the one approved two years earlier, due to changes in the design of subcomponents, the enlargement or reduction of the project area, or new decisions about construction technologies made during implementation. These costly and time-consuming changes often stem from inadequate attention to the social context of the project, which imposes constraints that therefore are not discovered until inappropriate designs are implemented.
- Resources of local counterparts are often insufficient or not readily available. In some cases local governments have underestimated costs and failed to allocate sufficient resources, causing delays in

resettlement programs and distrust toward the project. This, too, is often due to incomplete social and economic analyses of the actual situation on the ground. In addition, most projects experience delays because previously allocated local funds are, in effect, not available when needed, partly because constituencies for their expenditure have not been mobilized.

- Frequently the various states and municipalities involved in a project lack a housing policy or have different housing policies, which complicates coordination and creates disparities in resettlement procedures and outcomes. Conflicts between resettlement strategies and environmental or urban planning regulations can also arise when national or local legal restrictions create obstacles to obtaining environmental permits for urban renewal, slum improvement, and construction of new housing units (see section on legal difficulties).

- Despite the fact that on paper the resettlement plan is consistent with the project's general construction schedule, in reality, progress on the main project tends to create pressures that compromise the resettlement plan. This pressure sometimes leads to unsatisfactory measures such as offering monetary compensation as the only option, using transitional shelters when the new settlement is not finished, or occupying unfinished housing and settlements that lack operational public services. In some cases the water and sanitation agency is separate from the resettlement agency. This makes coordination difficult, especially when the resettlement component is considered a subordinate activity rather than an integral part of the project.

- All projects in the Latin American and Caribbean region involve numerous housing, urban, environmental, and public service agencies. This institutional complexity can result in a very slow process of coordination and decisionmaking.

- Political changes in local, state, and even national administrations during the course of project implementation cause revisions to projects and resettlement plans, and consequent delays and difficulties in negotiations with affected populations. Policy differences in successive administrations, the creation of new municipalities (such as in Paraná and Rio de Janeiro), and ongoing institutional reorganization and shifting of responsibilities have generated enormous difficulties.

- Inadequate social teams, sometimes without full-time commitment, plague many projects. In São Paulo, for example, six social workers are responsible for assisting 2,000 families (including both the displaced and others affected). If the work requires a minimum of two visits per family, each social worker must make about 600 visits, not counting the time required for census interviews, community meetings, preparing for the move, and accompanying the families during the move and the adaptation period.

- Weak management capability in some municipal administrations is sometimes aggravated by competing interests between different municipalities with differing stakes in the costs and benefits of a project. Centralization of budgeting and decisionmaking plays an important role, as well as lack of experience on the part of sanitation and public works agencies in resettlement of involuntarily displaced populations.
- Invasion by squatters, both in the areas affected by the projects as well as the new resettlement sites, generally falls into one of two basic categories: homeless families seeking housing opportunities and groups led by political or community leaders trying to gain electoral advantage. In the São Paulo project, the population to be resettled in the first seven slums under rehabilitation increased 16 percent in the year between the initial census and the actual move. In Rio de Janeiro (Strada do Paraiso), homeless people invaded 600 units designated for families displaced by the project. In the Yacyretá project the number of families in the urban area affected doubled in four years. While population pressures pose an additional problem and risk for urban resettlement, it is the responsibility of local public authorities, not the project, to control squatters.
- Lack of contingency plans aggravate the effects of natural disasters. The most significant case of this is the Paraná project, in which one of the resettlement sites, Renato Bonilaure, became partially uninhabitable due to flooding. As a result, an additional drainage project is required. The Rio de Janeiro and Yacyretá projects also have faced various emergencies during implementation. Such problems result in the social science teams constantly "putting out fires," which necessarily disrupts the resettlement schedule.

Legal Difficulties

BRAZIL: LEI DE PROTEÇÃO DOS MANANCIAIS. Perhaps one of the major legal difficulties confronted by the sanitation and rehabilitation projects in Brazil has been the requirements imposed by the Lei dos Mananciais, which regulates use of the space around bodies of water and springs. The law basically prohibits construction of human settlements within 50 meters of a body of water, which in many cases has impeded construction of housing developments already approved by the Bank and the borrower. Legal restrictions include rules on lot size and housing density that conflicted with housing plans for low-income families.

In São Paulo, the scarcity of lots complying with the regulations has led to proposals to amend the law, or to the search for semideveloped lots with licenses approved before the new law in order to meet the budgetary limitations of the implementing agency. In other cases land is available only at the city outskirts. In this case, two of the municipalities involved in the project, Itapecerica da Serra and Embu-Guacu, fall entirely within areas affected by the law, thus prohibiting construction of new housing within the town for the displaced families.

LACK OF LAWS ON EXPROPRIATION AND PUBLIC UTILITY. The absence of laws for expropriation and decrees of public utility have created special difficulties for resettlement operations, making it difficult to take possession of areas necessary for project construction and for relocating the displaced population. In the case of Yacyretá, the resettlement programs have faced innumerable legal obstacles (particularly on the Paraguayan side) due to nonexistent and/or inoperative processes for expropriation under declaration of public utility.

INADEQUATE LEGAL PROVISIONS FOR OCCUPANTS. No country in Latin America or the Caribbean has adequate provisions for dealing with cases of squatters: families that occupy public lands without legal title to those lands or the structures built upon them. Therefore there are no agreed rules for protecting the rights of families that have been living in an area for many years, even generations, prior to the government's decision to utilize that particular piece of land. As a consequence, in resettlement planning these families are often "invisible," and provisions are not made for their relocation to alternative sites and occupations.

Economic Difficulties

UNDERESTIMATING RESETTLEMENT COSTS. Failure to understand the nature and complexity of the resettlement process has caused chronic underestimation of its cost. The only resettlement costs usually included in the budgets of projects involving involuntary displacement are related to acquisition of land, construction of housing, and compensation for material losses. The 1993 *LAC Resettlement Review* showed that cost estimates for resettlement in Bank operations were 54 percent too low on average, and in many cases final costs were 300 to 400 percent higher than initial estimates. Urban resettlement projects in Latin America are not an exception in this regard. The original resettlement plan for the Paraná project estimated a unit cost of $2,500, even though the current price of a finished low-income housing unit in Curitiba was $7,500. In the Yacyretá Hydroelectric Project, resettlement costs doubled in the three years since the original estimate. Evidently not all costs were considered. Below is a list of some of the typical activities whose costs need to be recognized from the outset:

- Consultation and participation
- Field studies and gathering of census information
- Design of housing projects
- Land acquisition and construction of housing and service infrastructure
- Investment in expanding or improving existing services to meet the new demand created by the resettled population
- Transactions with the communities receiving the displaced populations
- Indemnification and compensation for material losses and adverse impacts on economic activities
- Moving the displaced population
- Social assistance and income restoration programs
- Title and registration
- Administrative costs and salaries of social researchers, workers, and related specialists
- Incremental costs due to urban land speculation
- Transaction costs between the institutions and agents involved
- Cost contingencies for miscellaneous activities not previously anticipated.

Furthermore, the rise in urban land and housing prices between the planning stage and the time of purchase generally tends to aggravate the insufficiency of local counterpart funds. In São Paulo, the costs estimated by the Housing and Urban Development Company had to be adjusted 69 percent to meet prevailing prices in the market for low-income housing.

Finally, administrative costs due to the institutional complexity of these projects are generally greater than predicted. Very frequently, arriving at agreements between institutions, creating interinstitutional coordinating committees, and overcoming the geographic and bureaucratic dispersion of the agencies involved leads to unforeseen costs.

UNIT COSTS OF RESETTLEMENT. Table 4.4 presents the unit costs for resettlement in eight active and in-preparation Bank-financed projects in Latin America and the Caribbean. The average unit costs are approximately $10,200. However, the characteristics of the solutions offered (such as location, lot and house size, services, and community facilities) vary, and actual costs range from a low of $1,700 for buying a flimsy, existing house in the same or another slum, to a high of $33,450 for building finished single-family units complete with services, community facilities, and socioeconomic assistance programs for urban, lower-middle-class families in Argentina.

Table 4.5 shows the total cost of the resettlement program as a percentage of total cost in seven projects. As mentioned, the real total cost of resettlement is higher due to the fact that the figures do not include all factors associated with resettlement. Necessary costs are much higher in projects that entail massive relocation and large urban upgrading components; for example, in the São Paulo project and the Rio Flood

Table 4.4. Resettlement Costs per Family

Country/project	Cost per family (US$)
Projects under implementation	
Brazil–Paraná Water Quality and Pollution Control Project	6,800
Brazil–Minas Gerais Water Quality and Pollution Control Project	
Contagem	6,780–7,300
Belo Horizonte	7,372–12,643
Brazil–São Paulo Water Quality and Pollution Control Project	1,700[a]–20,515
Brazil–Rio Flood Reconstruction and Prevention Project	6,502–13,980
Argentina–Yacyretá Hydroelectric Project II	10,105–17,122
Paraguay–Yacyretá Hydroelectric Project II	17,000–22,000
Brazil–Integrated Urban Transport Project	
Belo Horizonte	7,200
Recife	6,300
Projects in preparation	
Colombia–Santa Fe 1 Water Supply and Sewerage Rehabilitation and Private Sector Development Project	13,492
Brazil–Minas Gerais Urban Development (Ipatinga)	10,199

a. This is the maximum cost that is invested in the purchase of a slum house where intervention takes place.

Table 4.5.   Cost of Resettlement as a Percentage of Total Cost

Project	Total cost (millions of US$)	Cost of resettlement (millions of US$)	Resettlement as a percentage of total cost
Rio Flood Reconstruction	300	45.0	15.0
Programa de Saneamiento– Minas Gerais	307	15.0	4.8
Programa de Saneamiento– Paraná	223	14.4[a]	5.4
Programa de Saneamiento– São Paulo	260	70.0	27.0
BH-REC Metropolitan Transportation	204	12.3	6.0
Yacyretá Hydroelectric Project	8,500	218.6[b]	2.6
Santa Fe I Water Supply	641		0.2

Note: The costs of resettlement of various projects only include the housing replacement programs. Acquisition of land, compensation, and administrative costs are not included.
a. Through December 1993.
b. Total cost including semiurban, urban, and rural resettlement.

reconstruction project, resettlement costs rose to 27 percent and 15 percent of total project costs, respectively.

In most cases, however, resettlement costs are of little significance in relation to total project costs, and their effect on profitability is minimal (table 4.5). Economic studies carried out by the Bank on megaprojects that entailed resettlement have demonstrated the low sensitivity of the rate of return in relation to a significant increase in resettlement costs. A recent calculation made for Yacyretá showed that an increase of 500 percent in the cost of resettlement would be required to drive the internal rate of return below 12 percent (World Bank 1996).

RESETTLEMENT FINANCING. In most projects, local counterpart resources for resettlement have been insufficient due to underestimation of resettlement costs, changes in financing priorities due to changes in public administration, and changes in project design and expansion of the area to be affected. Furthermore, the funds that do exist and have been appropriated by the borrower are not always available when needed due to bureaucratic delays in moving the funds to the implementing agencies. Greater World Bank involvement in resettlement financing could help solve some of these problems.

Although Bank resources designated for resettlement have increased significantly in recent years, the financial participation of the Bank is still weak. In accordance with existing guidelines, the Bank cannot finance some important resettlement costs, such as land acquisition, salaries of government functionaries, compensation for goods other than land, or already-built housing units (Ninio 1995). Except for these items, the Bank can finance all investments related to resettlement, subject of course to the Bank's financing norms and prevailing procedures for bidding and contracting.

Initially, governments tend to have little interest, if any, in borrowing money for resettlement and prefer to finance resettlement operations by using local budgetary resources. However, these resources often are limited, and local agencies often employ a "mechanism" to deliberately understate the costs of resettlement. Other times, the budgetary allocation proves to be utterly insufficient in midstream, and resettlement is stalled. The Bank has other financial support instruments specifically directed toward project preparation through the Project Preparation Facility (PPF). Generally, the projects with resettlement in the portfolio for Latin America and the Caribbean have not used such financing.[5] It would be interesting to investigate the reasons why, and find ways to facilitate access to preparation funds, specifically for projects with resettlement.

Table 4.6 shows current Bank participation in resettlement financing of projects under implementation in Latin America and the Caribbean. Most of these projects did not include external resettlement financing when they were approved, but once the projects were under implementation (and at the request of the borrowing governments), the Bank expanded its participation by financing construction of housing units, infrastructure, and consultant salaries to carry out independent studies and evaluations. The most notable case is the Rio Flood Reconstruction Project, in which the Bank financed 60 percent of the resettlement program.

Obviously, we cannot postulate a direct correlation between external financing and the success of resettlement programs. But we can empirically document that in practice the availability of external resources creates a positive response and increases the commitment by governments to deliver local counterpart financing and thereby facilitate implementation of the program in accordance with agreed schedules.

Table 4.6. World Bank Participation in Financing Resettlement

Project	Bank participation	Comments
Paraná Water Quality and Pollution Control	Yes	Until now the state of Paraná has been responsible for 100 percent of resettlement costs. At the borrower's request, the Bank will finance the infrastructure and earthworks as well as water and sewage services for the lots.
São Paulo Water Quality and Pollution Control	Yes	The state of São Paulo, with the support of the municipality of São Paulo, is responsible for 98.7 percent of the resettlement costs. The Bank is financing the services infrastructure in the housing developments (1.3 percent of the total construction costs for the housing).
Rio Flood Reconstruction and Prevention	Yes	The Bank is financing 60 percent of the resettlement costs (state component), and the federal government is financing 40 percent.
Minas Gerais Water Quality and Pollution Control	Yes	Until now, the state of Minas Gerais and the municipality of Contagem have been responsible for 100 percent of resettlement costs. At the request of the state government, the Bank will finance the housing construction component.
Yacyretá Hydroelectric II	Yes	The Argentine government is responsible for resettlement financing, but the Bank is financing 6 percent of the total cost of the plan, including urban and rural relocation.
Belo Horizonte and Recife Metropolitan Transportation	No	The implementing agency will be responsible for 100 percent of the resettlement costs.
Santa Fe I Water Supply and Sewerage Rehabilitation and Private Sector Development	No	The implementing agency will be responsible for all resettlement costs.

RECUPERATION OF INVESTMENT IN RESETTLEMENT. Resettlement required by development investments need not be economically viable on its own, or subject to criteria of investment recovery—it is a project cost. However, it is expected that resettlement goals will be achieved at the optimal, if not the lowest, cost possible. In massive resettlement cases and those with high resettlement costs, all implicit costs should be identified and included as part of the overall project cost.

Both the costs and benefits of resettlement should be considered in the cost-benefit analysis of the main project. It is certainly possible to reflect the cost of resettlement and socioeconomic reestablishment of the displaced population in the price charged for services provided by the project. In this way the benefits of a project would pay for the resettlement necessary to implement it while ensuring more sustainable development. This clearly goes beyond mere cost considerations, and it involves a broad range of issues in the conception, design, and implementation of resettlement programs within the context of development and urban rehabilitation. These ideas should be explored by the social teams, along with economists, project managers, and urban planning specialists.

Relocation Impacts on Income-Generating Activities

It is widely recognized that the resettlement process does not end when the population has been moved to the new site (Partridge 1990). In fact, the work of ensuring the community's sustainability has just begun: adaptation to the new site and new housing, rebuilding social networks and the structure of the community, new relations with the host population, recovery of prior family income level, management and maintenance of new services, and so on. These challenges go far beyond the mere physical relocation of the population.

Successful budgeting, financing, recouping of resettlement investments, and sustainability are closely tied to the central issues of urban development itself. In other words, social and economic rehabilitation programs are the backbone of sustainable urban resettlement. Location of the new settlement is a key element in restoring productive activities and ensuring income opportunities and access to services. In resettling the urban poor it is important to move them the least distance possible from their original location. This is problematic, however, since many of the difficulties of urban resettlement are rooted in the relative scarcity of land and housing (especially for low-income groups), restrictions on land use, and the burden on municipal finances.

The impact of resettlement on economic activities has not been seriously considered and monitored in most Bank-assisted projects in Latin America. For many years, until recently, income restoration programs generally were not included in project design. This was due to the prevailing belief that resettlement of the urban poor does not seriously disrupt economic activities, and that with time families adapt and find other ways to subsist.

This erroneous belief persists, in part, because of the scarcity of data on the correlation between economic activities and place of residence.

One factor to consider in assessing the potential economic effect of resettlement is the degree to which families gravitate toward particular neighborhoods and how their economic activities are linked to that specific area. This will help to identify impacts on home-based businesses or survival strategies based on the informal sector and to design income restoration strategies at the new site. Among the families relocated by the El Salvador Earthquake Reconstruction Project, for example, field studies documented the decline or even disappearance of such activities as selling tortillas and tailoring that depended on proximity to the business generated by government workers in downtown offices.

In many of the Latin America and Caribbean urban resettlement projects it has been possible to obtain adequate lots near the current settlements, but in other cases budget limitations have forced implementing agencies to select sites relatively far away. In the projects reviewed, distances to the new sites range from less than 1 kilometer for most of the Yacyretá settlements to 60 kilometers for one of the communities displaced by the Paraná project.

But distance is not the only factor that poses a risk to the displaced families' income, economic opportunities, and survival strategies. Some other important factors are:

- Negative effects on the semirural survival patterns developed by poor families living in areas of urban expansion, especially activities that complement family income and nutrition, such as raising animals, maintaining home gardens, scavenging, and garbage recycling
- Family income erosion due to new financial burdens, such as additional transportation costs or having to pay for services that were previously free or subsidized
- Additional expenditures due to the rupture of community ties and interdependence that previously guaranteed services, such as child care and neighborhood security.

As mentioned earlier, there are no systematic and reliable data regarding the impact of completed Bank resettlement programs on family income in Latin America, or on local or home-based businesses. This problem is compounded by the general scarcity of research on informal sector economic activities, which are usually the largest source of income for residents in marginalized areas. Even in cases where postrelocation surveys have been carried out (as in Rio Flood) there has not been systematic monitoring of the economic welfare of the resettled families. Usually only a narrowly focused sample survey is carried out to determine the level of satisfaction of relocated families with housing and new services.

In the Minas Gerais project (municipality of Contagem) a survey was conducted recently in the new settlement of Camp Alto, located 20 kilometers from the old site, in which 68 families were resettled during 1993–94. The survey showed that 39 percent of the economically active population still were working in industries near the former site of the community, and 17 percent were self-employed in activities near the former site. In total, 56 percent depended on the physical and economic environment of the former site for their subsistence. Although the social team in charge of the resettlement concluded that there has not been a rupture of economic activities and that existing difficulties are minor and transitory, the survey signals potential problems that require attention:

- Of those surveyed, 58 percent cited problems related to distance, transportation, and scarce demand for labor in the area of the new settlement.
- Thirty-five percent said that lower wages and higher costs for services in the new settlement affected their family income.
- The community complained that insufficient education and health facilities forced them to use other schools and hospitals, thereby increasing transportation costs.

The El Salvador Earthquake Reconstruction Project is an exception to the usual absence of economic welfare monitoring. At the Bank's request a quick evaluation was carried out on the risks of impoverishment for families resettled in the Villa Italia District, 15 kilometers from the original settlement. The study showed that economic conditions had worsened for 6 percent of the resettled families because they had lost access to their usual sources of employment in the city's center, and also because of higher costs for transportation and services. A support strategy was designed and implemented for these families, with the support of a nongovernmental organization, consisting of a rotating fund for financing family microenterprises.

It should be recognized, however, that each case is different and that distance is not necessarily a negative factor. For example, in the case of Parque Libertad in the municipality of Caixas, the residents chose to be

resettled in the Bento Riviero Danta housing development in Rio de Janeiro. This was far from their former site but had the advantage of being
closer to the job market. Early consultation with affected families and participation in decisionmaking were key factors to the success of this case.

Finally, an independent evaluation and monitoring system has
been set up to assess income restoration and recovery of prior living conditions in Yacyretá. Monitoring will cover a postrelocation period of one
and a half years.

New Challenges and Practical Recommendations

The resettlement operations mentioned here, and many others, clearly
reflect the progress made by development agencies in understanding,
planning, and implementing projects that involve involuntary displacement of urban populations. Some of the most notable advances and positive results are briefly mentioned below.

- *Avoiding unnecessary displacement.* In all the projects borrowers
  have made serious efforts to minimize involuntary displacement,
  often by searching for better design options. Table 4.7 summarizes
  some cases of design optimization that significantly reduced displacement.

Table 4.7.   Project Optimization to Minimize Displacement

Country/ project	Optimization actions	Reduction in number of people displaced
Brazil– Rio Flood	The project (state component) has been opti- mized through changes in the layout of ditches and water treatment services and the adoption of new construction technologies to minimize the impact on affected neighborhoods	1,300
Brazil– PROSAM, Paraná	The project has been improved by changing the initial approach of moving the population away from bodies of water and into areas with access to services (to prevent contamination). Instead, appropriate technology was intro- duced to improve water and sanitation infra- structure at the existing settlements.	1,000
Colombia– Santa Fe 1	The project has been optimized by changing some of the areas to be affected.	1,800

- *Resettlement plans and policies.* All the projects have resettlement plans generally consistent with Bank policy and with the norms and regulations of each country.
- *Taking into account the views of the affected population.* Consultation and participation by the communities directly affected is a fundamental part of all resettlement operations currently in progress. In all cases, direct involvement of the population affected is a key element in the implementation phase.
- *Participation from the earliest stages.* Recent projects have shown progress in conducting consultation and participation from the first stages of planning, thereby contributing significantly to the social feasibility and acceptance of the project.
- *New initiatives.* Significant efforts have been made by the interdisciplinary technical teams of the projects to provide sound technical, economic, environmental, and social solutions to mitigate the impacts of the forced displacement. In several projects, innovative instruments have been developed for the replacement of housing, such as letters of credit, options to purchase, resident aid, contracting out services to third parties, and so on, which are more in harmony with the reality of major urban centers in Latin America.
- *Growing institutional capacity.* The technical capacity and accumulation of experience on the part of the social teams in charge of resettlement has slowly permeated and fortified the capacity of the borrowing institutions.
- *Interinstitutional coordination.* Important progress in inter-institutional coordination through adoption of formal agreements has permitted a clearer designation of responsibility among agencies involved in resettlement.
- *Best practices.* The process of analyzing and understanding past resettlement experiences, while still weak, has yielded important lessons that have been incorporated into current resettlement plans.
- *Financial support.* At the borrowers' request, the Bank has augmented its participation in financing resettlement and rehabilitation plans, greatly increasing cash flow availability.
- In summary, many resettlement projects have turned involuntary displacement from a solely negative experience into a source of positive benefits, such as:
  * Security and stability for the families removed from the areas at risk
  * Better housing, health, and sanitary conditions
  * Secure property rights
  * Increased value of family assets and access to basic services.

Notwithstanding the progress achieved, there are still many problems that must be studied and resolved to improve the planning, management, and social outcomes of urban resettlement programs. The conclusions and practical recommendations that follow will help to overcome the aforementioned operational problems.

Preparation

Design of urban projects should be optimized and should incorporate resettlement as an integral component from the very outset. Many difficulties result from failure to optimize project design and from viewing resettlement as an obstacle rather than an integral part of urban development and rehabilitation. Last-minute changes in the location and impact area of projects, for example, or the accommodation of civil works (and other components) to the detriment of resettlement has sometimes meant that populations are resettled into housing units without finished services, water, and electricity (Rio Flood, Yacyretá). It also can result in the use of temporary shelters that do not meet even minimal conditions of hygiene and habitability.

In Rio de Janeiro, due to the pressure imposed by progress in the main civil works, about 100 families were temporarily placed in rented houses before being moved to Missoes and Campo do America. Such measures usually involve high social costs, uncertainty, and discontent that could have been avoided if explicit designs and optimal technical solutions had been clearly defined before project approval or at the earliest possible stage.

EARLY RESETTLEMENT ARRANGEMENTS. Early preparation of institutional and financial arrangements and particularly the timely definition of mechanisms for participation appear to be critical prerequisites for successful resettlement operations.

SOCIAL ASSISTANCE AND ECONOMIC RECOVERY ACTIVITIES. These activities should be contracted to governmental or nongovernmental entities specializing in this type of program. It is especially important to design support programs for microenterprises and home-based economic activities. Such programs have proved to be effective tools in restoring income as well as facilitating the adaptation process and rebuilding of communities.

ADOPTION OF A RESETTLEMENT POLICY AT THE NATIONAL, STATE, AND SECTORAL LEVELS. This is particularly important in countries with numerous projects involving resettlement, because designing policies project by project is inefficient and time-consuming and can lead to inconsistencies that complicate project management. The Bank could offer technical assistance and help coordinate inter-institutional dialogue.

STAFFING PROJECTS WITH ADEQUATE SOCIAL SPECIALIST TEAMS. Along with engineers, economists, and planners, the central coordinating unit of the project should include from the outset a basic team of social specialists to evaluate the project and design of the resettlement plan. Before project approval the Bank and borrower should agree on a minimum number of social specialists to contract during the implementation phase of the project.

RESETTLEMENT AS A PLANNING PROCESS AND NOT JUST AS DOCUMENT PREPARATION. Designing the resettlement plan as phases included in the legal agreement—with clauses synchronizing civil works with resettlement progress, and authorization requirements for beginning construction of main civil works at each phase—will permit flexible management without unnecessary pressure on social programs and the pace of the work. Just as the resettlement plan needs to be flexible, so too must the civil works be responsive to the vicissitudes of the resettlement process, such as negotiation with the affected population, acquisition and preparation of new sites, availability of housing, new legislation, and political interference. All changes in the project should be submitted to the Bank for review and approval.

CARRY OUT A SOCIAL ASSESSMENT (SA) AND ANALYSIS OF STAKEHOLDERS. The SA will help identify the social actors affected by the project and ensure their participation in the planning and design of resettlement options as well as the distribution of associated costs and benefits. The findings of the SA will be a fundamental tool in designing socially feasible projects. They also should be a factor in defining criteria for distributing costs and benefits (including the displaced population), financial analysis and investment decisions, optimal use of project resources, and the price of services produced by the project.

MORE THAN JUST REPLACEMENT HOUSING. Urban displacement and resettlement requires an integrated vision not only of housing issues but also of economic and social impacts. Resettlement programs should include not just housing agencies, which possess enormous experience with low-income housing, but also other institutions responsible for addressing socioeconomic problems associated with forced displacement.

ADEQUATE ECONOMIC AND CULTURAL DATA. During preparation, information should be included about the social, economic, and political networks—the *modus operandi*—of the so-called poverty belts or slums. Likewise, urban planners and government agencies should know about the survival strategies, solidarity networks, and systems of power in those settlements. Indicators of poverty should include additional data such as literacy, marginalization, and people's representation in decisionmaking institutions. Resettlement plans should include programs for restoring productive activities. In selecting the resettlement site and planning income rehabilitation measures, it is important to assess the degree to which the economic activities of displaced families are linked to the community's original location.

IMPROVED ESTIMATION OF THE COSTS, FINANCING, AND TIME FRAME FOR RESETTLEMENT. Underestimation of costs and the resulting unavailability of resources have often led to poorer housing quality or to providing prepared lots rather than finished houses. There also is a tendency to underestimate the time necessary for implementation, particularly for acquiring and preparing resettlement sites, obtaining licenses, and carrying out renewal and rehabilitation projects. Bank resettlement programs in Latin America are typically 10 to 24 months behind schedule.

RESETTLEMENT FINANCING. Bank participation in resettlement financing has been a key element in the success of some operations, while reliance solely on local counterpart financing has contributed to delays and problems in others. It is strongly recommended that the Bank and borrowers study the pros and cons of increased financing from external sources and facilitate the availability of sufficient local funds.

INSTITUTION STRENGTHENING FOR IMPLEMENTING AGENCIES. Measures should also be taken to strengthen the commitment and participation of local governments in project planning and development. Specifically, the Bank should promote, and the borrower should be committed to, the sharing of experiences between projects and countries.

A RANGE OF ALTERNATIVES FOR THE AFFECTED POPULATION. This helps address the heterogeneity of displaced groups, recognizes their right to weigh different options and choose the most appropriate one, and permits more flexible management of the resettlement operation. The broader the range of alternatives for replacing land, housing, and services, and for restoring standards of living, the better the chance of reducing negative impacts and having a successful outcome. Special emphasis should be given to preparing viable social and economic alternatives for families in extreme poverty, even if that implies large subsidies.

CONTINGENCY PLANS. Projects in areas subject to frequent natural disasters such as flooding and earthquakes should have contingency plans for emergency evacuation of the displaced population. The plan should establish explicit institutional responsibilities and economic measures, and the corresponding economic resources should be contemplated within the project budget.

Implementation

Immediately after project approval, counterpart funds for resettlement should be transferred to a special account to guarantee timely availability of resources for the implementing agency. An interdisciplinary team should be in charge of resettlement during the entire implementation phase and should include, where possible, architects and specialists in social science, community participation, and social engineering. The principal civil works and resettlement activities should be developed in parallel, phase by phase, through a special project management unit. It is critical that the resettlement team be part of the project management unit.

Housing solutions involving costs to the resettled population should be studied carefully. Requiring those displaced to bear part of the resettlement cost, particularly when no other alternative is offered, can have serious negative effects on precarious family incomes. Such arrangements should be rigorously analyzed and monitored to avoid further impoverishing already marginalized populations.

Plans involving monetary compensation should be carefully evaluated and monitored and should include safeguards to prevent families from falling into poverty. Difficulties with housing availability and the advance of civil works make cash compensation an attractive option for project planners. While there is no systematic tracking of resettlement outcomes, experience throughout the world has shown that the cash payment alternative does not guarantee replacement of housing or previous living conditions. Indemnification in money may be an adequate option for groups with higher incomes and greater capacity to self-relocate, but it should not be an "easy out" for planners and managers to avoid finding viable solutions for vulnerable low-income families.

In general, there are no effective regulations or measures to control invasions by squatters in the project area or in the resettlement sites. One tactic is to start the civil works as soon as possible after the population is moved to prevent new squatters from taking over the abandoned site. Before resettlement takes place, the affected communities themselves can often help control invasions, in both the original site and the future site. Once a census has been conducted, and as long as there are no significant delays, the project area should be "closed" and agreement should be reached with residents that newcomers will not be entitled to resettlement or cash compensation.

A systematic monitoring program should be planned and put into place immediately after the census has been conducted. Indicators to measure restoration of social networks and economic activities, adaptation to the new environment, and improvement in living conditions should be clearly defined and routinely incorporated into all resettlement processes. Quarterly monitoring reports should include specific recommendations for fine-tuning policies, modifying housing alternatives and assistance, and avoiding emergencies in future phases of the resettlement.

Special attention should be given to field monitoring of economic activities, employment, and family income when the new site is far from the original settlement or job market, or is located in the urban outskirts or in a different municipality. Resettlement should be supervised, and the implementing agency should demand the necessary technical assistance during implementation. Supervisory support from the Bank must be planned to allow time for evaluating problems and designing solutions together with the agency.

In addition to the traditional indicators of success for urban resettlement—replacement of housing, quality of housing, access to services, improvement in quality of life, and degree of satisfaction—the completion report should evaluate whether the risks of impoverishment have been counteracted and to what degree economic activities have been recovered using such indicators as:

- Effects on home-based employment and economic activities
- New economic activities
- Evolution of family income
- Cost of basic family necessities in the new place
- New expenditures in services
- Value of family assets
- Changes in sociocultural behavior
- Sustainability of the new settlement.

Post-project evaluation of results is essential. With the exception of Yacyretá, there are no independent *ex post* evaluations of urban resettlement programs in the Latin American and Caribbean region. Few projects have been systematically evaluated; most reviews are only fragmentary. This is one of the reasons why decisionmaking related to resettlement policy is largely based on speculation and subjective interpretations—and why there has been an endless repetition of failures. It is especially important to include analysis of the living conditions of people who received monetary compensation and to adapt prevailing policy accordingly. The *ex post* evaluation of each resettlement should begin after the physical transfer of the families and establishment of services is completed. A detailed report of the results of resettlement should always be part of the project's completion report.

Acknowledgements

The author especially wants to thank Laura Mancini (Rio de Janeiro) for gathering the basic information, much of which was used in this chapter, as well as for her contribution to our understanding of urban resettlement procedures in Brazil; the resettlement coordinators—Paula Pini (São Paulo), Soraya Melgaco (Minas Gerais), and Angela Dias (Paraná)— for the information provided and their contributions to the development of the resettlement component in the urban renewal projects; the Yacyretá Department of Complementary Works for its contribution to the analysis of urban resettlement experiences in hydroelectric projects; Kathy Johns for her constant and valuable collaboration and assistance in the preparation of the study; Scott Guggenheim and William Partridge for their critical contributions to the ideas expressed in this chapter; Michael Cernea for his assistance and guidance; and Peter Brandriss for his help in editing the text.

Notes

1. Most of the data utilized here are drawn from sources (such as statistics and field reports) covering several years, through December 1995. By the end of 1996 there were 11 more urban operations entailing involuntary displacement in the Bank's Latin American portfolio, and additional projects were initiated in 1997. This chapter does not purport in any way to be a status report on these projects or a comprehensive review to date of their performance, because like all other projects, performance in these projects varies with better or weaker results in different implementation periods. Rather, this paper intends to highlight the specific nature and most typical issues of urban projects as a subcategory of projects entailing resettlement, using the data about the context and content addressed in these projects to illustrate successes, problems, and challenges.

2. *Sources*: Rio de Janeiro, Program Expectative-Ativa 1993; São Paulo, CDHU report March 1995; Minas Gerais (Contagem), SUDECOM report August 1993; Paraná (Curitiba), PARDES-COMEC reports 1, 2, and 3, 1994.

3. The objectives of the Bank's involuntary resettlement policy are set forth in Operational Directive 4.30 (World Bank 1990).

4. The economic and social vulnerability of each family is assessed through sociocultural and economic field research, and relocation is offered only to those with high vulnerability, especially those facing a serious risk of impoverishment and social trauma.

5. See World Bank Operational Directive 8.10 on the Project Preparation Facility (World Bank 1994).

References

The word "processed" describes informally reproduced works that may not be commonly available through libraries.

Burki, S. J., and S. Edwards. 1995. *Latin America after Mexico: Quickening the Pace.* Washington, D.C.: World Bank.

Cernea, Michael M. 1989. "Metropolitan Development and Compulsory Population Relocation: Policy Issues and Project Experiences." *Regional Development Dialogue* 10:4.

_____. 1992. *Urban Environment and Forced Population Relocation.* World Bank Working Paper 152. Washington, D.C.: World Bank.

_____. 1995. "Urban Settlements and Forced Population Displacement." In Hari Mohan Mathur, ed., *Development, Displacement, and Resettlement: Focus on Asian Experiences.* New Delhi: Vikas Publishing House.

_____. 1997. "The Risks and Reconstruction Model for Resettling Displaced Populations." *World Development* 25:10: 1569–87.

Davidson, Forbes, Mirjam Zaaijer, Monique Peltenburg, and Mike Rodell. 1993. *Relocation and Resettlement Manual: A Guide to Managing and Planning Relocation.* Rotterdam, Netherlands: Institute for Housing and Urban Development Studies.

Lomnitz, Larissa Adler. 1977. *Networks and Marginality: Life in a Mexican Shantytown.* New York: Academic Press.

Mejía, María Clara. 1996. "Economic Recovery of Brickmakers in the Yacyretá Project: Argentina and Paraguay." Presented at the conference "Reconstructing Livelihoods: New Approaches to Resettlement," Oxford University, United Kingdom. Processed.

Ninio, Alberto. 1995. "Reassentamento Involuntário em Projetos Financiados Pelo Banco Mundial: Requerimentos y Práticas." World Bank, Washington, D.C. Processed.

Partridge, William. 1990. "Involuntary Resettlement and Development Projects." *Journal for Refugee Studies*. October.

Peattie, Lisa Redfield. 1970. *The View from the Barrio*. Ann Arbor: University of Michigan Press.

Perlman, Janice. 1982. "Favela Removal: Eradication of a Lifestyle." In Art Hansen and Anthony Oliver-Smith, eds., *Involuntary Resettlement and Migration*. Boulder, Colorado: Westview Press.

United Nations–World Bank. 1993. "Guidelines for Managing Urban Relocation and Resettlement." World Bank, Washington, D.C. Processed.

World Bank. 1990. Operational Directive 4.30 "Involuntary Resettlement." Washington, D.C. Processed.

_____. 1993. "LAC Resettlement Review." Latin America Environment Unit Discussion Paper 152. Washington, D.C. Processed.

_____. 1994. Operational Directive 8.10 "Project Preparation Facility." Washington, D.C. Processed.

_____. 1995a. "LAC Annual Review on Portfolio Performance—Resettlement." Latin America and the Caribbean Regional Office, Technical Department, Environment Unit. Washington, D.C. Processed.

_____. 1995b. "LAC Regional Remedial Action Plan—Resettlement." Latin America and the Caribbean Regional Office, Technical Department, Environment Unit. Washington, D.C. Processed.

_____. 1996. "Resettlement and Development: The Bankwide Review of Projects Involving Involuntary Resettlement, 1986–93." Environment Department Paper 32. Washington, D.C. Processed.

5

Testing the Risks and Reconstruction Model on India's Resettlement Experiences

Lakshman K. Mahapatra

Editor's Note   This chapter offers a vast synthesis of resettlement experiences in India, centered on the economic risks and the socially adverse impacts of forced displacements, as well as on the main approaches for overcoming risks and impoverishment. To build this synthesis, Mahapatra employs a distinct theoretical framework—the impoverishment risks and livelihood reconstruction model—and reviews empirical findings from numerous field investigations of resettlement in India over the past four decades.

Within the conceptual and methodological framework adopted for his analysis, the author builds a broad socioeconomic panorama of resettlement processes in India. One by one he documents and emphasizes the loss of income-generating assets, employment, and common property; the declines in health levels and nutrition; and the loss of education and of social and human capital. Because the analysis of reconstruction processes found less empirical evidence than expected on successful recovery approaches, the author outlines the key directions in which such efforts should be further carried out.

The study also discusses the paucity of economic research on resettlement in India, in contrast with the vast anthropological and sociological literature. Unaddressed equity issues are highlighted, while neoclassical economic approaches and narrow cost-benefit analysis are criticized.

Mahapatra concludes by outlining the unfinished tasks in the practice and study of displacement and rehabilitation and by suggesting priorities for each. Those tasks include the elaboration of governmental policies for resettlement and for the effective reestablishment of income and livelihood, strengthening institutions for resettlement operations, supporting the work of NGOs, and focusing more economic research on resettlement in India.

In this study I am concerned with the economic and social content of involuntary population displacement in India, since it is induced primarily through infrastructure development. My interest in the economics of resettlement stems from my concern with global humanistic issues in the Indian context. These concerns have impelled me to engage in about three decades of independent anthropological studies of resettlement and rehabilitation. Therefore, I propose to undertake a comprehensive reexamination of the empirical evidence available from India's many resettlement operations, funded domestically or jointly with various donors, and to draw from this synthesis some key theoretical, policy, and operational conclusions. To this end I will employ and rely upon two main research tools:

- A conceptual model that encompasses both the risks of impoverishment through displacement and the strategies for reconstruction (Cernea 1990, 1996b, 1997)
- The rich thesaurus of empirical evidence and interpretations on resettlement generated by Indian researchers over the past four decades.

The theoretical model that I will test against empirical evidence is the "impoverishment risks and livelihood reconstruction model" developed by Michael Cernea. This model, itself a recent research product, is based on, and summarizes, findings on resettlement on a worldwide scale. The interest of India's resettlement researchers and practitioners in the model proposed by Cernea is substantial, as shown by three most recent books on resettlement published in India constructed around the analytical model of impoverishment risks (Ota and Agnihotri 1996, Pandey and associates 1998, Mathur and Marsden 1998). Thus it makes sense to apply this new model to, and explore in depth its validity for, the full scope of Indian experiences.

In turn, the factual source material on India represents probably the richest body of empirical data on resettlement available in any single country so far and can therefore provide grounds for either confirming or negating the proposed risks and reconstruction model. This vast store of seemingly diffuse findings on resettlement, accruing from numerous sites and produced by many different researchers, needs to be synthesized, unified, and structured along some key variable. The question is whether, or how, the theoretical model can assist in unifying these data. I will also review the main theoretical elaborations in economic and social research developed by India's resettlement scholars—not just the empirical findings—and examine the risks and reconstruction model against this body of theoretical interpretations

Though these may seem ambitious goals for a single study, the need to advance conceptualizing and modeling in Indian (and world) resettlement research is the best justification for at least a first step in such an undertaking. Our intention is also to nudge more Indian researchers— especially economists (and not just anthropologists)—into recognizing the seriousness of the economic risks inherent in resettlement and to call on them to elaborate in more detail the economics of reconstruction and rehabilitation. We trust that others will follow up, add to, and improve on what we can achieve through this study.

Estimates of India's displaced population from all projects over the past 50 years (1947–97) vary, but the total may be as many as 25 million since independence (Fernandes 1994 for the 1951–90 period only, with my extrapolation to 1997). For water resources development alone the world has already constructed 34,798 dams, of which India has built some 3 to 4 percent (Times of India 1997). India's Central Water Commission in March 1990 recorded 465 major dams of 30 meters and higher, while dams of 20 meters and above numbered 1,174 (Fernandes 1991). This clearly indicates the macroeconomic scale of displacements in India.

India is not the only country, of course, in which massive displacements take place. Every year since 1990, about 10 million people have been displaced involuntarily all over the world in the wake of infrastructural development projects alone (World Bank 1994, Cernea 1997). Of these, some 6 million have been displaced by urban development and transport programs.

Conceptual Frameworks and Theoretical Perspectives

Clarifying the key concepts from the outset will be useful. The voluntary migration of people, either within the nation state or outside, must be distinguished from *involuntary displacement*, where people are forced to leave their dwelling places—under physical threat, if not actual application of force, in the event they do not vacate.

Resettlement in the Western literature encompasses the processes of displacement and reestablishment. In India, however, the usual practice is to differentiate between *resettlement* and *rehabilitation*. Resettlement in India is taken to mean simple relocation after physical displacement from the original habitat. In turn, rehabilitation is defined as "grafting a community at a new place and nurturing it to ensure its steady and balanced growth" (Joshi 1987). Elsewhere, the concept of rehabilitation may be interpreted rather narrowly as referring to a household, or a section of the targeted groups, or even an individual such as an orphan or a displaced person who is physically handicapped. But the basic thrust remains: rehabilitation focuses on achieving sustained development for displaced people. Cernea pointed out that the distinction made in India captures the fact that

> Rehabilitation . . . refers to the fate of the displaced people after relocation and to the reconstruction of their patterns of socio-economic organization . . . In India, a country tested by much population displacement and distinguished by a vast social science literature about it, . . . two distinct concepts are used for the two post-displacement phases of this process: resettlement and rehabilitation (R&R). The Indian legal and sociological literatures uniformly emphasize that "rehabilitation" does not occur automatically just after relocation . . . *Indeed, resettlement may occur without rehabilitation, and unfortunately it often does* (Cernea 1996a, author's italics).

We emphasize further that *resettlement* and *rehabilitation* are two interrelated processes that form a continuum, partly overlap, and should not be seen necessarily as sequential "stages." On the contrary: to be successful, rehabilitation processes may be, and sometimes should be, initiated before physical displacement of people takes place.

As a sociological concept *risk* can be defined as "the potential that a certain course of action will trigger future injurious effect-losses and destruction" (Cernea 1997). Specific economic risks and other risks of impoverishment are embedded in all displacements.

Stages of Resettlement and Rehabilitation

Displacement-development dynamics have been studied and conceptualized by some scholars in terms of stages or phases, sequentially. Scudder identifies four stages in what he calls a "dynamic model of settlement processes," built upon the three-stage framework of Robert Chambers (Scudder 1985). Scudder's four stages are (1) planning and settlement recruitment, (2) transition, (3) potential economic and social development, and (4) handing over and incorporation. When they occur, the four stages cover at least one generation of the displaced people, beginning with the planning of resettlement after displacement. But Scudder notes frequent exceptions to this less-than-general model because "not all projects pass through all stages or pass through them in the order outlined here. . . A steady movement through the four stages is the exception rather than the rule" (Scudder 1985).

Scudder's model was formulated initially to reflect *voluntary* settlement schemes with four stages, then was extended to *involuntary* resettlement, despite the very different circumstances that characterize these two processes. Voluntary settlements, for example, rarely have transitional resettlement colonies, which are unavoidable in many projects involving resettlement and rehabilitation under involuntary displacement in developing countries. There are numerous other structural, cultural, and political differences between these two types of socioeconomic processes, which create inconsistencies if they are included in the same model.

Scudder's model has proved to be of limited value in the Indian context. As learned from predisplacement and postdisplacement studies in India, notably the remarkable resettlement in Orissa State during 1950–90 (Pandey and associates 1998), these four stages may go haywire, because there is no synchronization between government efforts and the initiatives taken by the ousted persons to plan and invest for their own rehabilitation. The process, as it unfolds on the ground, may differ significantly from the progression suggested by Scudder's four stages. This is especially so when land is not provided by the government or the project and the displaced persons themselves have to scout for land and assets to restore their livelihood.

In most cases the land provided by authorities is not fully reclaimed, is rocky, or is upland with no irrigation facility. It is no surprise then that there are large-scale reverse flows of ousted persons from the government-provided colonies to their old village sites—or to whatever remains above flood level, or to sites along the rim. As to resettlers' organization, posited by Scudder to belong to the second stage, or transition, we found that in many predisplacement villages ousted persons had organized during or even before stage one, in order to fight for higher compensation or better resettlement sites or amenities.

The Impoverishment Risks and Reconstruction Model

Displacement involves a long, complex process of human interactions. Each case has its own story rather than occurring in standard, sequential stages: its own economy, ecology, sociocultural disruptions (class and ethnic tensions), technological and bureaucratic constraints, and patterns of recovery and reconstruction.

The most frequent end result is that rich farmers, bureaucrats, and people with power become the "haves," at the expense of the "have-nots," who overnight become even more deprived—landless, jobless, homeless, and poor, perhaps begging for their food, vulnerable to increased morbidity and mortality, socially disoriented, and politically powerless. These processes of impoverishment and social disintegration, and the means of overcoming them through the rebuilding of a life-support system, are central issues and challenges in involuntary displacement and reconstruction.

Starting from this key point, and based on a bold comparative analysis of many resettlement experiences around the world (especially in the developing world, including China and India), Michael Cernea has formulated and proposed a complex and comprehensive model of "impoverishment risks and reconstruction of livelihood." This theoretical model has evolved over two decades of analysis, monitoring, and evaluation of involuntary resettlement. As a conceptual framework it has been outlined in several studies, first in a Harvard paper (Cernea 1990) and then in several other studies (World Bank 1994; Cernea 1995, 1996b, 1998, and, in a comprehensive and refined form, Cernea 1997. Further in this study, references will be made to the 1997 version).

The strength and methodological novelty of this model derives from its integration of impoverishment risk analysis with recovery analysis. This essential integration also equips the model with operational capacity as a *tool for action*, in addition to its explanatory or descriptive function. This is the main reason the model seems eminently suitable for understanding the forces, factors, and processes at work in the displacement-rehabilitation-development dynamics in India.

Cernea's model identifies the eight most important dimensions of impoverishment:

- *Landlessness* (expropriation of land assets)
- *Joblessness* (even when the development project ostensibly creates some temporary jobs)
- *Homelessness* (loss of not merely the physical house, but of the family home and cultural space, with resulting alienation and "placelessness")
- *Marginalization* ("downward mobility"—socially and psychologically, as well as economically)
- *Increased morbidity and mortality* (especially among the weakest segments of the population)
- *Food insecurity* (low daily calorie intake, malnourishment)

- *Loss of access to common property* (such as forests, bodies of water, and wastelands, which substantially supplement the food and income of lower-income groups)
- *Social disarticulation* (loss of social, economic, and moral support among kinsmen and members of community networks, leading to social anomie).

These basic risks have varying intensities, depending on local conditions and on the nature of the projects (Cernea 1997).

It is very important that the model also captures the key processes that could counteract the impoverishment risks and lead to the economic and social reestablishment of the displaced. These processes—based on land and employment, on restoration of social services for health and education, and on community reconstruction—will be examined later in the chapter. Whether these reconstructive processes occur is a matter of governmental policy, resource allocation by project initiators, and the initiative of resettlers themselves. The model is convincing and practical precisely because it offers a conceptual framework designed not only to explain but also to trigger reconstructive processes and policies.

Cernea's model is seminal, too, in that it is not a closed or finite framework. Appropriately, it offers scope for further thinking and conceptual development. Cernea rightly notes that the "eight impoverishment hazards are not the only ones that result in processes of economic and social deprivation, but rather the most important ones" (Cernea 1997). The model can accommodate and include other risk variables, for instance, to which I would add: *education loss* among displaced children. In a recent study Cernea agrees and notes, "Indeed, relocation often interrupts schooling and some children never return to school. After displacement, as a result of losses in family income, many children are drafted into the labor market earlier than what would otherwise occur" (Cernea 1997).

A refreshing aspect of this model is that Cernea is concerned not only with economic impoverishment, but also with the loss of social and cultural endowments. The model contends that during displacement people lose natural capital, manmade (physical) capital, human capital, and social capital. Cernea then builds a reconstruction model aimed at enabling and helping displaced people "to restore their 'capital' in all its multifaceted forms" (Cernea 1997).

The components in this reconstruction model would therefore require not only adequate compensation for property losses, but also adequate *rebuilding of the displaced people's income-generating capacity and livelihoods,* particularly in terms of the four lost "capitals" (World Bank 1990, 1994; Cernea 1997). What is needed, Cernea argues, "is a change in concept and method predicated on treating resettlement operations as *opportunities for development, as development projects in their own right.* This includes risk mitigation but goes beyond it to construct a new socioeconomic basis on which resettlers' livelihoods can first be restored and then improved, so that their 'income curve' could exceed predisplacement levels" (Cernea 1995, 1997; Shi and Hu 1994).

The eight components of the reconstruction process—land-based reestablishment, reemployment (through either self-employment or jobs created by or for the project), house reconstruction, social inclusion (status improvement), better health care, adequate nutrition, restoration of community assets (creation of new common property resources), and community reconstruction (social reintegration)—are designed to reverse eight impoverishment risks. To these one could add education restitution as a follow-up to the addition of the impoverishment risk of education loss. Cernea correctly adds that "it is important to repeat that the risks and reconstruction framework emphasizes their interdependence and synergy" (Cernea 1997).

Cernea's model, unlike Scudder's, is not tied to a rigid time frame or invariable stage sequence, nor is it weighed down by assumptions (sometimes unwarranted, arbitrary, or merely rhetorical) of social change, modernization, and irreversible progress.

The Social Actors in Resettlement

An essential complement to the overall model of resettlement is the identification of the key social actors who participate in this process. Based on the Indian experience with involuntary displacement and various field observations, my own view is that in the context of Indian society it is possible to differentiate the following social actors:

- Development agencies: state sector, private sector, and joint sector, especially in India, where the private sector is promoted, supported, and facilitated by the state sector in joint ventures because of its financial or technical inputs.
- Project beneficiaries: specific (for example, landowners in the command area, industrial enterprise, mining company), general (for example, the regional development, national biodiversity, or defense capability), and intermediaries (for example, ancillary industries, traders, service sector).

- Development operators: planners and executives at the implementation level (technocrats and bureaucrats in the field).
- Development facilitators: planners and policymakers (politicians, technocrats, bureaucrats), NGOs and activists who mobilize affected people, social analysts and resettlement researchers, people-sponsored institutions (for example, oustees' organizations, associations of affected ethnic groups, organizations of more vulnerable groups such as women).
- The adversely affected: these include persons, families, and villages *immediately affected*, both directly (for example, village displacees) and indirectly (individuals or groups upstream or downstream), and persons or groups affected because of their particular vulnerability (scheduled tribes, scheduled castes, women, children, the handicapped, service providers, artisans, the landless). It also includes those *secondarily affected*, such as host communities.

The above listing differs marginally from the general set of actors identified by Cernea (1996a), because in this study we are taking into account India's stratified social structure. But we similarly emphasize that all the key actors must deliberately participate in risk prevention and reconstruction management.

Essential in this respect is achieving adequate communication between planners and policymakers, on the one hand, and resettlers, on the other. When communication processes are absent or break down, the result is what Cernea calls "negative participation," that is, "active opposition movements against development" (Cernea 1997).

The common experience in India is that development operators and development facilitators—especially in the state sector, private sector, and joint ventures—usually overlook or underestimate the *indirect* impacts of the project on affected or vulnerable groups and the *secondary* impacts on host communities.

Indian researchers, such as Upendra Baxi, have correctly and frequently deplored the Indian pattern of "development without participation," using as particular examples projects that cause displacement. Baxi writes, "No consultation with the people in general or the affected constituencies is thought necessary in any single one of the following matters: the site of dams; size of dams; allocation of resources, including international aid; design, including safety designing; epidemiological impact analysis; contracts for construction; flow of benefits to certain classes/sectors; displacement; rehabilitation!" (Baxi 1989). As a matter of fact, there is no genuine consultation with the affected people even on such cultural issues as the desirability of a project or the selection of re-settlement sites after displacement.

Interestingly, the World Bank has sought in recent years to improve participation in resettlement by requiring its borrowers (since 1993) to make resettlement plans publicly available (in draft form in the project area) for review and comment by local NGOs and other local institutions and organizations. Encouraging and securing the active participation of the people involuntarily displaced in solving resettlement problems is essential—more important than fostering participation in many other types of projects (Cernea 1995). And participation of the host communities may similarly bring about a smooth transition to community reintegration, thus nipping conflicts in the bud.

The Economics of Resettlement: Missing Research in India

Economists have studied poverty and impoverishment in developing countries, including India. But there is little writing by Indian economists devoted to the specific types and processes of impoverishment arising because of expropriation and displacement for development projects.

There has been, however, a lot of thought, debate, and writing on the cost of irrigation projects and their cost-benefit ratio. In 1964 a special committee appointed to suggest ways and means of "improving the financial returns from irrigation projects" recommended that an economic benefit criterion be adopted in place of the financial productivity criterion for a selection of irrigation projects. The committee recommended a cost-benefit ratio of at least 1.5 for project approval, or more, if possible, to leave room for unanticipated cost escalations. When he evaluated the Tehri Dam by balancing its benefits and costs, economist Paranjpye noted that the cost-benefit ratio tries to weigh societal benefits and societal costs. "But since no distributional weights have been attached, the [cost-benefit] ratio does not tell us the distributional impact of this investment; though we get to know what benefit [can be obtained] at what cost, we cannot ascertain "whose benefit" at "whose cost" (Paranjpye 1988). Cost-benefit analysis does not aim to achieve balanced income distribution, or regional balance, or other forms of distributive equity. Only those costs or benefits that are amenable to monetization are included in cost-benefit ratio calculation. Paranjpye correctly noted, "The problem of rehabilitation of displaced persons is merely represented as a statistically insignificant value measured in terms of monetary compensation" (Paranjpye 1988). He goes on to assert that this leads to wrongly treating the demands of rehabilitation as just an "obstacle" to be brushed aside from the path of "national development."

Solid, extensive research by Indian economists on the economics of resettlement is sorely missing. It is surprising that, over several decades, when economists have undertaken special studies like the economic survey of Orissa State (Misra 1960), or produced reports on the benefits of Hirakud irrigation (Government of Orissa 1968), or when the National Council of Applied Economic Research prepared (in 1977) the Perspective Plan of Economic Development of Orissa from 1974 to 1984, they have shown no intellectual interest in the many forms of impoverishment experienced by project-affected persons. Nor are current mainstream economists concerned with the economic and financial dimensions of reconstructing displaced persons' livelihoods. It is as if the development projects they study did not result in the displacement of any people.

By contrast, India's noneconomist social scientists, primarily anthropologists and sociologists, but also some jurists and political scientists and many environmentalists, have given due importance to the forms of impoverishment, before and after expropriation, of project-affected persons. An important center of these studies in India has been the Department of Anthropology, Utkal University, where my colleagues and I began to look into these issues as early as the mid-1970s. Another noteworthy center is the Indian Social Institute, New Delhi, where Walter Fernandes (sociologist) and his colleagues have taken up, both academically and as NGO activists, impoverishment and reconstruction issues. Important research has been carried out by the Surat Center for Social Studies and particularly by researchers associated with the Tata Institute for Social Sciences in Mumbai. B. K. Roy-Burman, the eminent and most senior anthropologist in India, who carried out the pioneering displacement and impoverishment study on the persons displaced by the first post-independence steel mega-industry at Rourkela (Roy-Burman 1961), has recently compared the rehabilitation provisions of the 1950s with those of the Narmada Sardar Sarovar project policy. He notes that "the rehabilitation pattern as prescribed at Rourkela in the 1950s was certainly much more liberal and comprehensive and was inherently community-oriented" (Roy-Burman 1995).

The lack of adequate economic information on resettlement is both a cause and a consequence of the absence of economic research on resettlement. Like many other developing countries India has been bedeviled by a lack of reliable and transparent official information. The area to be acquired for a development project, and its structure by type of tenure and use, are often not made public in a clear manner. As to the proportion in the overall population of scheduled tribes, scheduled castes, or vulnerable groups such as the handicapped, artisans, landless laborers, service providers, and orphans, the information either is not available or differs from one official agency to another (Mahapatra 1990).

In the official documentation for projects only rarely can one find data about resettlement costs beyond compensation paid to the project-affected families. No rehabilitation expenses are computed and recorded (Government of Orissa 1991). The official data we examined from the IDA-funded projects in Orissa (1960–83) did not mention any expenses incurred apart from compensation paid, although some land-for-rehabilitation grants were given for house construction.

The lack of full economic information is, in part, attributable to the mindset of the officials in charge, who try to keep secret the information base on rehabilitation. They regard it as sensitive, with the potential of leading to agitations from the population and NGOs. Only since the late 1980s has there been better generation and sharing of the information base, thanks to international funding agencies' demands on the Indian government, as well as to pressures brought to bear by local NGOs.

The insufficiency of economic debate and analysis also obscures the profound issues of equity and sustainability that arise when development programs result not only in beneficiaries but also in new cohorts of impoverished people. I have treated this set of issues elsewhere, under the heading "Development for Whom?" (Mahapatra 1991). It is gratifying to see the issues of equity and sustainability with respect to resettlement taken up recently by an increasing number of scholars, including Indian and foreign students of India's resettlement experiences (for example, Fisher 1995, and on sustainability Morse and Berger 1992, Drèze, Sampson, and Singh 1997). A scholar with the reputation of M. S. Swaminathan wisely observed that "development which is not equitable, will not be sustainable in the long term" (1996). And in what they called a "class-benefit analysis," Singh, Kothari, and Amin noted, "In virtually every project it is seen that the primary costs are being paid by the poor and the tribals, while the benefits are flowing to big farmers and the urban elite. Those who are displaced by such projects are usually too poor and politically weak to safeguard their own interests" (1992).

Mathur, in turn, deplores the exclusion of the poor: "In sharing benefits from development, the poor lag behind the rich. The rich are quick to seize opportunities which open up with the inauguration of development projects. The new jobs go to those who have the requisite skills, but their lack among the poor is common" (Mathur 1995). Among the displaced, "the affluent groups do not lose so completely. They are in a better position to adjust to change. In fact, they prefer to resettle themselves with resources of their own rather than endure governmental administration of their lives. For them uprooting is certainly less traumatic (Mathur 1995). Many other field researchers in India corroborate this observation (Nayak 1986, Baboo 1992).

In neoclassical theory the problem of social costs has been dismissed with the rationale that in some instances remedial measures have been taken either by the government or by private organizations. Such social costs are treated as the inevitable price of economic development, and the social losses are justified as exceptional cases or minor disturbances.

We can only say that such neoclassical interpretation is clearly anachronistic today. Yet this view still guides practice and is not explicitly rejected by modern Indian economics. The net result is that painful types of social and human costs are not taken into account and effective remedial measures for rehabilitation are in most cases not taken. Moreover, involuntary displacement in the coming decades in both rural and urban areas in India is expected to continue on a considerable scale. Consequently, issues of equity and of the exclusion of persons displaced by development are bound to become even more pressing and galling in the near future (Reddy 1996, Cernea 1993).

Impoverishment Risks and Social Exclusion

We turn now to the typology of impoverishment as identified in Cernea's model of impoverishment risks and examine its eight elements directly, one to one, against empirical evidence from predisplacement and postdisplacement studies in India. This evidence, culled from research carried out by many Indian scholars, is only a fragment of the much richer evidence we found in their original studies.

Landlessness

Loss of land sets the level of impoverishment in involuntary displacement. The model correctly defines causality: "Expropriation of land removes the main foundation upon which people's productive systems, commercial activities, and livelihoods are constructed. This is the principal form of de-capitalization and pauperization of displaced people, as they lose both physical and man-made capital" (Cernea 1997).

In India, land is often lost, not only by those who are ousted, but also by people who are not physically displaced. When land lost reduces a landholding to an uneconomical size, impoverishment sets in, though households affected in this way are often denied the assistance that would be accorded to a displaced household. Landlessness also brings about change in occupation, and in the ability to hold assets (like livestock). This reduces the food supply and the resources base used to secure other necessities. An Indian peasant, for example, often sells part of his production to meet other needs, including payment of taxes and gifts of food (Pandey and associates 1996, 1998; Mahapatra 1997).

The state-owned industry and mining sectors have even experienced clear regression in rehabilitation policy. In the late 1950s, when the first steel mega-industry was established at Rourkela, the government of India provided the displaced with land for land rehabilitation, in addition to compensation and a resettlement colony (Roy-Burman 1961). Later, in 1967, the T. N. Singh formula promised one job per displaced family in industries and mines, but without any land for land rehabilitation. As most of the displaced belonged to tribal or to other largely illiterate, vulnerable groups and did not possess the skills required, only low-paid, unskilled jobs, if any at all, were made available to them, and most of these were temporary. Later, with the reduction of unskilled jobs because of mechanization, the Bureau of Public Enterprises abandoned this scheme (Fernandes and Asif 1997).

The Constitution of India, Section 31 A(1), provides for "payment of compensation at a rate which shall not be less than the market value thereof" (India 1993). But the procedures involved in setting compensation levels and the payment of compensation before displacement have led to impoverishment and destitution, rather than equitable restitution and reconstruction. One reason is that only immovable properties with title deeds or other valid evidence of absolute ownership entitled one to compensation, while many tribal groups own land customarily, without formal title deeds. Also, for many historic and current reasons land is undervalued in land records. The "market value," which is the standard for compensation under the Constitution as well as under the Land Acquisition Act, is very much on the low side. Compensation paid based on the capitalized value of the annual production of the land, as determined by the law courts, or based on the land's replacement value, would have been more realistic and fair to the displaced (Mahapatra 1996a). For trees the market value for compensation has been fixed absolutely arbitrarily, without any reference to the market. This has been studied in depth by Pandey (Pandey and associates 1996, 1998).

Payment of compensation in cash to tribal people, whose economy is largely nonmonetized, has invariably left most of the money in the pockets of brokers, bootleggers, gamblers, or confidence tricksters (Mahapatra 1994; Pandey and associates 1996, 1998; and Fernandes and Raj 1992, among others). Typically, "the money lenders cooperated with the local leaders in trying to convince the displaced persons to accept monetary compensation instead of land-based resettlement," for obviously self-serving purposes (Stanley 1996). And when compensation was paid very late, sometimes not even after 15 years, as in Natedi village under the Mahanadi Coalfields Project (Pandey and associates 1996, 1998), the displaced persons' movable assets were used up even as their land was inexorably swallowed up by the mine.

Furthermore, India's experience has confirmed time and time again that without replacement value as compensation, it is not possible for the landowning displaced persons and other project-affected persons to buy land. And landlessness has resulted not only in destitution, as it pushed more people below the poverty line (Reddy 1996), but also in enduring trauma and listlessness in many cases (Nayak 1986). It even caused some women to suffer mental disorientation because of their utterly helpless condition (Das, Das, and Das 1996; Baboo 1992). This trauma is compounded when joblessness, another grievous loss, is added to it.

Joblessness

Loss of employment by wage earners caught in the turmoil of forced displacement represents, as the model we examine correctly posits, a fundamental risk and, unfortunately, a widespread reality in India. And the risk of joblessness is particularly difficult to counteract, even if a job is secured. When rehabilitation is land-based, most members of a displaced family are likely to remain gainfully involved in work. But when rehabilitation is job-based, as in mining and industry projects, typically only one member of a family is given a job, while the other members are likely to remain unemployed. The landless, and other displaced persons who are not eligible for a job, are completely helpless. "The unemployed landless may lose in three ways: in urban areas, they lose jobs in industry and services, or other job opportunities; in rural areas, they lose access to work on land owned by others (leased or share-cropped) and the use of assets under common property regimes" (Cernea 1997).

After the employment boom caused by the construction phase of a dam or industry project, employment "severely drops toward the end of the project. This compounds the incidence of chronic or temporary joblessness among the displaced population" (Cernea 1996b). Although Cernea finds some hope in the new enterprises established by farmers after displacement, as in China, he warns, "New enterprises have high failure rates: often they are either unable to pay salaries for months in a row, or they soon go bankrupt leaving resettlers without either a job or land" (Cernea 1997).

Evidence from many displacements in India confirms this analysis. From the Ukai Project of Gujarat, Mankodi reported that, although two new areas of activity provided some new employment (cooperative marketing of milk and fish), this did not add up to sufficient employ-ment. "Apart from these, there simply was nothing for the people to do. This forced unemployment generated its own social problems" (Mankodi 1992). Mankodi found a high incidence of social ills (drunken-ness, gambling) attributed to the imposed idleness.

Unemployment and underemployment push displaced people to engage in seasonal migration, interstate migrant work, or bonded or child labor. Researchers have found that, lacking other income sources, large numbers of women, children, and even adult men collect firewood from India's shrinking forests to sell it in urban centers (Baboo 1991, Fernandes and Raj 1992, Mahapatra 1994, Mohanty 1983). This is often a last resort, before they fall into starvation. A study of the Rengali project (Ota 1996) clearly revealed the disruption in employment. Before dis-placement Rengali villagers got work for 290 days, but after resettle-ment work was available for only 119 days, on average.

A startling failure in employment rehabilitation is seen in the Vindhyachal Super Thermal Power Project (first phase) of the National Thermal Power Corporation (NTPC), with 2,330 affected families, of which only 1,298 (56 percent) could be traced, only 272 (or 21 percent) of those traced were rehabilitated with a job or self-employment (shops). "NTPC has not paid any serious attention to restoration of livelihood or training for appropriate skills improvement" (Thangaraj 1996).

M. S. Swaminathan (1982) wisely observed that famines in India are not famines of food but famines of work, with 7 million or more people entering the job market every year. Involuntary displacement, leaving many formerly productive people unemployed, only aggravates this sordid situation.

Homelessness

The family "home" is far more than a mere house; it enshrines and en-riches life. The loss of a family dwelling is tantamount to the loss of cul-tural space, which weakens identity and, ultimately, overlays economic loss with cultural impoverishment. "Loss of housing and shelter may be only temporary for many displacees, but for some homelessness re-mains a chronic condition. In a broader cultural sense, loss of a family's individual home is linked with the loss of a group's cultural space, re-sulting in alienation and deprivation" (Cernea 1997).

To substantiate the multifaceted character of impoverishment, Cernea relied considerably on empirical evidence from India. Indeed, such evidence is abundant. The emergency housing centers or tempo-rary relocation camps frequently used in India as fallback solutions (by projects that have not prepared housing alternatives in time) tend to make homelessness chronic rather than temporary and do not provide an acceptable "cultural space."

Poor people consider it more important to invest their money primarily in land rather than in house construction. It is thus contrary to people's strategies when project authorities require construction of a house up to a certain level before they will pay the next installment. I heard complaints about this from displaced people resettled in government colonies under the Hariharjore Project in Sonepur district in 1995. The poor people often eat up the house construction advance while preparing their land for cultivation. Pandey's studies (Pandey and associates 1996, 1998) also revealed a substantial decline over the years in the area allotted by projects in Orissa for homestead plots after resettlement—from 0.33 acres on average to 0.08 acre. Under these conditions there will be homelessness in a relative sense, in relation to need, and in the next generation.

Marginalization

The risks and reconstruction model conceptualizes marginalization as occurring "when families lose economic power and slide on a 'downward mobility' path: middle income farm-households do not become landless, they become small landholders; small shopkeepers and craftsmen downsize and slip below poverty thresholds. Many individuals cannot use their previously acquired skills at the new location and human capital is lost or rendered useless. The coerciveness of displacement also depreciates the image of self" (Cernea 1997).

Being uprooted often is perceived as a drop in social status in India. It can trigger a psychological downturn, a loss of confidence in society and the self, and it may be perceived as a form of injustice. The relationship among the model's building blocks is obvious, as marginalization may be seen also as a byproduct of the other processes of impoverishment, especially in the economic and social spheres, namely, landlessness, joblessness, homelessness, and social disarticulation.

At NTPC in Orissa "those who are aged or those who could not get jobs in the project have no other sources of earning and become marginalized. Again those who got jobs in the project have to manage the expenditure needs of their whole family based on a single income" (Pandey and associates 1996, 1998). Nayak reported that the displaced of the Rengali Dam Project had suffered public status devaluation by being dubbed *budiloka*, or "people of submerged areas." This is a derogatory term implying that the ousted people are not respectable. Daughters and sons from these families do not find bridegrooms and brides outside the *budiloka* category easily. This designation encompasses all the caste groups and other classes of farmers in Rengali. The stigma attached to the displaced of Rengali has affected their self-esteem and sense of group dignity. This is an extreme case of social marginalization (Nayak 1986, Baboo 1996).

Many young couples from among those displaced by Upper Krishna's Narayanpur reservoir migrated to Mumbai, Goa, and Ratnagiri for mining, agricultural wage labor, or construction work. Migration of families seeking work as construction labor to places with hard living conditions, such as Mumbai, hurts children and women most severely.

> Most child-and-women-related services like health care, pre-school, ration shops, schools and other important basic services are place specific. Construction work involved constant moves from site to site. During monsoon months the families were forced to return to the villages to work as agricultural laborers in the sowing season, only to move out in September. The whole process deprived women and children of services meant for them. Displacement pushed men and women into repetitive, unrewarding, seasonal migration for construction and other temporary work, and it marginalized not just them, but subsequent generations as well (Parasuraman 1996).

Increased Morbidity and Mortality

The serious risk to health associated with displacement has been much discussed recently in India. Empirical evidence testifies to the pervasiveness of relocation-related illnesses and outbreaks of parasitic and vector-borne diseases. Pandey's studies (Pandey and associates 1996, 1998) of the ITPS resettlement colony near Hirakud reservoir in Orissa revealed a high incidence of malaria and water-borne diseases, such as diarrhea and dysentery. Toxic effluents from the ITPS plant caused water pollution in the reservoir, leading to skin diseases and other illnesses. In a comprehensive study of morbidity, Savitri Ramaiah (1996) compared those who had been displaced in eight projects (three irrigation projects, two coal-based power projects, one hydroelectric power project, two coal mining projects) and those who had not (control group), totaling 110,000 families from rural and tribal areas. The findings showed that:

- The health status of a large number of affected people who were cultivators was adversely affected.
- A higher prevalence of malaria, fluorosis, guinea worm, and schistosomiasis was attributable to reservoir and irrigation projects,

which increase the subsoil water level and provide breeding places for mosquitoes and other vectors.

- The incidence of acute and chronic respiratory illnesses, as well as gastrointestinal disturbances, was higher among the project-affected persons of the Singrauli area as a result of decreased vegetable intake.

- The prevalence of acute illnesses was higher in seven resettlement groups, and of chronic diseases in five resettlement groups; the severity of acute illnesses among children up to six years old was higher in six resettlement groups (Ramaiah 1996).

Effects on mental health as a consequence of displacement have not been seriously studied in India, except for the clinical and ethnographic observation of traumatic and stressed behavior. Byron J. Good, through Harvard-sponsored research, has taken this up. He notes, "Given the extraordinary importance of place, of attachments to the most minute details of a community's environment, grief should be an expected part of adaptation. . . .When dislocation and resettlement are experienced as unjust, when compensation is viewed as inadequate or unfairly distributed, bitterness and a sense of 'relative deprivation' may prolong grieving, even for generations" (Good 1996). Nayak highlighted the same kind of grieving, brooding, and bitterness (Nayak 1986).

Food Insecurity

"Forced uprooting increases the risk that people will fall into chronic undernourishment, defined as calorie-protein intake levels below the minimum necessary for normal growth and work, and food insecurity. . . . Undernourishment is both a symptom and result of inadequate resettlement" (Cernea 1997).

As if in illustration of this risk becoming reality, Ota (1996) found recently that after 12 years of resettlement in colonies and villages under the Rengali irrigation and power project in Orissa, the displaced still experience acute food insecurity. People are often half-starved during the three-to-four-month lean season, when wage work is also scarce. This is primarily because the (paddy) food grains produced have drastically declined from an average of 16 quintals per family to just 7 quintals. The land allotted is of poor quality and has not been adequately reclaimed by the project. Moreover, the nontimber forest produce, an abundant supplementary food resource before displacement, is no longer accessible. Similar situations have been observed in many other resettlement locations (Nayak 1986, Baboo 1992).

Children in displaced families are particularly victimized by food insecurity. Ramaiah's research compared nutritional data for children in seven resettlement groups with data for children in control groups. Findings revealed that "mean energy intake among children below six years was lower in five resettlement groups," while the mean energy intake of female children 12 to 35 months old was lower in six resettlement groups. The prevalence of underweight children below six years was higher in four resettlement groups, and the prevalence of underweight female children 12 to 41 months old was higher in four resettlement groups. The "mean nutritional status score was poor in six resettlement groups, with calorie intake inadequate for up to 50 percent children below six years in all projects. More than 60 percent of children below six years were underweight in all seven resettlement colonies, as compared with the control groups (Ramaiah 1996). Of course, this inequity is compounded by skewed intrahousehold food distribution patterns. Ramaiah found that "in a majority of projects up to 50 percent households had calorie intake adequate at the household level but inadequate at the child level, indicating that the ability to buy adequate food for the family did not ensure equal distribution of food among all household members" (Ramaiah 1996).

Food insecurity in terms of inadequate calorie-protein intake is endemic in certain parts of India, as demonstrated by Rath's findings of undernourishment (less than 2,250 calories) (Rath 1996). We note that undernourishment is particularly prevalent in those Indian states where much involuntary resettlement has taken place in recent decades: Gujarat (74 percent of the minimal required intake), Andhra Pradesh and Maharashtra (79 percent each), Orissa (70 percent), Karnataka (69 percent), Bihar (65 percent), and Madhya Pradesh (61 percent). Food insecurity due to forced displacement is still neglected, in my view, by Indian scholars and NGOs active in predisplacement and postdisplacement contexts.

Loss of Access to Common Property

This component of the impoverishment process is probably the most ignored by governments. Yet for poor people, particularly those without assets, loss of access to common (nonindividual) property assets (forest lands, bodies of water, grazing lands) results in significant deterioration in income and livelihood. And loss of common property assets is usually not compensated under government relocation schemes. Cernea derives his argument for this feature of the risks model primarily from empirical evidence in India. Indeed, this evidence fully supports the model. In various semi-arid regions of India between 91 and 100 percent of firewood and 66 and 89 percent of poor households' grazing needs are supplied by lands held under common property regimes. Another important common property asset in India is burial grounds.

Food, nutrition, and income patterns in India make gleanings from common property lands essential for many. Gleanings range from food, fuel, and raw materials (for tools, construction, and medicines) to forest produce that can guarantee income. Examples include roots; yams; fruits; flowers; honey; edible resin; sago palm (for food and wine); birds and wild animals; deadwood and brush for fuel; fodder; thatching grass for making house roofs; bamboo and wood for building; herbs for medicines; and forest produce sold for cash, such as oil seeds, medicinal fruits, firewood; leaves for making leaf platters and brooms; resin leaves for making country cigars and cigarettes (*bidi*); detergents and preservatives; raw materials for artisans—rope fiber, carpenter's materials, charcoal (for blacksmiths); leaves for matmaking; bamboo and cane for basket making; potter's clay and ochres; and bark and plant dyes for textiles.

Fernandes and Raj (1992) observe,

> A comparison with the past . . . shows that even in recent projects, the availability of forest produce was better before the displacement/loss of land of the respondents than after it. Today many displaced and affected people, particularly those from Koraput, continue to depend on it. But no provision is made by project authorities to replace the resource that has been lost. . . . Consequently, like many others who have been deprived of their livelihood without alternatives, they have to resort to destructive measures like cutting trees for sale as firewood. It is this dynamic of impoverishment that boomerangs back on the environment and compounds the costs of displacement, with repercussions on a much wider societal scale.

Social Disarticulation

The social-anthropological approach to resettlement compels us to explore not only how displacement threatens individuals with impoverishment, but also how society may be affected as a whole, in its structure and fabric. Integrating the previously discussed risks at the societal level, Cernea writes: "Forced displacement tears apart existing communities and structures of social organization, interpersonal ties, and the enveloping social fabric. Kinship groups tend to get scattered. Life-sustaining informal networks of mutual help, local voluntary associations, and self-organized service arrangements are dismantled. The

destabilization of community life is apt to generate a typical state of anomie, crisis-laden insecurity, and loss of a sense of cultural identity"
(Cernea 1997).

Nayak's research has contributed to identification and analysis of
the parameters of social disarticulation centering on and within the kinship system. He found that payment of compensation money to the father as head of the displaced family has led to "altercations between
father and married son and between married brothers. . . . Consequent
upon this estrangement in the family . . . father and son and also joint
brothers have chosen to resettle in separate villages. . . . The *biradari*
group relationship and the lineage tie at the level of 'cas te group' [have]
been broken off, for the families have been spread out in different resettlement sites. . . . Now the displaced persons are not being properly
served by the traditional service-caste men; they have been relegated to
lower social status position" (Nayak 1986). A distinct trend has developed to contract endogamous marriages within resettlement of displaced oustee populations. Kinsmen do not interact or help whole-
heartedly anymore, as the impoverished displaced persons cannot
reciprocate (Nayak 1986).

Mahapatra (1960) showed how poor tribal villagers depended on
their kinsmen during crises and also at the time of marriages and funer-
als, which required deployment of substantial resources, beyond the capacity of a family. Kinsmen also included ritual kinsmen, who
sometimes belonged to other ethnic groups in the region. Mahapatra
calls this interdependence among kinsmen "social insurance" which
corresponds to the "social capital" in Cernea's conceptualization.

In one example of this mutual support among kinsmen, a Hill
Bhuiyan family providing for a marriage (in 1956) was given what was,
in that economy, an astounding array of goods: 580 kilos of rice, 7 kilos
of *biri* pulses, seven goats, two bolts of cloth, and one pot of rice beer.
These goods, in addition to the manpower and ritual skills required at
the time of the wedding, constituted the fruits of social insurance offered with the understanding that the family would reciprocate later on
(Mahapatra 1960).

Patnaik (1996) contrasts the social networking, dignity, self-assur-
ance, and command over their resources that characterized the people
of Paraja before their displacement by the Upper Kolab Project with the
sense of inferiority, insult, impoverishment, and powerlessness that
overwhelmed them when they shifted to resettlement colonies and
found themselves subservient to the host tribal group and to the Bhatra
and Hindu caste groups of the locality. As the Paraja were beefeaters
and killed cows, they were felt to be ritually impure, bringing

defilement to the community. In all senses the displaced of Paraja were completely unwelcome immigrants into the area. They had already lost their social base and power and dignity during the displacement, and now they were denied a social anchor and articulation with other groups in the resettlement area, which might have been extended to other ethnic groups more acceptable to the Bhatra and Hindu castes. In this inhospitable climate, and because of the impoverishment of their better-off Paraja kinsmen who had lent them money or food grains at low interest, the Paraja now had to depend on an exploiting *sundi* (distillers and moneylenders) group, which had no compunction about impoverishing them further.

In light of such experience, anthropologists and other social scientists, as well as the World Bank guidelines, plead for resettling tribal groups as village communities in an effort to maintain the power of their community life, social network, social capital, and social insurance. With this power, the displaced may better withstand the cultural, economic, and power shocks in the new environment after relocation.

The lower castes, especially the scheduled castes, historically have been dominated by the higher castes. But for the educated, younger generations in the weaker classes this has become intolerable. Hence displacement and the consequent opportunity for a resettlement of one's own choosing offered an avenue of escape from the constraints and predetermination of caste. One thus finds that castes belonging to a lower position without dominance in a village "have chosen sites together so they can avoid recreating the confines of their low status position" and establish themselves in resettlement villages as members of relatively unstratified caste groups (Behura and Nayak 1993). Thus there was social disruption in the resettlement phase, when considered from the perspective of the old village, but there was also an unprecedented opportunity for regeneration of dignified community life.

Cernea speaks of the significance of social disorganization in the overall impoverishment scenario: "Overall, if poverty is not only an absence of material means or basic services such as shelter, work, food, health, or education but also powerlessness, dependency, and vulnerability, then the disorganization of communities and the loss of reciprocity networks are significant factors in aggravating poverty" (Cernea 1997).

Loss of Education

The children of the tribal groups displaced by the IDA-funded Salandi Major Irrigation Project in Orissa (around 1965) suffered a serious setback in education when displacement schools were not provided at the relocation sites. Only after about 10 years were schools established in the government resettlement colonies. During those years, the children mostly worked for the family, either collecting and selling firewood or earning daily wages (Mohanty 1983). Fernandes and Raj (1992) found that out of 184 children only 57 (31 percent) were going to school and out of 90 girls only 10 (11 percent) were in school—and this was after the schools had been established for nearly 20 years. The children in nearby villages, by contrast, were receiving regular education either in government schools or in village-sponsored schools (Mahapatra 1996a, Mohanty 1983).

Beyond India itself, calculations suggest that if 10 million people are displaced worldwide every year, mostly in Africa, Asia, Central America, and South America, there could be at least 3 million children up to 14 years old, or at least 2 million school-age children, affected by relocation (calculating with a ratio lower than for India's growing population). The sample-based registration system in India puts children up to 14 at 36 percent and children aged 5 to 14 at 22.9 percent of the total population in 1992 (IIPS 1995). Conservatively estimated, well over 1 million primary school–aged children of displaced and project-affected families will be affected. The educational lag is already heavy in developing countries compared with levels in industrialized countries: 66 percent of school-age children are expected to reach grade five in Central America and the Caribbean, 50 percent in South Asia, 48 percent in South America, and 48 percent in Sub-Saharan Africa (UNICEF 1994). To this we have to add the loss in human capital that results when school-aged children must go to work to help out in displaced families who have migrated to cities (Parasuraman 1996) or who have been relocated in villages and tribal areas (Fernandes and Raj 1992; Baboo 1991, 1992; Mohanty 1983; Mahapatra 1996a). If a child is withdrawn from school and compelled to work and loses the opportunity to receive a general education, it is a loss with repercussions not only for that child but for future generations of the displaced.

With this in mind I suggest that Cernea's solid theoretical model be expanded to include education loss as a major impoverishment risk. Children of the displaced and other project-affected persons in India and around the world face this severe risk and threat to their development. Indeed, Cernea's recent discussion of the model acknowledges that "relocation often interrupts schooling and some children never return to school. After displacement, as a result of losses in family income, many children are drafted into labor market earlier than what would otherwise occur" (Cernea 1997).

Reconstructing the Livelihoods of Resettlers

Perhaps the main attribute of the impoverishment risks and reconstruction model is that it analytically points to resettlement operations as opportunities for development. Its internal logic places reestablishment processes under the same analytical lens as the risks of impoverishment in order to model the key dimensions of reconstruction.

Thus the model's logic supports the proposition that involuntary resettlement either should be programmed as development operations in themselves or should not be deliberately caused to begin with.

We now ask whether the recovery variable and processes of the general model are substantiated by the empirical findings of India's resettlement research. The issue is economic, social, and cultural rehabilitation of resettlers' lives. We discuss the elements of reconstruction by grouping the economic dimensions (income generation), the social dimensions (social services and welfare), and the community restoration dimensions. These are not a series of elements but rather the complex pieces of a single mosaic that must become the new socioeconomic basis of resettlers' existence. The pieces are internally linked and integrated, and as we shall see, countering each risk has a cumulative and synergistic effect in mitigating other risks.

Countering Landlessness and Joblessness

India's resettlement experiences, despite the numerous cases of impoverishment without rehabilitation, nonetheless reveal significant instances of adequate postdisplacement recovery, including land-based recovery.

Cernea rightly stated that "placing displaced people . . . back on cultivable land or in income-generating employment/self-employment activities is the heart of the matter in reconstructing livelihoods" (1997). The case reviewed below, some of which I studied firsthand, confirms the risks and reconstruction model's reliance on land or employment, more than any other variable, as the key to recovery.

We have seen that not all resettlement risks are equal in their intensity and effects; similarly, not all remedies for recovery are equal. Central strategies that provide an economic basis for recovery through land or employment are best, and Indian experience confirms that if these are followed, the other variables of the reestablishment process are strongly and positively influenced.

In earlier projects, like the Machhkund Hydroelectricity Project in south Orissa, the mostly tribal resettlers were given a generous amount of land: 8 acres of largely fertile land, on average, in Malkangiri, where forests and common property resources were abundant and there was no conflict with host people (Mahapatra 1990). Moreover, the displaced could move there with many of their relatives from the same village or from villages near the displacement site. Hence the people affected were able to reknit their cultural and social fabric rather comfortably in a new location. Fernandes and Raj also wrote of this case as a "successful rehabilitation" (1992). It is nonetheless difficult to confirm that the displaced have achieved development. To assess a situation as "successful," the linear scale of a single component of recovery—in this case reconstruction of livelihood—is not sufficient; we must consider the other reconstruction variables, including education.

Thangaraj correctly noted that "Orissa is a state that very seriously implemented the land for land option and provided either irrigated or unirrigated land of various sizes to displaced persons. But the quantum of land provided gradually declined over a period" (Thangaraj 1996). Responding to protests by a politically organized group of persons displaced by the Rengali Project in the early 1970s, the government of Orissa decided to allocate to each displaced family, whether land-owning or landless, up to 6 acres. The terms were either 3 acres of reclaimed irrigated land or 6 acres of reclaimed unirrigated land, free of *salami* (land price), along with compensation. Besides this, each displaced family, including the landless, was granted half an acre of land as homestead land.

The practice of giving land to the landless, on par with land grants to those who had lost land, enabled not only recovery, but also development of the landless people's livelihood. The provisions went further than the Maharashtra Act of 1976 and the Narmada Water Disputes Tribunal award for the displaced of Sardar Sarovar.

If providing a job is a criterion for success in employment-based rehabilitation, NALCO-Angul has done well (Samal 1995). One hundred percent of the persons displaced from their land have been given NALCO jobs. The others have been employed either by NALCO or by its contractors (see also Reddy 1996). Reservoir-related employment has also been, at times, a success. Mahapatra (1996a) found that persons displaced by a reservoir organized a cooperative of fish workers, consisting of 287 members drawn from 24 villages. This fishing cooperative was originally initiated by project authorities. Most of the cooperative's members were scheduled tribes and displaced persons who had fished occasionally in the Salandi River before reservoir impoundment. Now fishing has become an occupation for them. Thus some of the project-affected persons also became project beneficiaries.

Planning for human resource development—by assessing the growth potential of relocation sites, including host communities, over the next 10 years or more—can permit appropriate skills development for the next generation, enabling people to take up new types of jobs or pursue avenues of self-employment.

Moving from Homelessness to House Reconstruction

Resettlement housing can take two forms. In one the project authority provides a resettlement colony or village with some infrastructure, civic amenities, and developed plots; most often it is up to the resettler to construct a house, while in relatively fewer instances built-up houses are provided. In the other the resettler decides to relocate to a place of his or her choosing and to construct a house there. In the Upper Indravati Project, for example, the displaced selected for their resettlement 560 different locations in small clusters (Ravindran 1996).

The provision of substantial financial assistance for house building that typifies government of Orissa irrigation projects makes it possible to construct a good house, but some projects offer only a pittance—such as the Rs2,000 given by Coal India (Mahanadi Coalfields in Talcher) or the Rs3,000 given by NTPC for the construction of temporary sheds—and a good house cannot be built. Housing after resettlement is usually improved for the poorer classes, who most often receive a house plot of their own.

There is strong evidence of the importance displaced people put on replacing housing. Fernandes and Raj (1992) looked at the spending patterns and found that when displaced persons in Orissa spent their compensation money, they gave house construction third priority. Indeed, "improving shelter conditions is one of the relatively easier achievable improvements in reconstructing resettlers' livelihoods, even though it is still far from occurring widely" (Cernea 1997). Ota (1996) showed that in the Rengali project, only 64 percent of families had their own house before displacement, while after resettlement 93 percent of the displaced families had houses. More families (53 percent) had two-room houses compared with before displacement (37 percent); 10 percent of families now had three-room houses (7 percent before displacement); and there were even more four-room houses (5 percent postdisplacement, 3 percent predisplacement). Homelessness most certainly has been countered by house reconstruction.

In India we have examples of urban resettlement of slum dwellers in such large cities as Mumbai, Calcutta, and Madras (Reddy 1996). Squatters and pavement dwellers in Mumbai have been offered the replacement cost of their meager structures and, most important, a free housing plot of 25 m^2; shops and other small business establishments have been given 16.75 m^2 free. Besides this compensation, house owners, lessees, and lessee tenants can buy floor space of up to 70 m^2 at the actual cost of construction (Reddy 1996).

In the resettlement colonies of the Ramial project in Orissa (Mahapatra 1997) the houses have been constructed at the displaced persons' expense, but they are invariably of better quality than the houses left behind in their old villages. All have homestead land of 0.3 acres, which leaves space for kitchen gardens. Experience indicates that for effective house reconstruction in projects where house plots, but no house-building grants, are given, it is essential to make house-building loans from financial institutions available to displaced persons who become residents of officially recognized villages.

Reconstructing Living Communities

Economic recovery must be complemented by the social reconstruction of living communities. Three strategies are interdependent as components of social reintegration:

- Moving from social disarticulation to community reconstruction
- Moving from marginalization to social inclusion
- Moving from expropriation to restoration of community assets.

Widespread underestimation of these sociocultural and psychological processes still persists among both social researchers and planners in India. Cernea rightly argues that addressing each of these partly overlapping dimensions of reconstructing livelihoods is mutually reinforcing and can achieve synergistic effects.

Social reintegration depends not only on the relationships and interdependence among the resettlement colony or cluster groups and the neighboring communities, but also on the relationships and network building within the resettlement colony. Resettlement colonies are most often heterogeneous, with families drawn from various villages, ethnic groups, and religions. Establishing a new leadership structure, facilitating colony interactions, and tackling community tasks all require a lot of adaptation, accommodation, and mutual trust, which can only be built up over time, withstanding the bumps and setbacks.

Analyzing the social reintegration processes in the rehabilitation colonies of the Ramial irrigation project, Mahapatra (1997) argued that there were three levels of integration to aim for in this specific case, which brought together colonies with heterogeneous ethnic composition. The displaced had re-created the wards of their old villages, with more or less ethnic homogeneity, and had resettled largely en bloc since 1979–80. The three levels of integration Mahapatra cites are intracolony community regeneration, pancolony social reconstruction, and pancolony host villages' social rearticulation. These three levels dovetail and reinforce one another. In seeking to carve out a niche in the social ecology of the adopted resettlement region, the displaced seek to retain a strong sense of the social and moral world they came from (intracolony community regeneration).

Mahapatra found eight bases for positive bonding in support of this first level of social reintegration. One of these involved committees in each colony, constituted to represent all the ethnic groups in the colony, entrusted with the responsibility of maintaining harmony and peace as well as the traditional intercaste/intertribe division of secular and ritual labor. (For more details about this social rearticulation case, see Mahapatra 1997).

Interestingly, in this context many displacement villages in the Talcher Coal Mining Project and in other project areas have been found to have functioning, traditional village leadership, with village councils acting in indifferent coexistence with the modern, statutory *panchayat* (multivillage) leadership systems (Pandey and associates 1996, 1998). In the Madhuban Nagar rehabilitation colony under the Ib Valley coal mining project, the predisplacement village structure has been transplanted, with the old village committee still functioning and attending to postresettlement village issues. The old leaders are still village spokesmen for problem solving and decisionmaking with regard to rehabilitation claims and options (Pandey and associates 1998). Similarly, discussing the displaced of Hirakud, Baboo observed that "it was gathered that people usually wanted to go en bloc to a particular locality. . . . In a few villages the villagers did not want to go along with a particular cast groups, if the latter was crooked and exploitative, or if they were a divided lot" (1996). In the Rengali project, people adopted group-based strategies, and these have been "the resettlers' most effective means for adapting to the new settlements, as well as the most positive and enduring response to the involuntary displacement stimulus" (Behura and Nayak 1993).

Thus we find that displaced people themselves had tried hard to re-create as much as possible harmonious groupings of resettlers in new rehabilitation sites, in both Hirakud and Rengali and in other projects. However, in those host villages where land was purchased by the displaced but there were no kinsmen (that is, by the standards of endogamy practiced by some castes or tribes), mistrust or estrangement over resource sharing (especially, common property resources and civic amenities) was likely, and harmony difficult to achieve.

From Hunger and Morbidity Risks to Adequate Nutrition and Better Health Care

Resettlers' nutrition levels and health care will depend largely on their economic recovery (through land or employment). But in the short run sudden disruption in food supply and adverse health effects of resettlement require specific and immediate action, even before economic recovery, in order to prevent increases in morbidity and mortality rates.

In Upper Indravati Project about 96 percent of the displaced have been enabled to purchase up to 1.25 acres of irrigated land or up to 2.50 acres of unirrigated land. Moreover, the resettlement and rehabilitation unit is to provide irrigation, productive assets, and linkages with other sources of finance. There is, in this case at least, reason to think that food insecurity will be substantially reduced. In other projects as well, where the lands allotted or purchased have been developed over the years, there is hope of mitigating shortages in food supply.

Ramaiah's study revealed that 70 percent of resettler households achieved adequate energy intake at the household level. Also, it was clear that more and more of the displaced were taking modern medicines and that there was a greater awareness of government programs. These localized improvements are few and far between, however, and what is needed is a generalized effort in this area. Of some significance, though still an isolated case, were the measures taken in Orissa in 1994, extending medical care to pregnant women in the villages to be evacuated. These measures taken by the government of Orissa required that medical facilities "be provided at least for a period of 15 days in the resettlement area. . . .The hospital/dispensary . . . programmed to function in resettlement areas" was to be set up immediately (Ramaiah 1996).

The evidence we found about effective concerted strategies for resettlers' health protection and nutritional security in India is limited, and it is our conviction that many innovative approaches are necessary in these areas.

From Educational Loss to Educational Restitution

We have emphasized the significance of education loss by displaced school-age children as a risk of resettlement. What is Indian experience, if any, with remedies for this type of impoverishment? How can such loss of human capital be preempted or counteracted?

Two examples—drawn from opposite ends of the vast spectrum of education scenarios in India—may capture the essence of the problem. The first involves the resettlers from Machhkund. Parents in this village were promised at the time of their displacement that a new school for their children would be rebuilt soon. But the promised school was built and opened by the state only after 30 years! During this time an unaccountable number of children were deprived of the education due them by law. Thus they became impoverished by default, and the community was denied any growth in human capital.

The second example, equally eloquent, involves educational recovery. In the Ramial resettlement colonies the residents themselves acted to prevent educational impoverishment from hurting their children. Without project or government support, the resettlers organized and funded a high school, over and above the limited educational facilities the government had provided.

The lesson is clear, in our view: human capital growth can easily be stunted for long years if education is overlooked in India's approaches to resettlement. But the remedy is not to be sought in the government alone. Reestablishment—and even improvement—of regular education services can be accelerated if resettlers mobilize their collective will and resources and act jointly to protect the interest of their children.

Institutional Mechanisms for Rehabilitation

Although resettlement and rehabilitation is a pervasive, and mostly problematic, process all over India, the government of India has no institutional mechanism at the central level to address it. There is neither a national policy nor constitutional prescriptions. As of 1985 there was perhaps only one state, Maharashtra, that had a department of rehabilitation to look after the resettlement and rehabilitation of persons displaced by irrigation projects.

By the late 1980s and mid-1990s some states, Gujarat and Orissa among them, had established directorates of rehabilitation to deal with the rehabilitation of only those persons displaced by irrigation projects. There is still no coordinated institutional arrangement to take care of rehabilitation matters for projects in wildlife conservation or in the energy, industry, or mining sectors.

Most Indian scholars studying resettlement issues are convinced that integrated institutional mechanisms to oversee rehabilitation must be set up at the national and state levels. Gujarat has set up a resettlement and rehabilitation organization directly under the state's chief minister, to make it more effective.

The World Bank must be given credit for requesting and insisting that the government of India and the state governments create rehabilitation machinery for irrigation and other projects supported by the World Bank in Orissa, Gujarat, Madhya Pradesh, and a few other states.

Acts and Policies Are Not Enough

In overpopulated India, where agriculture is still the most important occupation and source of livelihood, power, and status in rural areas, land is extremely scarce. So-called government land, often encroached upon by both the haves and have-nots, has not been easily available for occupation, even for allotment by the authorities for resettlement purposes. After passage of the Forest Conservation Act of 1980, the forest land could not be used to resettle displaced communities. The land that was available could be allotted on a land-for-land basis to displaced persons who owned land. And since 1977, in response to sustained protests and agitations by the nontribal displaced (for example, in the early 1970s in Orissa's Rengali project) the landless could get the same rehabilitation package as given to land-owning families in Orissa.

There was no government policy on resettlement. Decisions were made through government resolutions on an ad hoc basis. Between 1973 and 1983 as many as 24 such resolutions were adopted in response to periodic agitations by displaced persons and political leaders. Similarly, where the market value of land had to be established because land sale records in a project-affected village or its neighboring villages were not available, this was done by government resolution. This greatly helped the displaced in the Upper Kolab and Upper Indravati projects, in the tribal, interior areas. The displaced in the Rengali project were promised land in 1973, and many of them eventually received reclaimed irrigated land or land in the command area.

All of this only highlights the point that government policy or no, if the government of the day is forced to make decisions in the interest of displaced persons, it can do so. Tribal and other vulnerable groups, isolated in remote interior areas and without political support, cannot wrest such decisions from the government, however, unless, as in the Sardar Sarovar project, it becomes a national issue.

The multilateral funding agencies, and the World Bank in particular, have been instrumental in bringing about a sea change in many practices, regulations, and acts governing the resettlement and rehabilitation of displaced persons (see Patel and others 1991 on the history of the Sardar Sarovar project). Indian scholars, activists, and NGOs have been active in this process since the 1970s, and in the 1980s they formulated policy guidelines (Fernandes and Asif 1997, Mahapatra 1991,

Fernandes and Thukral 1989). Yet only in response to the added pressures brought to bear by resistance and international agencies has the government of India taken up formulation of national policies on resettlement and rehabilitation (Indian Ministry of Rural Development 1994, Indian Ministry of Water Resources 1996).

My reading of the situation in India is that acts and policies are not enough! A proper humane attitude toward displaced populations, adequate provisions for rehabilitation built into development programs, transparent and people-friendly institutional mechanisms, and the active participation of the affected people in promoting their own development are absolutely essential prerequisites for successful rehabilitation.

Conclusions: Unfinished Tasks

Our detailed examination of India's resettlement experiences confirms empirically and theoretically the validity of the conceptual model of risks and reconstruction as an analytical, explanatory, and strategic tool.

Several other policy planks and intellectual contributions on resettlement in India have converged with the theoretical model discussed here. Indian NGOs, scholars, environmentalists, and activists have formulated and proposed to the government a Draft National Policy on Developmental Resettlement of Project-Affected People, which requires an objective assessment of the overall adverse impacts (risks) of resettlement on people and their environment and the preparation of rehabilitation plans that include benefit sharing (Fernandes and Thukral 1989). Such plans would have to be approved by project-affected people in any given case, for their "welfare and development," and would become an inseparable part of the project itself. This approach is called "developmental resettlement."

The thinking behind these policy proposals is fully convergent with Cernea's model for impoverishment risks and reconstruction of livelihoods. This model is to be credited with placing resettlement issues squarely in the context of a development framework. It brings together coherently both the impoverishment risks of resettlement, which are demonstrably preventable, and the planning, strategy building, and preventive actions necessary to avoid or mitigate these risks and promote the development of uprooted people.

Scholars and others in India have contributed much to the measurement and analysis of these impoverishment risks. They have been incisive and creative in this endeavor. The same cannot be said, however, about the empirical study and analysis of the modes of reconstructing livelihoods in India. This has seldom been done, and on the whole, it has been done insufficiently.

One reason may be that rehabilitation programs in India, which are still evolving, have rarely had sufficient resources allocated to them. Moreover, it takes at least 10 years to assess the success or failure of a rehabilitation program. Few projects have been studied longitudinally with such hindsight. The strategic recovery activities suggested by the livelihood reconstruction model provide useful guidance, not just for social science research, but for government and corporate (private sector) action. When the policy for resettlement in India is adopted, the hope is that such strategic recovery activities will be followed and tested in a systematic, rather than an occasional, manner.

In light of the integrated conceptualization of Cernea's model and of India's own experience with resettlement and rehabilitation, it appears that we in India have just begun to unravel the total reality—to find the best means to gauge problems and develop solutions to them. In this far-from-finished task, India's academic research community, the NGOs, the civil society, state governments and various agencies all have roles to play and contributions to make.

As noted earlier, Indian scholars have made significant contributions to compiling, analyzing, and conceptualizing rehabilitation-development scenarios involving all the aspects Cernea developed in his reconstruction of livelihoods model. Now that rehabilitation programs in many projects are more than 10, even 20, years old, there are many opportunities for independent evaluators to learn from the failures and successes. Toward that end Indian scholars should develop indicators of success in such areas as:

- Trauma management
- Compensation, savings, and utilization-land purchase committees
- Predisplacement impoverishment and coping activities
- Evacuation and resettlement
- Economic reconstruction processes: land, jobs, shared benefits.

Together, economic rehabilitation, sociocultural reestablishment, and environmental rehabilitation may form the components of an integrated approach to enhancing the development of project-affected people, and indicators for each may be developed.

I have attempted to develop overall indicators of success based primarily on the ultimate goal of reconstructing livelihood, which implies *sustained development not only of the first generation of displaced persons, but also of their progeny in the second generation.* The analysis of impoverishment risks and the formulation of action programs to counter them, adequately and in an appropriate time frame, together with substantial follow-up and institutions to ensure maintenance and development of infrastructure and amenities, will provide viable means of reaching this ultimate goal.

The indicators I would propose for evaluating development within the first 10 years of resettlement (whether in project-sponsored resettlement colonies or in self-sponsored resettlement clusters) are as follows: (a) the quality of life in the majority of households, including physical quality of life, is higher than in the old community; (b) vulnerable groups (women, children, the elderly, tribal and backward castes and classes) have adequate provisions; (c) the displaced participate fully and freely in local development programs; (d) the displaced are integrated into the region, treated equitably, and empowered; (e) amity is established with the host community and a network of interdependence is established with neighboring communities; (f) the displaced have retained or rebuilt their identity; (g) the resettlement community engages in self-regulation, self-management of common property, and ecoconservation.

A further task for Indian scholars might be a comparative study of the whole gamut of displacement-rehabilitation-development Indian experiences with experiences in other countries.

NGOs and Civil Society

The NGOs have lent their voice to radically modify the Draft National Policy for Rehabilitation, as proposed by the government of India (Indian Ministry of Rural Development 1994). But their role is crucial in bringing about a rapprochement between the displaced in resettlement clusters and rehabilitation colonies and the neighboring villages in host areas, whose infrastructure and common property resources are often shared by the displaced. Since competition, rather than collaboration, characterizes the initial relations between these groups, areas of cooperation must be widened.

Projects should identify educated, younger persons from among colony residents, as has been done in some NTPC projects, so that they may learn how to look after the affairs of colony life. NGOs may make a lasting contribution to resettlers through capacity and institution building in the community, so that after the project is completed or closed, the people will be able, through their own skills and institutions, to manage the maintenance and development of infrastructure and amenities.

If more awareness of the sacrifices required from project-affected people can be built, the attitude of the civil society toward them may change. The civil society—for example, the political parties—can, given sufficient reason, persuade authorities or companies to change either dam sites, height, or other project parameters to reduce displacement. The civil society may also put pressure on the government to pay the project-affected people the replacement value of land and other assets, so that they may build their production base elsewhere on their own.

Central and State Governments

The government of India should heed the warning sounded by the Supreme Court of India: "No development project, however laudable, can possibly justify impoverishment of large sections of people and their utter destitution" (Supreme Court of India, Civil Original Jurisdiction, MP No. 16331 of 1982, Lanchand Mahto and others versus Coal India Ltd.).

In our view, it is high time to amend the Constitution of India, Article 31A (Fundamental Rights), by substituting *replacement value* for the term "market value" (as it occurs in the second proviso), and to replace in the Land Acquisition Act of 1894 "market value" with *replacement value*, wherever the former is mentioned. With such a step, the single most frequent manner of deprivation and of impoverishment would be kept in better check. It would protect not only the land-owning project-affected people, but also the landless laborer, whose rehabilitation package is also defined in terms of land or cash in lieu of land, as in Orissa. (For other suggested amendments to the Constitution and the Land Acquisition Act, see Pandey and associates 1998). Such amendments would standardize the concepts of rights which could then be brought to bear on the interpretation of other instruments, for example, ILO Convention No. 107 of 1957, ratified by the government of India.

A second important legal change would have substantial impact on people's participation in consultation over land acquisition for government or private projects. For tribal (scheduled) areas, the Panchayats Acts of 1996 (Extension to the Scheduled Areas) has empowered the Gram Sabha, Gram Panchayat, Block-level Panchayat, or Zilla Parishad (at the district level) to be "consulted before making the acquisition of land in the Scheduled Areas for development projects and before resettling or rehabilitating persons affected by such projects in the Scheduled Areas." Similar empowerment may be achieved in favor of other, more numerous, panchayats outside the Scheduled Areas, through the general Panchayat Act. This would immediately put a brake on the often excessive acquisition of land for development projects, which displace many more families than necessary.

Similarly, the central government needs to amend the Land Acquisition Act of 1894 and require that a certain portion of the ex gratia payment (over and above the price paid for land and the solatium of 50 percent of the compensation) be contributed by the responsible agency or private company to be used as a deposit. Such a deposit would yield interest for infrastructure maintenance and development in the resettlement colony after the project closes.

Further, as provided in the Modified Draft National Policy for Resettlement (Indian Ministry of Water Resources 1996), there should be further amendment to the Land Acquisition Act of 1894, to the effect that an independent body shall make a strict assessment of the land requirements of the project. Firm provisions are needed to make sure that land acquired but not used for 10 years or more shall revert to the state and be distributed to the former landowners without compensation.

Indian states should each enact legislation in line with the amendments proposed to the Constitution and the Land Acquisition Act. Further, state governments should constitute a Department of Resettlement and Rehabilitation, under a secretary, to formulate binding rules and procedures for acquiring land, issuing compensation, establishing eligibility and amount of rehabilitation grants, and setting standards for amenities and services in resettlement colonies and clusters. This body should also set standards for infrastructure development in colonies and neighboring host villages, so that the compensation and rehabilitation benefits accorded to displaced people will not be discriminatory among sectors (industry, energy, water resources, mining, urban development) within the same state. The proposed Department of Resettlement and Rehabilitation should have sufficient personnel to monitor and ensure that the laws and regulations are being observed by state and private sector programs.

Testing the impoverishment risks and reconstruction framework against the vast amount of empirical findings communicated by academic and applied studies of R&R in India has not only confirmed the model itself, but also enabled this author to organize a huge and disparate volume of field data into a broader picture. With the considerable new factual information now "loaded" onto the general matrix of the risks and reconstruction model, we now hope that a structured synthesis of *concepts* and *facts* can be constructed from the perspective of processes in the Indian subcontinent.

We hope that this synthesis will give additional impetus to further research, in India and elsewhere, particularly to joint economic and anthropological studies of resettlement. We also hope that this study would serve advocacy and policy purposes, as an argument for improving resettlement practice and for providing better development opportunities to the downtrodden oustees.

Acknowledgements

The author wishes to thank Michael M. Cernea for his kind interest in and comments on this study and for his critical and valuable suggestions regarding the complexities of resettlement programs in India. Thanks are also due to A. B. Ota, anthropologist, Directorate of Rehabilitation, Water Resources Department, Government of Orissa, for encouragement and assistance. Rita Ray, Department of Sociology, Utkal University, and R. M. Mallick and N. C. Choudhury, Center for Development Studies, in Bhubaneswar, Orissa, also have the author's gratitude for facilitating this work.

A debt is also due to Hari Mohan Mathur, anthropologist consultant, EDIEN, the World Bank, and P. M. Mohapatra, I.A.S., Director General, Gopabandhu Academy of Administration, Orissa, for their encouragement. The author thanks his daughter, Sheela Mahapatra, an anthropologist, for correcting the manuscript; C. Das, for putting the manuscript on diskette; and P. Sahoo, for undertaking the arduous typing of the manuscript.

References

The word "processed" describes informally reproduced works that may not be commonly available through libraries.

Baboo, Balgovind. 1991. "Big Dams and the Tribals: The Case of the Hirakud Dam Oustees in Orissa." *Social Action* 41(3).

———. 1992. *Technology and Social Transformation: The Case of the Hirakud Multipurpose Dam in Orissa.* Delhi: Concept Publishing House.

———. 1996. "State Policies and People's Response: Lessons from Hirakud Dam." In A. B. Ota and A. Agnihotri, eds., *Involuntary Displacement in Dam Projects.* New Delhi: Prachi Prakashan.

Baxi, Upendra. 1989. "Notes on Constitutional and Legal Aspects of Rehabilitation and Displacement." In Walter Fernandes and E. G. Thukral, eds., *Development Displacement and Rehabilitation.* New Delhi: Indian Social Institute.

Behura, N. K., and P. K. Nayak. 1993. "Involuntary displacement and the Changing Frontiers of Kinship: A Study of Resettlement of Orissa." In M. M. Cernea and S. E. Guggenheim, eds., *Anthropological Approaches to Resettlement: Policy, Practice, Theory.* Boulder, Colo.: Westview Press.

Cernea, Michael M. 1990. *Poverty Risks from Population Displacement in Water Resources Development: Policy and Operational Issues.* DDP 335. Cambridge, Mass.: Harvard University, HIID.

———. 1993. "Anthropological and Sociological Research for Policy Development on Population Resettlement." In M. M. Cernea and S. E. Guggenheim, eds., *Anthropological Approaches to Resettlement: Policy, Practice, Theory*. Boulder, Colo.: Westview Press.

_____. 1995. "Understanding and Preventing Impoverishment from Displacement: Reflections on the State of Knowledge." Keynote address at the International Conference on Development-Induced Displacement and Impoverishment, Oxford University. Processed. (See also Chris McDowell, ed., *Understanding Impoverishment*. Providence: Berghahn.)

_____. 1996a. "Public Policy Responses to Development-Induced Population Displacements." *Economic and Political Weekly* (June 15).

_____. 1996b. "The Risks and Reconstruction Model for Resettling Displaced Populations." Keynote Address, International Conference on Reconstructing Livelihoods. University of Oxford, Refugee Studies Programme. Processed.

_____. 1997. "The Risks and Reconstruction Model for Resettling Displaced Populations." *World Development* 25(10).

_____. 1998. Impoverishment or Social Justice? In H. M. Mathur and D. Marsden, eds., *Development Projects and Impoverishment Risks*. New Delhi: Oxford University Press.

Das, A., V. Das, and B. Das. 1996. "Involuntary Displacement in Upper Indravati Hydroelectricity Project." In A. B. Ota and A. Agnihotri, eds., *Involuntary Displacement in Dam Projects*. New Delhi: Prachi Prakashan.

Drèze, J. P., M. Sampson, and S. Singh, eds. 1997. *The Dam and the Nation: Displacement and Resettlement in the Narmada Valley*. Delhi: Oxford University Press.

Fernandes, Walter. 1991. "Power and Powerlessness: Development Projects and Displacement of Tribals." *Social Action* 41(3).

_____. 1994. *Development-Induced Displacement in the Tribal Areas of Eastern India*. New Delhi, Indian Social Institute.

Fernandes, Walter, and Mohammed Asif. 1997. *Development-Induced Displacement and Rehabilitation in Orissa, 1951 to 1995: A Database on Its Extent and Nature*. New Delhi: ISI.

Fernandes, Walter, and S. Anthony Raj. 1992. *Development, Displacement, and Rehabilitation in the Tribal Areas of Orissa*. New Delhi: Indian Social Institute.

Fernandes, Walter, and Enakshi Ganguly Thukral, eds. 1989. *Development, Displacement, and Rehabilitation*. New Delhi: Indian Social Institute.

Fisher, William F. 1995. *Towards Sustainable Development? Struggling over India's Narmada River*. Armonk, N.Y.: Sharpe.

Good, Byron J. 1996. "Mental Health Consequences of Displacement and Resettlement." *Economic and Political Weekly* (June 15).

Government of Orissa, Bureau of Statistics and Economics, Department of Planning and Coordination. 1968. "Report on the Benefits of Hirakud Irrigation." Bhubaneswar. Processed.

Government of Orissa, Water and Land Management Institute. 1991. "Irrigation in Orissa." A. C. Nayak, ed. Bhubaneswar. Processed.

India. 1993. *The Constitution of India. With Short Notes and Subject Index*. 13th ed. Lucknow: Eastern Book Company.

India, Ministry of Rural Development. 1994. "The Draft National Policy for Rehabilitation of Persons Displaced as a Consequence of Acquisition of Land: Cabinet Note." New Delhi. Processed.

India, Ministry of Water Resources, Central Water Commission. 1996. "Modified Draft National Policy for Resettlement and Rehabilitation of Persons Affected by Reservoir Projects." New Delhi. Processed.

IIPS (International Institute for Population Studies). 1995. *National Family Health Survey, 1992–93*. Bombay.

Joshi, Vidyut. 1987. *Submerging Villages: Problems and Prospects*. Delhi: Ajanta Publications.

Mahapatra, L. K. 1960. "A Hill Bhuiyan Village: An Empirical Socio-Economic Study." Hamburg University, Germany. Processed.

_____. 1990. "Rehabilitation of Tribals Affected by Major Dams and Other Projects in Orissa." In A. P. Fernandez, ed., *Report on Workshop on Rehabilitation of Persons Displaced by Development Projects*. Bangalore: Institute for Social Economic Change.

_____. 1991. "Development for Whom? Depriving the Dispossessed Tribals." *Social Action* (July-September). (Original version presented at World Congress of Anthropology, Vancouver, 1983).

_____. 1994. *Tribal Development in India: Myth and Reality*. New Delhi: Vikas Publishers.

_____. 1996a. "Good Intentions or Policy Are Not Enough: Reducing Impoverishment Risks for the Tribal Oustees." Presented at the World Bank Workshop on Impoverishment Risks in Involuntary Resettlement, New Delhi. Processed.

_____. 1996b. "Rehabilitation by the Government and the People: A Case Study of Impoverishment of Salandi Major Irrigation Project Oustees." Presented at the Training Seminar on Resettlement and Rehabilitation, Gopabandhu Academy of Administration, Bhubaneswar. Processed.

_____. 1996c. "Society in Orissa." In Mishra and Samal, eds., *Comprehensive History and Culture of Orissa*. Delhi: Kaveri Publishers.

_____. 1997. "Social Rearticulation and Community Regeneration among the Resettled Oustees of Ramial Medium Irrigation Project, Dhenkanal District." Presented at the Training Seminar on Resettlement and Rehabilitation, Gopabandhu Academy of Administration, Bhubaneswar. Processed.

Mankodi, Kashyap. 1992. "Resettlement and Rehabilitation of Dam Oustees: A Case Study of Ukai Dam." In E. G. Thukral, ed., *Big Dams, Displaced People*. New Delhi: Sage Publications.

Mathur, Hari Mohan. 1995. *Anthropology and Development in Traditional Societies*. 2nd ed. New Delhi: Vikas Publishing House.

Mathur, Hari Mohan, and David Marsden, eds. 1998. *Development Projects and Impoverishment Risks.* New Delhi: Oxford University Press.

Misra, Sadasiv. 1960. *Economic Survey of Orissa,* vols. 1 and 2. Bhubaneswar: Government of Orissa, Finance Department.

Mohanty, B. P. 1983. *A Socio-Economic Investigation on the Displaced Families of Salandi Riverdam, Hadgarh.* Anandapur: Antyodaya Chetana Kendra.

Morse, Bradford, and Thomas R. Berger. 1992. *Sardar Sarovar: Report of the Independent Review.* Ottawa: Resource Futures International, Inc.

Nayak, P. K. 1986. "Displaced Denizens of Rengali Dam Project: A Study of Their Socio-Economic Conditions, Resettlement Problems and Ameliorative Action Measures." OXFAM, Bhubaneswar. Processed.

Ota, A. B. 1996. "Countering the Impoverishment Risk: The Case of the Rengali Dam Project." In A. B. Ota and A. Agnihotri, eds., *Involuntary Displacement in Dam Projects.* New Delhi. Prachi Prakashan.

Pandey, Balaji, and associates. 1996. *Development, Displacement and Rehabilitation in Orissa, 1950–1990.* Bhubaneswar: ISED.

_____. 1998. *Depriving the Underprivileged for Development.* Bhubaneswar, Orissa: Institute for Socio-Economic Development.

Paranjpye, Vijay. 1988. *Evaluating the Tehri Dam: An Extended Cost Benefit Appraisal.* New Delhi: Indian National Trust for Art and Cultural Heritage.

Parasuraman, S. 1996. "Development Projects, Displacement, and Outcomes for Displaced: Two Case Studies." *Economic and Political Weekly* (June 15).

Patel, Anil, and others. 1991. "Rehabilitation and Resettlement in Sardar Project: Are the Critics Right?" *Social Action* 41(3).

Patnaik, S. M. 1996. *Displacement, Rehabilitation, and Social Change: The Case of Paraja Highlanders.* New Delhi: Inter-India Publications.

Ramaiah, Savitri. 1996. "Impact of Involuntary Resettlement and Rehabilitation on Level of Living of Project-Affected Persons (PAPs)." Presented at the World Bank Workshop on Impoverishment Risks in Involuntary Resettlement. New Delhi. Processed.

Rath, Nilkantha. 1996. "Poverty in India Revisted." *Indian Journal of Agricultural Economics* 51(1, 2, January-June).

Ravindran, Latha. 1996. "Resettlement and Rehabilitation: From Policy Guidelines to Practice—A Case Study." In *Theme Papers of the First Training Seminar on Resettlement and Rehabilitation.* Bhubaneswar: Gopabandhu Academy of Administration.

Reddy, I. U. B. 1996. "New Approaches in Involuntary Resettlement in Urban Infrastructure Projects in India." Presented at the International Conference on Reconstructing Livelihoods. Oxford University. Processed.

Roy-Burman, B. K. 1961. *Social Processes in the Industrialization of Rourkela.* New Delhi: Census of India.

_____. 1995. "Rourkela Steel and Sardar Sarovar Project Oustees: Rehabilitation Policies Compared." *Main Stream* (March 26).

Samal, K. C. 1995. *Socio-Economic Impact of NALCO Angul Sector: Involuntary Displacement and Adjustment*. Bhubaneswar: NC Centre for Development Studies.

Scudder, Thayer. 1985. "A Sociological Framework for the Analysis of New Land Settlements." In M. M. Cernea, ed., *Putting People First*. New York: Oxford University Press.

Shi, Guoqing and Hu Weison. 1994. "Comprehensive Evaluation and Monitoring of Displaced Persons' Standards of Living and Production." Hohai University, National Research Centre of Resettlement, Nanjing. Processed.

Singh, Sekhar, Ashish Kothari, and Kulan Amin. 1992. "Evaluating Major Irrigation Projects in India." In E. G. Thukral, ed., *Big Dams: Displaced People*. New Delhi: Sage Publications.

Stanley, William. 1996. "Machhkund, Upper Kolab, and NALCO Projects in Koraput District, Orissa." *Economic and Political Weekly* (June 15).

Swaminathan, M. S. 1982. "Irrigation and Our Agricultural Future." A. N. Khosla Memorial Lecture. New Delhi. Processed.

_____. 1996. "Science and Technology for Sustainable Food Security." *Indian Journal of Agricultural Economics* 51(1, 2).

Thangaraj, Sam. 1996. "'Impoverishment Risks in Involuntary Resettlement: An Overview." Presented at the World Bank Workshop on Impoverishment Risks in Involuntary Resettlement. New Delhi. Processed.

Times of India. 1997. "Snapshot World: Four Countries with the Most Dams." June 28, 1997.

UNICEF (United Nations Children's Fund). 1994. *The State of World's Children, 1994*. India ed. New Delhi: Oxford University Press.

World Bank. 1990. Operational Directive 4.30. "Involuntary Resettlement." Washington, D.C. Processed.

_____. 1994. "Resettlement and Development. The Bankwide Review of Projects Involving Involuntary Resettlement, 1986–1993." Environment Department. Washington, D.C.

6

Sharing Project Benefits to Improve Resettlers' Livelihoods

Warren A. Van Wicklin III

Editor's Note
Any attempt to develop an economics of recovery and development, as this volume advocates, would certainly have to reexamine the rationale of benefit distribution patterns in the projects that involve forced resettlement. These patterns are too often too skewed, dividing the affected people into net gainers and net losers, with some sharing the gains and some only the pains of development.

Contrary to what the vast majority of resettlement studies do—namely, reporting the deprivations people suffer through displacement—the study by Warren Van Wicklin explores the circumstances under which displaced people also can participate, through deliberate project design, in *sharing the gains* from the projects that caused their relocation. Such studies are seldom done.

The author has reviewed a large number of projects under implementation between 1987 and 1997, using both the *ex ante* and the *ex post* project documents. The purpose is to identify if, and how, the stream of benefits generated by the project can be channeled to resettlers as well, rather than relying only on up-front project financial allocations for resettlement. A typology of benefits is constructed, all resulting from project *outputs* rather than *inputs*. This typology includes both in-kind benefits (such as access to electricity) and various forms of access to newly created revenues based on project experiences from the Philippines, China, India, Mexico, Indonesia, and many other countries.

One, partly unexpected, finding of the study is that there is a significant number of projects in which displaced people also share in some of the project benefits, in one form or another. This finding is important in itself. But even more revealing is the demonstration that projects of various types, and in different sectors, contain within their own fabric options to direct project benefits to the resettlers, either during project implementation or afterwards. Effective ways and cases of channeling project-created benefits towards reconstructing resettlers' livelihoods are discussed, citing projects in Indonesia, China, and Latin America.

Yet this potential to rechannel resources remains unused in many projects. This is both inequitable and unjustifiable. Often, such potential is overlooked because of trivial, not structural, reasons: lack of commitment and concern of project decisionmakers, poor methodologies of economic and financial analysis at the project planning level, poorly designed resettlement components, a lack of creativity and inventiveness in using resources available to the project, and so on. Van Wicklin emphasizes, however, that such apparently trivial reasons also have deeper roots: the absence of national policies and of legally compelling regulations that would make it mandatory for developers from the public or private sector to deliberately open access for those displaced to the project's stream of benefits. National policies for making benefit sharing a *standard* would always reach further and deeper than only discrete, project-specific initiatives to promote such approaches.

A public debate is going on about whether restoring resettlers to their prior standards is sufficient or if they must necessarily be assisted to reach, sooner rather than later, improved levels. Surely, development is insufficiently served when only restoration is achieved, and restoration of prior *poverty* levels is not a great accomplishment, to say the least. This only highlights the importance of the distributional issues raised in this study, for it is only through much more generous benefit sharing, that improving rather than only restoring resettlers' livelihood will become possible.

The World Bank's resettlement policy emphasizes benefit sharing and recommends to all countries that undertake projects entailing resettlement to adopt and apply in practice benefit-sharing policies and procedures. Benefit-sharing and forward-looking developmental approaches (rather than only asset compensation) are the most constructive and progressive dimensions in resettlement policy.

Toward such goals, the study that follows provides policymakers and planners with an inspiring inventory of good practices, able to mitigate to a significant extent the sacrifices of those affected by development-induced displacements. Policies and projects that are not predicated on benefit sharing misuse the potential for resettlers' recovery: they have much to learn from policies and projects that do this effectively.

One of the most difficult aspects of reconstructing the livelihoods and incomes of displaced people is finding the financial resources necessary for this complex endeavor. As the other chapters in this volume make clear, the costs of resettlement and rehabilitation are often not internalized in project budgets. Typically, initial project budgets tend to provide little more than compensation payments for land acquisition. Too often this undercompensates the displaced, who may lack legal title to their land or sustain losses other than land. It also underestimates the actual replacement cost of land in situations where there is a sudden increased demand for it and a shrinking supply. As the recent OED study on involuntary resettlement associated with eight large dam projects found, "Land prices spiral beyond all reasonable budget limits in situations with large numbers of resettlers taking unrestricted cash packages and competing for the same limited land pool" (World Bank 1998d).

Because resettlement costs tend to be underestimated and externalized (see Cernea, this volume, chapter 1), corrections in current practice are necessary to recognize and generate the necessary financial resources for rehabilitating displaced people. This chapter argues that sharing project benefits with resettlers is an effective—yet underutilized—approach, providing numerous examples illustrating its merits.

Arguments for Sharing Benefits

Empirical evidence informs that compensation alone is usually insufficient to relaunch resettlers on a sustainable income path (World Bank 1994g, World Bank 1998d). Proper socioeconomic reestablishment requires more than paying the fair market value of the condemned land. Reconstructing livelihoods implies reestablishing the income flows that the displaced people had prior to resettlement. New income streams, or investments that can produce these income streams, must be developed. As a rule of thumb, appropriate resettlement budgets on a per family basis need to be a multiple (four or more) of the lost income streams (World Bank 1994g). Therefore successful resettlement requires financial resources commensurate to this difficult task. In every single project the means to generate them need to be identified or created.

One way to help alleviate financial constraints on resettlement budgets is to deliberately design projects so that involuntarily displaced people receive some of the benefits created by the projects displacing them. This means that in addition to allocating resources from the up-front project budget for the purpose of resettlement and reconstruction, the stream of benefits created by the project should also be tapped to provide direct benefits and resources for resettlers. This is one of the most important issues in the economics of involuntary resettlement operations, though so far it has received scant attention in the economic literature.

Besides the economic and financial rationale, there are also major equity arguments for sharing benefits. Giving up one's home and land is much more than an economic transaction: it has profound social, cultural, and psychological ramifications. Communities and neighborhoods, with their mutual support and labor exchange networks, are often broken up and dispersed as a consequence of forced relocation. Cultural losses include ties to the land, ancestral sites, indigenous knowledge of local production systems, and other forms of cultural heritage. Among the psychological costs and consequences of relocation are isolation, alienation, anomie, substance abuse, higher rates of prostitution and divorce, and other signs of social disarticulation (Pandey and associates 1996). Since resettlers are called upon to make sacrifices for the general good by giving up their habitats and their income-generating assets, it is only equitable that they should share in the benefits of the project displacing them.

There is also a political rationale for projects to share benefits with resettlers. Typically, the displaced and the project beneficiaries are largely separate groups. Resettlers bear the burden for someone else's benefit. Displaced people are frequently the "losers" while "project beneficiaries" are the "winners" of development (Cernea 1997). Many beneficiaries live at a great distance from the project area, while many in the project area are the first to suffer the adverse effects, and therefore often oppose the project.

Recent research on resistance to involuntary resettlement documents the extent to which people will go to avoid displacement and impoverishment (Cernea 1995c, Gray 1996, Oliver-Smith 1996, and Posey 1996). Lack of benefits from the project commensurate with the sacrifices the displaced people make is part of the rationale for their resistance and opposition to the projects. Various communities threatened with resettlement and many nongovernmental organizations (NGOs) have mounted vigorous public campaigns against the Itaparica (Brazil), Narmada Sardar Sarovar (India), Arun III (Nepal), Nam Theun (Laos), Pak Mun (Thailand), Kedung Ombo (Indonesia), Bakun (Malaysia), and Katse (Lesotho) dams, among others. In turn, political opposition tends to increase the cost of projects and to delay their benefits. It even threatens their sustainability (Fisher 1995). Learning from extensive experience, World Bank strategies for promoting participation and public involvement encourage governments to develop collaborative relationships with those to be displaced and to be more sensitive to their needs and rights. One important form of participation is to make resettlers direct beneficiaries of the project so that they gain a vested interest in the project, instead of having only an adversarial relationship.

Sharing project benefits is not just a way to gain acceptance of displacement, or to generate more resources; it provides an opportunity to do resettlement better. Yet many projects have not availed themselves of this opportunity. Part of the reason has been a narrow—or lack of—understanding of the economics of involuntary resettlement. This is manifested in the design of rehabilitation packages that are not linked to the benefits and resources generated by the main project. This is often due to the weak economic analysis and projections characteristically performed for involuntary resettlement components, compared with the design of voluntary resettlement projects where resettlement is integrated into regional development strategies. As Eriksen has documented (this volume, chapter 3), not only are involuntary resettlement components more often poorly prepared, they are not fully integrated into the economic design of the project and are seen as "add-ons."

The Bank's original goal with resettlement was to mitigate adverse impacts on resettlers. Since the World Bank's initial policy on involuntary resettlement was first promulgated, in 1980, increasing attention has been given to procedures and mechanisms for achieving this mitigation. The Bank's first published policy and operational paper on resettlement (Cernea 1988) analyzed many of the practical pitfalls leading to resettlement failure, including inadequate financial resources, and suggested strategies and methodologies to avoid them. In the Bank's subsequent formulations of its original policy (World Bank 1986, Cernea 1988, World Bank 1990), what was previously implicit in the Bank's policy was made explicit. Indeed, the new text states that *all involuntary resettlement should be conceived and executed as development programs, with resettlers provided sufficient investment resources and opportunities to share in project benefits* (World Bank 1990).

Thus since the mid-1980s the concept of sharing project benefits with resettlers was repeatedly formulated, explicitly and normatively (Cernea 1995a). The Bank went on record as encouraging governments to use benefit sharing as a strategy for mobilizing financial resources for relocation, in order to improve resettlement performance.

Rather than emphasizing only the mitigation of losses, the revised policy took a forward-looking stance and stated that projects should be deliberately designed in ways that would directly benefit resettlers, in addition to the economic rehabilitation they might receive. Some Bank-assisted projects had already adopted benefit sharing, and in 1990 provisions were made to translate this "good practice" into a "mainstream" approach to resettlement. This coincided with some of the first literature focusing on impoverishment risks, recommending stronger, proactive strategies to counteract, and not merely mitigate, such risks (Cernea 1990).

Indeed, the norm of sharing project benefits with resettlers requires radically improving the project design and planning process, because benefit sharing has to be planned for at the outset. Given this requirement, this chapter inquires to what extent development projects plan to, and actually do, share benefits with resettlers, and how they do it.

To answer these questions, we reviewed a large set of Bank-assisted projects that involved involuntary resettlement during the past 10 years; that is, projects under implementation between 1987 and 1997. The information is derived from staff appraisal reports (the principal project document at the time a project is approved), implementation or project completion reports (the principal project document when Bank financing of a project is completed), and performance audit reports (another postproject document prepared for about half of all Bank-assisted projects). It is possible that some projects might have shared project benefits with resettlers, either by design or otherwise, without the main project documents reporting on this, but it is unlikely that this happened often.

We complemented written sources with interviews with project task managers and others knowledgeable about the project. The author supplemented the desk review with field research carried out during 1996–97 under OED auspices at seven projects in Asia and Africa (World Bank 1998a-g). Only about half of the projects reviewed were approved after 1990, when sharing project benefits with resettlers was explicitly recommended for the first time. Thus, the purpose of this chapter is not to ascertain whether or not specific projects shared project benefits with resettlers, but to identify methods of sharing benefits.

The approach used for this analysis was to determine whether there was benefit sharing of direct outputs of the project's main components. For example, if the project was an urban upgrading project creating new housing as one of its core outputs, and resettlers were given priority for this new housing, then the resettlers would be seen as sharing directly in the benefits. Similarly, if an irrigation dam moved displaced people into the "command area," that is, onto land where they would receive water from the reservoir or the irrigation canal that displaced them, they would be directly sharing in the benefits.

A remarkable new practice is that some development projects are specifically designed to rehabilitate resettlers displaced by a separate infrastructure project. For example, in 1994 the Bank approved the first "pair" of projects that treated the resettlement component of infrastructure building as a full-fledged, freestanding project: this pair was the China Xiaolangdi Dam Project and the Xiaolangdi Resettlement Project (box 6.1). Another, more recent example of a pair of projects is the India Coal Sector Rehabilitation Project and the India Coal Sector Environmental and Social Mitigation Project, approved in 1997. In such cases all the outputs of the resettlement project go to the resettlers (and their hosts), so none of those outputs is considered benefit sharing. The issue is to determine whether and how the benefits of the associated infrastructure project are shared with resettlers.

National Policy Provisions for Sharing Benefits

National policies with provisions for benefit sharing have far broader impact than discrete, project-specific decisions to promote such approaches. National policies provide legal frameworks and make benefit sharing standard, rather than leaving it to the discretion of each project planner. So far the most progress made in putting into practice national policies mandating benefit sharing has been in the energy sector. Some hydroelectric and thermal projects allocate a percentage of their electricity sales revenues to resettlers and local administrative units, in response to legal and policy frameworks that were adopted to institutionalize this practice. Among the projects using this approach are the Lubuge, Yantan, Shuikou, and Ertan hydroelectric projects in China; the Rio Grande Hydroelectric Project in Colombia; and the Leyte-Cebu and Leyte-Luzon geothermal projects in the Philippines. Of course, this approach is used in other, non-Bank-assisted projects in those countries.

Brazil developed a specific policy for benefit sharing with people affected by energy sector projects. Brazilian Law 7990/89 mandates that 6 percent of electricity sale revenues are to be returned to affected municipalities. This created a significant source of funds in the Itaparica projec that will, among other things, permit the relocated rural population to receive a higher grade of irrigation technology and the relocated urban population to obtain upgraded services (Serra 1993).

Colombia developed a similar policy on sharing the benefits of hydroelectric projects with locally affected people. Law 56/91 of 1991 requires that 4 percent of annual electricity revenues generated by a hydroelectric plant be allocated to municipalities in that plant's area. Specifically, 2 percent of the revenues are for reforestation and other environmental mitigation activities, and 2 percent for social infrastructure such as schools, roads, rural electrification, and so forth. In the first year expenditures are for improvements in the area closest to the reservoir. As the needs of those most immediately affected are met, additional revenues are shared more broadly.

Box 6.1   Financing Separate Projects for Resettlement

In 1994 the Bank helped design and approved the first pair of "twinned" projects where the resettlement component of an infrastructure project is separated into a parallel, stand-alone project. The China Xiaolangdi dam and reservoir project will displace about 182,000 people. The dam will provide substantial irrigation, hydropower, and flood control benefits. To ensure that resettlers also benefit, a a parallel and distinct $571 million Xiaolangdi Resettlement Project was created, with its major objective being "to restore and improve the livelihoods of 154,000 resettlers and 300,000 host people affected by the construction and operation of the Xiaolangdi multipurpose dam, and to minimize the adverse effects of their social adjustment to their new environments" (World Bank 1994c). The resettlement project will construct all infrastructure including housing for 276 villages and 10 towns for the resettlers. It will also develop 11,100 hectares of land, of which 7,000 will be irrigated, principally by the reservoir. A total of 252 small industries and mines will be relocated, and the workers will move with these industries. An additional 84 industries will be established, employing some 20,500 resettlers. All the financial and human resources dedicated to this project will benefit resettlers and their hosts.

Already the benefits of "twinning" are clear. This project is one of the most detailed resettlement efforts ever designed. The budget, timetable, and resettlement plan are unparalleled in their detail. Thus far not only the planning but the implementation is successful. Incomes for the first group of 2,000 resettlers exceeded their previous incomes by 10 to 60 percent 14 months after relocation. Independent monitoring found that more than 95 percent of the first 7,000 resettlers were satisfied with their relocation sites and the facilities provided.

* * *

In 1996 the Bank approved a full-scale project that would address resettlement problems for an infrastructure project that had already closed, but where the resettlement component was not satisfactorily completed. The India Coal Sector Environmental and Social Mitigation Project is the twin project to the Coal Sector Rehabilitation Project (World Bank 1996a). The social mitigation project is undertaken to reestablish incomes not only for people displaced by 25 coal mines being financed by the current coal sector rehabilitation project, but for people displaced by four mines in previous World Bank–financed coal mining projects. Economic rehabilitation for displaced people revolves around training and employment with the coal companies themselves.

China has applied the principle of sharing project benefits with resettlers to the greatest number of projects. Practically all of the recent Bank-assisted projects in China include the applicable Chinese legal frameworks for sharing project benefits. This applies not only to resettlers but to host communities. To make this possible, many incentives are included for the receiving population.

Chinese legal frameworks for benefit sharing were first developed in large reservoir projects. In June 1981 the Ministry of Electric Power issued the "Circular on Collection of Reservoir Maintenance Fund from Power Generation Revenue of Hydropower Stations." This act established a "reservoir maintenance fund" for each reservoir to (a) compensate those relocated for both lost livelihood and, if needed, lost means of production, after completion of the reservoir; (b) maintain reservoir structures; and (c) maintain structures for drinking water supply, irrigation, and transportation used by the relocated. This fund, one yuan (Y) per thousand kilowatt-hours (kWh), is collected from the hydropower revenue of power stations under the Ministry of Electric Power.

In July 1986 the General Office of the State Council issued the "Circular on Transmitting the Report of Paying Close Attention to Reservoir Resettlement" prepared by the Ministry of Water Resources and Electric Power. This document stipulated that (a) additional resettlement funds for reservoirs begun in 1986 or later should be allocated in the total capital construction costs, and (b) the additional funds would have three sources—hydropower revenue, water tariffs, and ministry or local government budgets.

In 1991 the State Council issued the "Regulation on Compensation of Land Requisition and Resettlement for the Construction of Big and Medium-Sized Water Resources and Hydropower Projects." It states that the support period for resettlement would be the first five to 10 years after completion of resettlement. Recently the hydropower revenue tariff was increased from Y0.001/kWh to Y0.0045/kWh. This approach provides significant revenues for benefit sharing and codifies the method in the legal policies of the governing national authorities.

There are at least two major advantages to this sort of benefit sharing. First, because it takes the form of a revenue stream, it is very flexible in providing financial resources for whatever is needed. Revenues have been used for community facilities, training and job creation, and stimulation of the local economy. Second, tapping future revenue streams ensures postproject financial resources for sustaining resettlement. Resettlement is rarely completed at the same time as project completion. As Eriksen's chapter in this volume suggests, resettlement requires a system establishment phase of four to six years and then a system

Box 6.2   Enabling Reservoir Displacees to Benefit from Irrigated Command Areas

Several dam projects in India, where large numbers of people have been displaced, shared direct project benefits with resettlers by moving displaced people into the newly irrigated areas. These include the Andhra Pradesh II and III, Gujarat Medium II, and Maharashtra III Irrigation projects.

In the Orissa Water Resources Consolidation Project, "over 75 percent of displaced and affected people would be direct beneficiaries of new irrigation provided under the project. As with other beneficiaries of new irrigation, their incomes would thus be expected to increase significantly under the project" (World Bank 1995j).

The Tamil Nadu Newsprint Project is very relevant as a second-phase project that remedied resettlement problems from an earlier project. As the implementation completion report explained:

> Although expansion of the [Tamil Nadu] paper mill did not involve any new displacement of the population, the operation of the first mill had adversely affected 102 families in an adjacent village as a result of seepage from the plant's effluent lagoon and settling of coal dust from the plant. Resettlement and rehabilitation was therefore required. Tamil Nadu Newsprint and Papers Ltd., with the support of farmers residing in villages adjacent to the mill site, implemented a unique lift irrigation system to fully exploit the treated effluent discharges from the plant. The scheme irrigates about 1,400 acres of formerly arid land and potentially another 3,000 to 4,000 acres, allowing local farmers to now harvest two or even three crops a year compared to only a single crop previously (World Bank 1996c).

Many reservoir projects outside India also share irrigation benefits with involuntary resettlers, such as the Brazil Ceara Water Resources, China Daguangba Multipurpose, Lubuge Hydroelectric, and Iran Irrigation projects. Plans for the China Daguangba Project estimated that "approximately half of the [displaced] people will move to new settlements which will be provided irrigation from the canals [constructed by the project]. New paddy fields will be irrigated on reclaimed lands now utilized by the affected people for rainfed crops." The Brazil Ceara Water Resources Project staff appraisal report noted that: "Those families which cannot be relocated on the same properties will be re-established in planned resettlement areas situated in the immediate vicinity of the reservoir, granted land tenure (independently of whether they possessed tenure of their former lots prior to resettlement) and direct access to water for agricultural production purposes" (World Bank 1995a).

stabilization phase of at least an additional five years. Guaranteed revenue streams during this longer time horizon help facilitate successful stabilization and sustainability of reconstruction.

A Typology of Project-Level Benefit Sharing

Projects create several kinds of benefits that can be directed to the displaced. For example, the outputs of a multipurpose dam that can be shared by resettlers include water for irrigation or drinking; electricity from hydroelectric plants; fishing rights in the reservoir; flood control; inland, waterborne transportation; and revenues from sales of electricity and water. Other types of infrastructure project benefits include improved roads and other transportation systems, health clinics, schools, and so on. Besides facilities, projects offer employment directly generated by the project, either temporary or permanent. Urban redevelopment projects provide housing, or serviced sites or plots for building, so that resettlers improve the quality of their housing and benefit from more secure tenure arrangements and community facilities.

The following typology of benefits, with project examples, is by no means exhaustive, but it shows the range of experiences in the set of projects we examined. Furthermore, when only one example is cited for a project, that does not mean that other forms of benefit sharing did not take place in that project. Of course, benefit sharing is usually only one of the provisions for economic rehabilitation, and each project also requires other measures to restore incomes and reconstruct livelihoods.

Irrigation

Dams—whether for irrigation, hydropower, drinking water, flood control, inland transportation, or a combination of these—have traditionally been the largest cause of displacement in Bank-assisted projects. The World Bank resettlement review found that 63 percent of people being involuntarily resettled in ongoing projects were being displaced by dams (World Bank 1996g). Many of the large Bank-financed irrigation projects in India, which as a group have displaced more than a million people in the past 15 years, have moved at least some of the displaced into command areas so they benefit directly from the project (box 6.2). With the increased yields arising from irrigation, these people can earn more than they did before they were displaced.

Electricity

Since many of the dams generate hydroelectric power, the opportunity is usually created to provide involuntary resettlers with electricity at their new sites. Hydroelectricity is often added to an existing power grid, but local connections are also technically feasible and cheaper if they are incorporated into project design from the outset. The Yantan, Shuikou, and Ertan hydroelectric projects in China did this. Thermal power projects also can provide electricity to resettlers. The China Zouxian Thermal will provide electricity to resettlers from the transmission component of the project, and the India Farakka II Thermal project has already done this (World Bank 1996e).

Several projects earmark a portion of their electricity revenues for the benefit of those displaced by the dam. In the Philippines' Leyte-Luzon Geothermal Project, "1 [percent] of the gross revenues from project electricity sales will be distributed among the province, the barangay, and the local community" (World Bank 1994f). This will result in significant funds for the area, and the resettlers and their hosts will be among those benefiting.

The China Lubuge Hydroelectric Project set aside one yuan for every thousand kilowatt-hours generated by the Lubuge plant to establish a reservoir maintenance fund, 80 percent of which is used by local governments for reforestation, fishery, and agricultural development activities. Twenty percent is retained by the power station for reservoir cleaning, maintenance works, and so on. The China Ertan, Yantan, and Shuikou hydroelectric projects also earmarked a portion of the revenues from electricity sales to benefit resettlers. Yantan Hydro "provides 1 yuan per 1,000 kilowatt-hours from power plant revenue towards development in the reservoir area, for the life of the project," generating a substantial financial flow (World Bank 1995c).

Fishing

One income-producing resource that can be allocated to resettlers is fishing rights in the newly created reservoir. Often these benefits have been allowed to go to outsiders, but a much better approach is to reserve these benefits, primarily or exclusively, for those displaced by the reservoir. This is a good example of transforming the cause of displacement or hardship into a source of new employment and income.

Reservoir fisheries have proved to be a more successful means of sharing benefits and reconstructing livelihoods than expected. In the Aguamilpa reservoir, part of the Mexico Hydroelectric Project, fishing represented only 4.1 percent of productive activities among the displaced people prior to the project (1989), but by 1995 that figure had risen to 60.8 percent (Johns 1996). The Cirata and Saguling reservoirs in Indonesia provide an even more dramatic example: cage aquaculture employed 7,500 families directly and another 21,000 in secondary enterprises, through production of 24,500 tons of fish a year, compared with the 10 tons produced annually in the original river fishery. Final production revenues are estimated to be seven times the value of the lost production from the submerged farms (box 6.3). In the 1998 OED review of eight large dam projects, six projects developed reservoir fisheries (World Bank 1998a-g). Yet it was found that only the two reservoirs in China developed fisheries into anything close to their real potential, using a combination of fish cages, netted areas of tributaries, fish ponds, and oyster beds. It appears that dissemination of the adequate technologies to aggressively stock the reservoirs with fish and shrimp could generate very substantial benefits for resettlers and surrounding populations.

Transport

Reservoirs create new possibilities and needs for water transport services, both for passengers and cargo. In both the Shuikou and Yantan hydro projects in China, previously less accessible villages are now on the shores of 100-kilometer-long reservoirs. Displaced people took advantage of the opportunity to establish ferrying services, with the support of local resettlement authorities. In the China Wanjiazhai Water Transfer Project, some affected farmers have seen the opportunity in the transport business and have opted for self-employment; 76 displaced people will be engaged in either private or collective transport business (World Bank 1997b). This phenomenon has been observed at other reservoirs in India and Africa. When displacement creates a need for new services or products, proactive resettlement planners examine these needs to see if displaced people can provide them and thereby create new income sources.

Employment

The benefit generally valued most by resettlers is wage employment, which yields a steady income flow and a sense of control over their lives. Even temporary employment by the project can provide much-needed income during the transition period, as well as skills, experience, and other benefits.

The most feasible form of employment is in the activity the project is supporting. Several projects have given displaced people priority for

Box 6.3   Diverting Benefits Away from Resettlers

Using reservoir fisheries for the economic rehabilitation of displaced people provides an enlightening example of benefit sharing with resettlers. Indonesia's Saguling dam (completed in 1984) and Cirata dam (1987) displaced more than 115,000 people living in the Citarum River basin in Western Java. Initial planning made overoptimistic assumptions about resettlers' willingness to join the transmigration program and the suitability of cash compensation. Studies carried out shortly after displacement found that incomes for farmers resettled on land had declined 40 to 50 percent.

Many displaced families, however, with support from a program launched by the government of Indonesia, the World Bank, and ICLARM (International Center for Living Aquatic Resources Management), took advantage of the newly created reservoirs to develop an innovative fisheries enterprise using fish culture technologies designed especially for small farmers. By 1992 cage aquaculture systems in the two reservoirs employed 7,500 people, produced 8,000 tons of fish—up from 10 tons produced in the original river fishery—and provided 25 percent of the total fish supply entering the Bandung district, an area with about 3 million people. By 1996 total aquaculture production was 24,500 tons. Total production could increase further if appropriate methods were utilized.

Indonesia's Institute of Ecology reports that landless resettlers hired for cage aquaculture earn more than rice field workers in nearby areas. By 1996 fishery revenues from the two reservoirs exceeded $24 million a year, almost five times the $5.1 million a year lost by the regional economy from submerged rice fields. Cage aquaculture created an additional 21,000 jobs for resettlers in secondary small enterprises, such as fish feed farms, cage maintenance, and marketing. Current estimates suggest that final production revenues will level off at about $34.5 million a year, nearly seven times the value of the lost rice production from the submerged farms. A recent follow-up study of Cirata found that 59 percent of the resettlers believed they were better off than before displacement. Both reservoirs have become sources of economic growth for surrounding communities.

However, the sustainability of benefit sharing in these projects is now at risk. The gains from cage aquaculture are so attractive that they draw nonresettlers. By the end of 1996, 52 percent of the cages were owned by competing nonresettlers who had paid resettlers or bribed officials for cage permits. These "outsiders" also had wrested almost complete control over marketing of the fish produced through aquaculture. Poor location of cages contributes to water pollution due to waste feed and nitrogen discharges. Furthermore, industrial discharges upstream cause fish kills. Therefore social, political, technical, economic, and environmental factors must be closely monitored and adaptations must be made to preserve resettlers' priority access to these benefits.

Source: Costa-Pierce and Soemarwoto (1990), Costa-Pierce (1998).

employment with the project—temporary, permanent, or both. For example, in the Pakistan Ghazi-Barotha Hydropower Project, "WAPDA [the Water and Power Development Authority] will give priority in employment to the affectees in the construction phase and in filling openings in all job categories in the permanent operations and maintenance staff" (World Bank 1995n). In the Karnataka Power Project, "KPC [the power company] has absorbed 43 project affected persons in its regular workforce" (World Bank 1995i). In the Vietnam Power Development Project, the agency managing construction and operation of the thermal plant will present displaced people seeking employment to the contractors. Electricity of Vietnam has recently started a two-year residential course for power plant operators, and suitable displaced people have been accepted (World Bank 1996h).

Numerous coal mining and thermal power projects in India offer jobs to the people they displace, when feasible, at the rate of one job per household (box 6.4). These jobs are highly prized and often are passed on as inheritances within families. Difficulties arise when not all the displaced can be employed in the new plants and alternative options must be found. For example, the Jharia Coking Coal Project "provided employment for 247 project-affected people. At this point, a deadlock has been reached since the remaining 551 project-affected families refuse to vacate their houses on the project site unless BCCL [Bharat Coking Coal Ltd.] offers employment to every person above 18. BCCL, however, has a significant overstaffing and low productivity problem. The company, therefore, decided not to resettle the remaining families and to reduce the mining area." Production reached only 24 percent of the target (World Bank 1996b).

Many projects in China have deliberately allocated jobs to involuntary displacees. This has been facilitated by China's rapid economic expansion and the shift in the labor force from agriculture to industry. Local authorities can grant preference to resettlers, who are often eager to receive the higher and more reliable incomes found in industry. The Sichuan Power Transmission Project will give resettlers priority for employment as transmission line maintenance workers and temporary construction workers (World Bank 1995b). This provides employment both during the construction phase and after the project is complete. The Shanghai Environment Project will recruit displaced people as operation and maintenance staff at the pumping station for which the displacees' land is being acquired (World Bank 1994b). The Southern Jiangsu Environmental Protection Project is retraining farmers to work at the wastewater treatment plants that are displacing them. The company implementing the water supply component of the Shandong Environment Project has agreed to provide some construction jobs to the

Box 6.4   Coal Companies That Employ People Whose Land They Acquire

Some of the coal mines and thermal power plants constructed under projects have offered jobs to some of the people displaced when their land was taken to be used for mines, plants, and ash ponds. Coal India has a company policy of giving resettlers preference for unskilled and semiskilled jobs. "Considering that wages in the coal industry are 8 to 10 times the prevailing minimum wage, most project-affected people opt for employment with the coal companies" (World Bank 1995f, 1995h). Coal company jobs are seen as much more reliable sources of income, compared with the vagaries of smallholder agriculture.

Several projects in India have used this method of benefit sharing. In the Dudhichua Coal Project "NCL [Northern Coalfields Ltd.] has employed 225 out of the 378 project-affected people" (World Bank 1995f). The Coal Mining and Coal Quality Improvement Project provided employment to 1,828 members of the 968 families displaced by the Gevra mine, employing 363 people directly and 1,500 indirectly (through contractors) of the 3,303 people displaced by the Sonepur-Bazari mine (World Bank 1997c). The Talcher Thermal Power Project employed 251 people directly and another 350 on a permanent basis under maintenance contracts for the main plant, the coal handling plant, lighting, sanitation and township maintenance, housekeeping, and so on. All 207 of the entitled families in the Chandrapur Thermal Project were provided one job per family with the state electricity board (World Bank 1995e). In the Second Farakka Thermal Power Project "449 PAPs (project affected people) have been employed by NTPC [National Thermal Power Corporation]. Another 165 PAPs opted to become contractors for NTPC. In addition, about 2,075 PAPs obtained temporary jobs with the contractors" (World Bank 1996e).

Other countries also use this strategy. The Indonesia Suralaya Thermal Project will offer displaced families employment with the state electricity company. Both the Leyte Cebu and Leyte Luzon Geothermal projects in the Philippines contained plans to employ resettlers in the geothermal or power plant, which would not only increase their present income, but provide them with training, health care, and retirement benefits (World Bank 1994e, 1994f). These are highly prized positions, and resettlers are eager to receive such opportunities.

affected persons, as well as technical assistance for the construction of piped water systems for the affected villages, thereby combining jobs and infrastructure services for resettlers (World Bank 1997a). The Second Red Soils Area Development project will offer one permanent job per household in the construction and operation of the agroprocessing enterprise acquiring their land (World Bank 1994a). In the Lubuge

Hydro Project 100 resettlers were assigned to reservoir maintenance and other development activities by the local governments. Most of these projects are displacing relatively small numbers of people, thus facilitating reestablishment through employment opportunities with the project.

The India Upper Krishna II and Maharashtra Composite III Irrigation projects employed displaced people as laborers in the construction of canals in developing the command areas (World Bank 1998g). In the Maharashtra case, many of the displaced people resettled in the command areas, thus linking their temporary employment and source of permanent means of livelihood. Temporary employment with the project during the critical reestablishment phase should be offered even when the people being resettled cannot receive permanent employment from the project. Of course, temporary employment is not a substitute for complete, long-term reconstruction of livelihoods. Additional investments are therefore necessary.

Quite often projects that require preparation of relocation sites allocate that work to the displaced people themselves. This may have a double benefit: paying wages to the displaced during a particularly vulnerable period in the resettlement process, and helping ensure that preparation at the new site reflects the preferences of the resettlers. The India Karnataka Power Project mandated that displaced families do all the manual work in the land preparation process and be paid a daily wage. The China Ertan Hydroelectric Project is paying a salary to family members working on development of the resettlement sites. Although this labor is necessitated by the resettlement operation, and thus is not strictly a project output, it is work that could be given to outsiders, so paying the resettlers is directing a project resource to them.

Housing

Many urban-upgrading projects build new housing, so it makes sense that those displaced by a project should be among the first to receive new housing generated by that project. The Mozambique Urban Rehabilitation Project planned to allocate 380 core units to be built in the first phase of the project to house families moved out of decaying (but high-quality) apartments that will be rehabilitated. The Ethiopia Second Addis Ababa Urban Development Project, though displacing only a few households, also planned to provide them with newly constructed housing units that are part of the project.

Many urban projects provide serviced plots or a core unit (walls and a roof). The owners can then build or complete houses according to their own preferences and resources. Resettlers often use part of their compensation money for this purpose and almost always can obtain better housing than they had before the project. This is the case in the Brazil Rio Flood Reconstruction and Prevention Project. The component that provides serviced sites for low-income families will create 11,000 serviced lots, of which 8,280 are to be allocated to families relocated because of the project's civil works (drainage, slope stabilization, and reforestation) components.

Similar examples come from the Middle East and North Africa. The Jordan National Urban Development Project will give relocated households first preference for newly serviced plots in either the infill or overspill areas adjacent to or near the upgrading scheme. In the Tunisia Third Urban Development Project, about 600 of the 1,600 newly serviced plots would be used to rehouse families that have been displaced to reduce overcrowding or as a result of necessary demolition in the project areas. The Tunisia Fourth Urban Project calls for families whose houses are demolished because of the infrastructure works to receive first priority for lots. And in the Morocco Land Development Project for Low-Income Families, *bidonville* dwellers are offered such highly desirable, subsidized lots that no one refuses in favor of remaining in the shantytown. The project executes the resettlement operation as de-densification to alleviate overcrowding in the slum areas and to provide improved services.

Some projects do not restrict resettlers to choosing only from among the housing or serviced plots created by the project. Instead, they offer vouchers or other in-kind credit toward housing of the resettler's choice. Although such projects add to the stock of housing, those specific houses or apartments may not go to resettlers. The project relies more on a free market solution. Resettlers get the chance to express their own preferences by obtaining credit toward any new housing they select, not just project-constructed housing. This method has been used successfully in several urban projects in China, most notably in Shanghai (World Bank 1996g).

Access to Improved Infrastructure

Besides housing or serviced plots, urban development projects often provide those they displace with access to improved infrastructure. The Sierra Leone Freetown Infrastructure Rehabilitation Project plans to set aside two tracts of government land in the rehabilitated Kroo Bay area in order to provide those relocated with access to water supply, solid waste disposal, upgraded markets, roads, and footways. The Kenya Export Development Project gave people displaced by the export processing zone (EPZ) titled plots next to the EPZ so that "they will be in the future connected [by] the same water and sewerage mains as the EPZ worker housing sites" (World Bank 1995l). In the Guinea Second Urban Project, sites near the infrastructure works are rehabilitated for resettling displaced people who will benefit from improved servicing and access to employment opportunities. Transportation and relocation costs are also kept to a minimum.

Some urban projects provide benefits that are aimed at the entire affected population, not only at resettlers. The China Liaoning Urban Project is providing clean water to all project area residents, including resettlers. The China Henan Provincial Highway Project—as is true in many transport projects in China—is paying land compensation fees and resettlement subsidies to county, township, or village governments, which use them collectively for area development. In many resettlement projects in China, benefits that are provided to host communities receiving resettlers wind up being shared with resettlers. In turn, nonresettlers often share a part of the land they have been using (through redistribution) with families who have lost their land completely. Everyone thus shares the costs (through land adjustment) for the greater good of all.

Some of the preceding examples, especially in urban rehousing projects, demonstrate how projects can be designed with resettler benefits as a central objective. In the Korea Ports Development and Environment Project, which is developing a new industrial-commercial complex, owners of displaced seafood eateries are offered the opportunity to participate in the project and reestablish their small shops as restaurants once the new complex is completed (World Bank 1994d). In this way the main project creates opportunities for those it displaces.

There are many other examples of project benefit sharing. The ones presented are sufficient to illustrate the validity of the strategy and the diversity of approaches. These should be a source of inspiration for project planners and decisionmakers to expand the use of benefit sharing in forthcoming projects.

Replicating Good Practices in Benefit Sharing for Income Recovery

Judging from the evidence presented above, we can conclude that sharing project benefits with resettlers is a relatively recent practice. Nonetheless, our survey of projects receiving World Bank assistance over the past 10 years has revealed dozens of projects adopting a benefit-sharing approach to reconstructing resettlers' livelihoods. The projects doing this most frequently are those constructing dams and reservoirs, irrigation systems, coal mines, and urban infrastructure. However, almost any kind of project can share benefits with resettlers if an orientation toward this strategy exists and there is the political will to implement it.

Projects that combine multiple forms of benefit sharing hold the greatest promise for restoring and improving resettler living standards. Although the use of such approaches became more frequent after the Bank instituted explicit policy support, benefit sharing is still far from standard practice. Some projects utilize a single method of benefit sharing, when several methods could have been used in combination. If more than the restoration of resettlers' prior livelihood levels is pursued, and if improvements over these levels is to be achieved through resettlement with development, strategies based on deliberate benefit-sharing designs become imperative.

Of great concern should be the consistent evidence that benefit sharing is seldom used in projects financed domestically without assistance from international donors. This chapter focused almost entirely on projects the Bank partially finances in order to signal some of their best practices. The need for generalizing them is acute. A broad review of resettlement (World Bank 1996g) found that the Bank is currently involved in relatively few projects, accounting for less than 3 percent of all the people displaced worldwide by development projects. Only several countries so far have been willing to establish resettlement policies with standards that match those recommended by the World Bank. Even a large country, such as India, with hundreds of domestically financed projects causing displacement, has not issued a national policy on involuntary resettlement.

As it has been well argued, the absence of policy responses to the perverse effects of forcible displacement is a cause of development distortions in many developing countries that must be overcome (Cernea 1995a, 1995b). Worldwide, the majority of resettlers are displaced in projects not subject to World Bank resettlement policies or to policies with similar standards. The available documentation shows that the majority of those resettlers do not share in project benefits, largely because national policies do not yet direct planners to pursue this goal and because private entrepreneurs rarely have such objectives.

The sectoral and national policy approaches to benefit sharing described near the beginning of this chapter demonstrate the advantages of systematizing the practice. Many of the project examples came from projects that were subject to national and sectoral policies, illustrating the synergy of project-specific and policy-mandated approaches. For governments to use the Bank's resettlement policy in Bank-financed projects but not in domestically financed projects is short-sighted. Similarly, to adopt Bank policy and then to ignore the critical dimension of benefit sharing is an unfortunately limited and restrictive adoption of the policy (Cernea 1995a, 1995b). Benefit-sharing and developmental approaches are the most forward-looking dimensions in resettlement policy.

Projects that are not predicated on benefit sharing have much to learn from projects that are. Benefit sharing generates resources beyond those already budgeted for resettlement. The provision of direct project outputs and benefits gives resettlers a positive, vested interest in the project, because beneficiaries and resettlers both benefit. Most important, resettlement is more effective and sustainable when an ongoing stream of benefits can be tapped for resettlers. Resettlement budgets are often insufficient to achieve lasting rehabilitation, but benefit sharing can provide continuous streams of benefits that are more secure and sustainable.

Although this chapter focuses primarily on positive examples of benefit sharing—in order to document the advantages of this approach in improving resettlers' livelihoods—the important converse message is that cost and harm will result if this approach is not utilized. The chapter contains a few examples of projects that failed to share benefits or did so ineffectively. Many more examples are available and could have been included. During the research we came across dozens of projects that could have shared benefits but failed to do so. All too often the difference between satisfactory and unsatisfactory resettlement performance was the failure to share benefits. This is symptomatic of the larger failure to seize resettlement as a development opportunity. This was mainly due to a failure of imagination or resolve on the part of project planners to "put resettlers first" when they targeted project benefits.

Most significant are the cases where project authorities adopted benefit sharing after initial resettler resistance to the project. As benefit sharing yielded tangible benefits to resettlers (and project authorities) and increased their incomes and living standards, resettlers gained an interest in the project. An adversarial relationship was transformed into one of mutual benefits. Managers of these resettlement operations became effective champions of a more enlightened approach to resettlement planning and implementation.

Our conclusion is that most projects cannot afford to treat benefit sharing as merely an act of goodwill; sharing benefits is necessary for good resettlement. The potential for this strategy is well established, even though interesting questions remain. For example, how to treat benefit-sharing issues in the economic and financial justification of project investments? How much additional resources can be raised? How to channel both project funds and project benefits accruing to resettlers toward new investments by the resettlers themselves? Which benefit-sharing methods are most successful, efficient, and sustainable? And which ones do resettlers themselves value the most? Much more research is needed if we are to become adequately informed about this important resettlement strategy, which could improve performance in a wide range of projects.

Acknowledgements

The author would like to thank Michael Cernea for initiating the writing of this chapter, and Gloria Davis for providing time in my work program to draft this chapter. Michael Cernea offered extensive suggestions and ideas during numerous drafts, which significantly improved the quality of the chapter. Dan Aronson, Daniel Gibson, Maninder Gill, and Scott Guggenheim provided valuable comments on an earlier paper that were incorporated into this chapter. Youxuan Zhu, María Clara Mejía, and Maria Teresa Serra explained to me the Chinese, Colombian, and Brazilian laws (respectively) that allocate hydroelectric revenues to people displaced by hydropower reservoirs. Robert Picciotto, Edward B. Rice, and Andres Liebenthal reviewed the chapter and contributed to my understanding of the economic and financial issues.

References

The word "processed" describes informally reproduced works that may not be commonly available through libraries.

Cernea, Michael M. 1988. *Involuntary Resettlement in Development Projects: Policy Guidelines in World Bank–Financed Projects.* Technical Paper 80. Washington, D.C.: World Bank.

_____. 1990. *Poverty Risks from Population Displacement in Water Resources Development.* Development Discussion Paper 355. Cambridge, Mass.: Harvard Institute for International Development.

_____. 1995a. "Public Policy Responses to Development-Induced Population Displacement." *Economic and Political Weekly* 31 (24): 1515–23.

_____. 1995b. "Social Integration and Population Displacement: The Contribution of Social Science." *International Social Science Journal* 143 (1): 91–112.

_____. 1995c. "Understanding and Preventing Impoverishment from Displacement: Reflections on the State of Knowledge." *Journal of Refugees Studies* 8 (3): 245–64.

_____. 1997. "The Risks and Reconstruction Model for Resettling Displaced Populations." *World Development* 25 (10): 1569–87.

Costa-Pierce, Barry. 1998. "Constraints to the Sustainability of Cage Aquaculture for Resettlement from Hydropower Dams in Asia: An Indonesian Case Study." *Journal of Environment and Development* 7 (4).

Costa-Pierce, Barry, and Otto Soemarwoto, eds. 1990. *Reservoir Fisheries and Aquaculture for Resettlement in Indonesia*. Manila: ICLARM.

Fisher, William F., ed. 1995. *Toward Sustainable Development? Struggling over India's Narmada River*. Armonk, N.Y.: M. E. Sharpe.

Gray, Andrew. 1996. "Indigenous Resistance to Involuntary Relocation." In Christopher McDowell, ed., *Understanding Impoverishment: The Consequences of Development-Induced Displacement*. Oxford, U.K.: Berghahn Books.

Johns, Kathryn. 1996. "Final Report of the Resettlement Program of the Aguamilpa Hydroelectric Project." World Bank, Washington, D.C. Processed.

Oliver-Smith, Anthony. 1996. "Fighting for a Place: The Policy Implications of Resistance to Development-Induced Resettlement." In Christopher McDowell, ed., *Understanding Impoverishment: The Consequences of Development-Induced Displacement*. Oxford, U.K.: Berghahn Books.

Pandey, Balaji, and associates. 1996. *Development, Displacement, and Rehabilitation in Orissa 1950–1990*. Bhubaneswar, India: Institute for Socio-Economic Development.

Posey, Darrell A. 1996. "The Kayapo Indian Protests against Amazonian Dams: Successes, Alliances, and Unending Battles." In Christopher McDowell, ed., *Understanding Impoverishment: The Consequences of Development-Induced Displacement*. Oxford, U.K.: Berghahn Books.

Serra, Maria Teresa Fernandes. 1993. "Resettlement Planning in the Brazilian Power Sector: Recent Changes in Approach." In Michael M. Cernea and Scott Guggenheim, eds., *Anthropological Approaches to Resettlement: Policy, Practice, and Theory*. Boulder, Colo.: Westview.

World Bank. 1980. Operational Manual Statement 2.33. "Social Issues Associated with Involuntary Resettlement in Bank-Financed Projects." Washington, D.C. Processed.

_____. 1986. Operations Policy Note 10.08. "Operations Policy Issues in the Treatment of Involuntary Resettlement in Bank-Financed Projects." Washington, D.C. Processed.

_____. 1990. Operational Directive 4.30. "Involuntary Resettlement." Washington, D.C. Processed.

_____. 1993a. "Early Experience with Involuntary Resettlement: Overview." OED Report 12142. Operations Evaluation Department, Washington, D.C. Processed.

_____. 1993b. "Early Experience with Involuntary Resettlement: Impact Evaluation on India Karnataka Irrigation Project." OED Report 12132. Operations Evaluation Department, Washington, D.C. Processed.

_____. 1993c. "Early Experience with Involuntary Resettlement: Impact Evaluation on India Maharashtra Irrigation II Project." OED Report 12133. Operations Evaluation Department, Washington, D.C. Processed.

_____. 1994a. "China: Second Red Soils Area Development Project." Staff Appraisal Report 12394. Washington, D.C. Processed.

_____. 1994b. "China: Shanghai Environment Project." Staff Appraisal Report 12386. Washington, D.C. Processed.

_____. 1994c. "China: Xiaolangdi Resettlement Project." Staff Appraisal Report 12527. Washington, D.C. Processed.

_____. 1994d. "Korea: Ports Development and Environment Improvement Project." Staff Appraisal Report 12998. Washington, D.C. Processed.

_____. 1994e."Philippines: Leyte-Cebu Geothermal Project." Staff Appraisal Report 11449. Washington, D.C. Processed.

_____. 1994f. "Philippines: Leyte-Luzon Geothermal Project." Staff Appraisal Report 12568. Washington, D.C. Processed.

_____. 1994g. "Resettlement and Development: The Bankwide Review of Projects Involving Involuntary Resettlement, 1986–1993." Environment Department, Washington, D.C. Processed.

_____. 1995a. "Brazil: Ceara Urban Development and Water Resource Management Project." Staff Appraisal Report 12527. Washington, D.C. Processed.

_____. 1995b. "China: Sichuan Power Transmission Project." Staff Appraisal Report 13468. Washington, D.C. Processed.

_____. 1995c. "China: Yantan Hydroelectric Project." Implementation Completion Report 14773. Washington, D.C. Processed.

_____. 1995d. "Colombia: Rio Grande Multipurpose Project." Project Completion Report 14663. Washington, D.C. Processed.

_____. 1995e. "India: Chandrapur Thermal Power Project." Project Completion Report 15246. Washington, D.C. Processed.

_____. 1995f. "India: Dudhichua Coal Project." Project Completion Report 13938. Washington, D.C. Processed.

_____. 1995g. "India: Gujarat Medium II Irrigation Project." Project Completion Report 14768. Washington, D.C. Processed.

_____. 1995i. "India: Karnataka Project." Implementation Completion Report 15184. Washington, D.C. Processed.

_____. 1995j. "India: Orissa Water Resources Consolidation Project." Staff Appraisal Report 14888. Washington, D.C. Processed.

_____. 1995k. "Indonesia: Kedung Ombo Multipurpose Dam and Irrigation Project." Project Completion Report 14636. Washington, D.C. Processed.

_____. 1995l. "Kenya: Export Development Project." Project Completion Report 13886. Washington, D.C. Processed.

_____. 1995m. "Pakistan: Ghazi-Barotha Hydropower Project." Staff Appraisal Report 14587. Washington, D.C. Processed.

_____. 1996a. "India: Coal Sector Environmental and Social Mitigation Project." Staff Appraisal Report 15405. Washington, D.C. Processed.

_____. 1996b. "India: Jharia Coking Coal Project." Project Completion Report 15238. Washington, D.C. Processed.

_____. 1996c. "India: Renewable Resources Development Project; Tamil Nadu Newsprint and Papers Limited Papermill Expansion Component." Implementation Completion Report 15619. Washington, D.C. Processed.

_____. 1996d. "India: Second Andhra Pradesh Irrigation Project." Implementation Completion Report 15708. Washington, D.C. Processed.

_____. 1996e. "India: Second Farakka Thermal Power Project." Project Completion Report 15243. Washington, D.C. Processed.

_____. 1996f. "India: Upper Indravati Hydropower Project." Implementation Completion Report 15676. Washington, D.C. Processed.

_____. 1996g. "Resettlement and Development: The Bankwide Review of Projects Involving Involuntary Resettlement, 1986–1993" (second edition). Environment Department, Washington, D.C. Processed.

_____. 1996h. "Vietnam: Power Development Project." Staff Appraisal Report 14893. Washington, D.C. Processed.

_____. 1997a."China: Shandong Environment Project." Staff Appraisal Report 16065. Washington, D.C. Processed.

_____. 1997b. "China: Wanjianzhai Water Transfer Project." Staff Appraisal Report 15999. Washington, D.C. Processed.

_____. 1997c. "India: Coal Mining and Coal Quality Improvement Project." Implementation Completion Report 16518. Washington, D.C. Processed.

_____. 1997d. "India: Coal Sector Rehabilitation Project." Staff Appraisal Report 16473. Washington, D.C. Processed.

_____. 1997e. "India: Third Andhra Pradesh Irrigation Project." Staff Appraisal Report 16336. Washington, D.C. Processed.

_____. 1998a. "Recent Experience with Involuntary Resettlement: Brazil—Itaparica." OED Report 17544. Operations Evaluation Department, Washington, D.C. Processed.

_____. 1998b. "Recent Experience with Involuntary Resettlement: China—Shuikou (and Yantan)." OED Report 17539. Operations Evaluation Department, Washington, D.C. Processed.

_____. 1998c. "Recent Experience with Involuntary Resettlement: Indonesia—Kedung Ombo." OED Report 17540. Operations Evaluation Department, Washington, D.C. Processed.

_____. 1998d. "Recent Experience with Involuntary Resettlement: Overview." OED Report 17538. Operations Evaluation Department, Washington, D.C. Processed.

———. 1998e. "Recent Experience with Involuntary Resettlement: Thailand—Pak Mun." OED Report 17541. Operations Evaluation Department, Washington, D.C. Processed.

———. 1998f. "Recent Experience with Involuntary Resettlement: Togo—Nangbeto." OED Report 17543. Operations Evaluation Department, Washington, D.C. Processed.

———. 1998g. "Recent Experience with Involuntary Resettlement: Upper Krishna (Karnataka and Maharashtra)." OED Report 17542. Operations Evaluation Department, Washington, D.C. Processed.

About the Contributors

Michael M. Cernea joined the World Bank in 1974 as its first in-house sociologist and worked as the Bank's Senior Adviser for Sociology and Social Policy beginning 1997. He has carried out social research and operational project work in many countries in Asia, Africa, the Middle East, Europe, and Latin America. Mr. Cernea has a Ph.D. in sociology and social philosophy and has taught and lectured in universities in Europe and the United States. He is Honorary Professor for Resettlement and Social Studies at Hohai University in Nanjing, China, was appointed Visiting Scholar at Harvard University, and is a Member-correspondent of the Academy of Sciences, Romania. For his research and applied work, he received the *Solon T. Kimball* Award for Public Policy and Applied Anthropology, offered by the American Anthropological Association, and the *Bronislaw Malinowski* Award, conferred by the Society for Applied Anthropology "in recognition of scholarly efforts to understand and serve the needs of the world through social science." He has written and edited numerous books and articles on development, social change, population resettlement, social forestry, grassroots organizations, and participation, including *Putting People First: Sociological Variables in Development* (1985, 1991), *Anthropological Approaches to Resettlement: Policy, Practice, Theory* (ed. with Scott E. Guggenheim, 1993), *Social Assessments for Better Development* (ed. with Ayse Kudat, 1997), and *Resettlement and Development*, vols. I and II (in Chinese, 1997 and 1998).

John H. Eriksen (1939–February 1999). (As this volume was prepared for publication, we received the sad news of John Eriksen's untimely death, in February 1999. All the co-authors of this volume express their sympathy to John's family for their, and our, tragic loss).

John Eriksen was a founder and principal Executive Officer with Ithaca International Limited, an international development consulting firm. He consulted extensively for the United Nations Agency for

International Development (USAID) and the World Bank throughout Asia and Africa. Prior to his international consulting career, he was a country director in the Peace Corps and a regional agricultural economist for USAID. He obtained his M.S. and Ph.D. in agricultural economics from Cornell University. John Eriksen published numerous studies on agriculture, livestock, natural resource management, and related fields.

Lakshman K. Mahapatra. Emeritus Professor and former Head (1967 to 1989), Department of Anthropology, Utkal University, Bhubaneswar, Orissa, India; Visiting Professor at Hamburg University; Visiting Fellow of the Ford Foundation in Indonesia; former Vice-Chancellor of Utkal and Sambalpur Universities; former Director of Nabakrushna Centre for Development Studies, Bhubaneswar. Awards: Swami Pranavananda Award, University Grants Commission, 1994; R. P. Chanda Centenary Memorial Medal, Asiatic Society, 1995. At present, Member, International Commission on Anthropology in Policy and Practice, and Member of International Commission on Anthropological Aspects of Global Environmental Change; President, Anthropological Society, Orissa. Main publications: over 150 scientific papers published in India or abroad; several books, including *Swidden Cultivation in Asia* (co-author); *Tribal Development: Myth and Reality,* Vikas Publishers, 1994; and *Resettlement, Impoverishment, and Reconstruction in India,* Vikas Publishers, 1999. (Address: 16, Satyanagar, Bhubaneswar 751007, Orissa, India).

María Clara Mejía is a resettlement specialist in the Environment Unit for the Latin America and Caribbean Region of the World Bank and has worked in many countries throughout Latin America. Prior to joining the World Bank, she was Head of the unit of planning and socioeconomic studies in the Environment Office of the National Electricity Authority of Colombia. Ms. Mejía was trained in economics and energy planning at the Universidad de Medellín, Colombia, and the Instituto de Economia Energetica in Bariloche, Argentina. Her M.A. in anthropology is from Catholic University in Washington, D.C. Ms. Mejía has written several papers on social and environmental aspects of development projects in Latin America.

David W. Pearce is Professor of Environmental Economics at University College, London, and Associate Director of the Centre for Social and Economic Research on the Global Environment (CSERGE). He has been Personal Adviser to the United Kingdom Secretary of State for Environment, Chairman of the United Nations Economic Commission for Europe (ECE), Economics Group on Acid Rain, and a Member of the Scientific and Advisory Panel of the Global Environment Facility (GEF). He has been a consultant to the World Bank, European Commission, International Union for the Conservation of Nature, Arab Fund, Overseas Development Administration, United Nations Conference on Trade and Development, International Labor Organization, and the World Health Organization. Mr. Pearce obtained his M.A. from Oxford University and is a recipient of the United Nations Global 500 Award for services to the world environment. He is the author or editor of more than 40 books, including *Blueprint for a Green Economy* (1989), *Economics of Natural Resources and the Environment* (1990), *Sustainable Development* (1990), and *World Without End* (1993).

Warren A. Van Wicklin III is a social scientist in the Operations Evaluation Department at the World Bank. Prior to joining the World Bank, he was a consultant to USAID, the United Nations Centre for Human Settlement, and various government agencies and foundations. He has conducted fieldwork and evaluations in several countries in Asia and in Latin America. Mr. Van Wicklin earned his Ph.D. in political science at MIT. His publications include several articles on the contribution of beneficiary participation to development project effectiveness and project evaluation.